TO CARL FRIEDAN
AND
TO OUR CHILDREN —
DANIEL, JONATHAN, AND EMILY

Contents

Preface and Acknowledgements

GRADUALLY, without seeing it clearly for quite a while, I came to realize that something is very wrong with the way American women are trying to live their lives today. I sensed it first as a question mark in my own life, as a wife and mother of three small children, half-guiltily, and therefore half-heartedly, almost in spite of myself using my abilities and education in work that took me away from home. It was this personal question mark that led me, in 1957, to spend a great deal of time doing an intensive questionnaire of my college classmates, fifteen years after our graduation from Smith. The answers given by 200 women to those intimate open-ended questions made me realize that what was wrong could not be related to education in the way it was then believed to be. The problems and satisfaction of their lives, and mine, and the way our education had contributed to them, simply did not fit the image of the modern American woman as she was written about in women's magazines, studied and analysed in classrooms and clinics, praised and damned in a ceaseless barrage of words ever since the end of the Second World War. There was a strange discrepancy between the reality of our lives as women and the image to which we were trying to conform, the image that I came to call the feminine mystique. I wondered if other women faced this schizophrenic split, and what it meant.

And so I began to hunt down the origins of the feminine mystique, and its effect on women who lived by it, or grew up under it. My methods were simply those of a reporter on the trail of a story, except I soon discovered that this was no ordinary story. For the startling pattern that began to emerge, as one clue led me to another in far-flung fields of modern thought and life, defied not only the conventional image but basic psychological assumptions about women. I found a few pieces of the puzzle in previous studies of women; but not many, for women in the past have been studied in terms of the feminine mystique. The Mellon study of Vassar women was provocative, Simone de Beauvoir's insights into French women, the work of Mirra Komarovsky, A. H. Maslow, Alva Myrdal. I found even more provocative the growing body of new psychological thought on the question of man's identity, whose implications for women seem not to have been realized. I found further evidence by questioning those who treat women's ills and problems. And I traced the growth of the mystique by talking to editors of women's magazines, advertising motivational researchers, and theoretical experts on women in the fields of psychology, psychoanalysis, anthropology, sociology, and family-life education. But the puzzle did not begin to fit together until I interviewed at some depth, from two hours to two days each, eighty women at certain crucial points in their life cycle – high-school and college girls facing or evading the question of who they were; young housewives and mothers for whom, if the mystique were right, there should be no such question and who thus had no name for the problem troubling them; and women who faced a jumping-off point at forty. These women, some tortured, some serene, gave me the final clues, and the most damning indictment of the feminine mystique.

I could not, however, have written this book without the assistance of many experts, both eminent theoreticians and practical workers in the field, and, indeed, without the cooperation of many who themselves believe and have helped perpetuate the feminine mystique. I was helped by many present and former editors of women's magazines, including Peggy Bell, John English, Bruce Gould, Mary Ann Guitar, James Skardon, Nancy Lynch, Geraldine Rhoades, Robert Stein, Neal Stewart, and Polly Weaver; by Ernest Dichter and the staff of the Institute for Motivational Research; and by Marion Skedgell, former editor of the Viking Press, who gave me her data from an unfinished study of fiction heroines. Among behavioural scientists, theoreticians, and therapists in the field, I owe a great debt to William Menaker and John Land-graf of New York University, A. H. Maslow of Brandeis, John Dollard of Yale, William J. Goode of Columbia; to Margaret Mead; to Paul Vahamian of Teachers College, Elsa Siipola Israel and Eli Chinoy of Smith. And to Dr Andras Angyal, psychoanalyst, of Boston, Dr Nathan Ackerman of New York, Dr Louis English and Dr Margaret Lawrence of the Rockland County Mental Health Center; to many mental-health workers in Westchester County, including Mrs Emily Gould, Dr Gerald Fountain, Dr Henrietta Glatzer, and Marjorie Ilgenfritz of the Guidance Center of New Rochelle, and the Rev. Edgar Jackson; Dr Richard Gordon and Katherine Gordon of Bergen County, New Jersey; the late Dr Abraham Stone, Dr Lena Levine, and Fred Jaffe of the Planned Parenthood Association, the staff of the James Jackson Putnam Center in Boston, Dr Doris Menzer and Dr Somers Sturges of the Peter Bent Brigham Hospital, Alice King of the Alumnae Advisory Center and Dr Lester Evans of the Commonwealth Fund. I am also grateful to those educators valiantly fighting the feminine mystique, who gave me helpful insights: Laura Bornholdt of Wellesley, Mary Bunting of Radcliffe, Marjorie Nicolson of Columbia, Esther Lloyd-Jones of Teachers College, Millicent McIntosh of Barnard, Esther Raushenbush of Sarah Lawrence, Thomas Mendenhall of Smith, Daniel Aaron, and many other members of the Smith faculty. I am above all grateful to the women who shared their problems and feelings with me, beginning with the 200 women of Smith, 1942, and Marion Ingersoll Howell and Ann Mather Montero, who worked with me on the alumnae questionnaire that started my search.

Without that superb institution, the Frederick Lewis Allen Room of the New York Public Library and its provision to a writer of quiet work space and continuous access to research sources, this particular mother of three might never have started a book, much less finished it. The same might be said of the sensitive support of the American publisher, George P. Brockway, editor, Burton Beals, and agent, Marie Rodell. In a larger sense, this book might never have been written if I had not had a most unusual education in psychology, from Kurt Koffka, Harold Israel, Elsa Siipola, and James Gibson at Smith; from Kurt Lewin, Tamara Dembo, and the others of their group then at Iowa; and from E. C. Tolman, Jean Macfarlane, Nevitt Sanford, and Erik Erikson at Berkeley – a liberal education, in the best sense, which was meant to be used, though I have not used it as I originally planned.

The insights, interpretations both of theory and fact, and the implicit values of this book are inevitably my own. But whether or not the answers I present here are final – and there are many questions which social scientists must probe further – the dilemma of the American woman is real. At the present time, many experts, finally forced to recognize this problem, are redoubling their efforts to adjust women to it in terms of the feminine mystique. My answers may disturb the experts and women alike, for they imply social change. But there would be no sense in my writing this book at all if I did not believe that women can affect society, as well as be affected by it; that, in the end, a woman, as a man, has the power to choose, and to make her own heaven or hell.

Grandview, New York,
June 1957–July 1962

12

THE FEMININE MYSTIQUE

CHAPTER I

The Problem that Has No Name

THE problem lay buried, unspoken, for many years in the minds of American women. It was a strange stirring, a sense of dissatisfaction, a yearning that women suffered in the middle of the twentieth century in the United States. Each suburban wife struggled with it alone. As she made the beds, shopped for groceries, matched slipcover material, ate peanut butter sandwiches with her children, chauffeured Cub Scouts and Brownies, lay beside her husband at night, she was afraid to ask even of herself the silent question: 'Is this all?'

For over fifteen years there was no word of this yearning in the millions of words written about women, for women, in all the columns, books and articles by experts telling women their role was to seek fulfilment as wives and mothers. Over and over women heard in voices of tradition and of Freudian sophistication that they could desire no greater destiny than to glory in their own femininity. Experts told them how to catch a man and keep him, how to breastfeed children and handle their toilet training, how to cope with sibling rivalry and adolescent rebellion; how to buy a dishwasher, bake bread, cook gourmet snails, and build a swimming pool with their own hands; how to dress, look, and act more feminine and make marriage more exciting; how to keep their husbands from dying young and their sons from growing into delinquents. They were taught to pity the neurotic, unfeminine, unhappy women who wanted to be poets or physicists or presidents. They learned that truly feminine women do not want careers, higher education, political rights – the independence and the opportunities that the old-fashioned feminists fought for. Some women, in their forties and fifties, still remembered painfully giving up those dreams, but most of the younger women no longer even thought about them. A thousand expert voices applauded their femininity, their adjustment, their new maturity. All they had to do was devote their lives from earliest girlhood to finding a husband and bearing children.

By the end of the nineteen-fifties, the average marriage age of women in America dropped to 20, and was still dropping, into the teens. Fourteen million girls were engaged by 17. The proportion of women attending college in comparison with men dropped from 47 per cent in 1920 to 35 per cent in 1958. A century earlier, women had fought for higher education; now girls went to college to get a husband. By the mid fifties, 60 per cent dropped out of college to marry, or because they were afraid too much education would be a marriage bar. Colleges built dormitories for 'married students', but the students were almost always the husbands. A new degree was instituted for the wives – 'Ph.T.' (Putting Husband Through).

Then American girls began getting married in high school. And the women's magazines, deploring the unhappy statistics about these young marriages, urged that courses on marriage, and marriage counsellors, be installed in the high schools. Girls started going steady at twelve and thirteen, in junior high. Manufacturers put out brassières with false bosoms of foam rubber for little girls of ten. And an advertisement for a child's dress, sizes 3–6x, in the *New York Times* in the fall of 1960, said: 'She Too Can Join the Man-Trap Set.'

By the end of the fifties, the United States birthrate was overtaking India's. Statisticians were especially astounded at the fantastic increase in the number of babies among college women. Where once they had two children, now they had four, five, six. Women who had once wanted careers were now making careers out of having babies. So rejoiced *Life* magazine in a 1956 paean to the movement of American women back to the home.

In a New York hospital, a woman had a nervous breakdown when she found she could not breastfeed her baby. In other hospitals, women dying of cancer refused a drug which research had proved might save their lives: its side effects were said to be unfeminine. 'If I have only one life, let me live it as a blonde', a larger-than-life-sized picture of a pretty, vacuous woman proclaimed from newspaper, magazine, and drugstore ads. And across America, three out of every ten women dyed their hair blonde. They ate a chalk called Metrecal, instead of food, to shrink to the size of the thin young models. Department-store buyers reported that American women, since 1939, had become three and four sizes smaller. 'Women are out to fit the clothes, instead of vice versa,' one buyer said.

Interior decorators were designing kitchens with mosaic murals and original paintings, for kitchens were once again the centre of women's lives. Home sewing became a million-dollar industry. Many women no longer left their homes, except to shop, chauffeur their children, or attend a social engagement with their husbands. Girls were growing up in America without ever having jobs outside the home. In the late fifties, a sociological phenomenon was suddenly re-marked: a third of American women now worked, but most were no longer young and very few were pursuing careers. They were married women who held part-time jobs, selling or secretarial, to put their husbands through school, their sons through college, or to help pay the mortgage. Or they were widows supporting families. Fewer and fewer women were entering professional work. The shortages in the nursing, social work, and teaching professions caused crises in almost every American city. Concerned over the Soviet Union's lead in the space race, scientists noted that America's greatest source of unused brainpower was women. But girls would not study physics: it was 'unfeminine'. A girl refused a science fellowship at Johns Hopkins to take a job in a real-estate office. All she wanted, she said, was what every other American girl wanted – to get married, have four children, and live in a nice house in a nice suburb.

The suburban housewife – she was the dream image of the young American women and the envy, it was said, of women all over the world. The American housewife – freed by science and labour-saving appliances from the drudgery, the dangers of childbirth, and the illnesses of her grandmother. She was healthy, beautiful, educated, concerned only about her husband, her children, her home. She had found true feminine fulfilment. As a housewife and mother, she was respected as a full and equal partner to man in his world. She was free to choose automobiles, clothes, appliances, supermarkets; she had everything that women ever dreamed of.

In the fifteen years after the Second World War, this mystique of feminine fulfilment became the cherished and self-perpetuating core of contemporary American culture. Millions of women lived their lives in the image of those pretty pictures of the American suburban housewife, kissing their husbands good-bye in front of the picture window, depositing their stationwagonsful of children at school, and smiling as they ran the new electric waxer over the spotless kitchen floor. They baked their own bread, sewed their own and their children's clothes, kept their new washing machines and dryers running all day. They changed the sheets on the beds twice a week instead of once, took the rug-hooking class in adult education, and pitied their poor frustrated mothers, who had dreamed of having a career. They gloried in their role as women, and wrote proudly on the census blank: 'Occupation: housewife'.

For over fifteen years, the words written for women, and the words women used when they talked to each other, while their husbands sat on the other side of the room and talked shop or politics or septic tanks, were about problems with their children, or how to keep their husbands happy, or improve their children's school, or cook chicken, or make slipcovers. Nobody argued whether women were inferior or superior to men; they were simply different. Words like 'emancipation' and 'career' sounded strange and embarrassing; no one had used them for years. When a Frenchwoman named Simone de Beauvoir wrote a book called *The Second Sex*, an American critic commented that she obviously 'didn't know what life was all about', and besides, she was talking about French women. The 'woman problem' in America no longer existed.

If a woman had a problem in the 1950s and 1960s, she knew that something must be wrong with her marriage, or with herself. Other women were satisfied with their lives, she thought. What kind of a woman was she if she did not feel this mysterious fulfilment waxing the kitchen floor? She was so ashamed to admit her dissatisfaction that she never knew how many other women shared it. If she tried to tell her husband, he didn't understand what she was talking about. She did not really understand it herself. For over fifteen years women in America found it harder to talk about this problem than about sex. 'I don't know what's wrong with women today,' a suburban psychiatrist said uneasily. 'I only know something is wrong because most of my patients happen to be women. And their problem isn't sexual.' Most women with this problem did not go to see a psychoanalyst, however. 'There's nothing wrong really,' they kept telling themselves. 'There isn't any problem.'

But on an April morning in 1959, I heard a mother of four, having coffee with four other mothers in a suburban development fifteen miles from New York, say in a tone of quiet desperation, 'the problem'. And the others knew, without words, that she was not talking about a problem with her husband, or her children, or her home. Suddenly they realized they all shared the same problem, the problem that has no name. They began, hesitantly, to talk about it. Later, after they had picked up their children at nursery school and taken them home to nap, two of the women cried, in sheer relief, just to know they were not alone.

Gradually I came to realize that the problem that has no name was shared by countless women in America. As a magazine writer I often interviewed women about problems with their children, or their marriages, or their houses, or their communities. But after a while I began to recognize the telltale signs of this other problem. I saw the same signs in suburban ranch houses and split-levels on Long Island and in New Jersey and Westchester County; in colonial houses in a small Massachusetts town; on patios in Memphis; in suburban and city apartments; in living-rooms in the Midwest. Sometimes I sensed the problem, not as a reporter, but as a suburban housewife, for during this time I was also bringing up my own three children in Rockland County, New York. The groping words I heard from other women, on quiet afternoons when children were at school or on quiet evenings when husbands worked late, I think I understood first as a woman long before I understood their larger social and psychological implications.

Just what was this problem that has no name? What were the words women used when they tried to express it? Sometimes a woman would say 'I feel empty somehow ... incomplete.' Or she would say, 'I feel as if I don't exist.' Sometimes she blotted out the feeling with a tranquillizer. Sometimes she thought the problem was with her husband, or her children, or that what she really needed was to redecorate her house, or move to a better neighbourhood, or have an affair, or another baby. Sometimes, she went to a doctor with symptoms she could hardly describe: 'A tired feeling ... I get so angry with the children it scares me ... I feel like crying without any reason.' (A Cleveland doctor called it 'the housewife's syndrome'.) A number of women told me about great bleeding blisters that break out on their hands and arms. 'I call it the housewife's blight,' said a family doctor in Pennsylvania. 'I see it so often lately in these young women with four, five, and six children, who bury themselves in their dishpans. But it isn't caused by detergent and it isn't cured by cortisone.'

Sometimes a woman would tell me that the feeling gets so strong she runs out of the house and walks through the streets. Or she stays inside her house and cries. Or her children tell her a joke, and she doesn't laugh because she doesn't hear it. I talked to women who had spent years on the analyst's couch, working out their 'adjustment to the feminine role', their blocks to 'fulfilment as a wife and mother'. But the desperate tone in these women's voices, and the look in their eyes, was the same as the tone and the look of other women, who were sure they had no problem, even though they did have a strange feeling of desperation.

A mother of four who left college at nineteen to get married told me:

I've tried everything women are supposed to do – hobbies, gardening, pickling, canning, being very social with my neighbours, joining committees, running P.T.A. [Parent–Teacher Association] teas. I can do it all, and I like it, but it doesn't leave you anything to think about – any feeling of who you are. I never had any career ambitions. All I wanted was to get married and have four children. I love the kids and Bob and my home. There's no problem you can even put a name to. But I'm desperate. I begin to feel I have no personality. I'm a server of food and a putter-on of pants and a bedmaker, somebody who can be called on when you want something. But who am I?

A twenty-three-year-old mother in blue jeans said:

I ask myself why I'm so dissatisfied. I've got my health, fine children, a lovely new home, enough money. My husband has a real future as an electronics engineer. He doesn't have any of these feelings. He says maybe I need a vacation, let's go to New York for a weekend. But that isn't it. I always had this idea we should do everything together. I can't sit down and read a book alone. If the children are napping and I have one hour to myself I just walk through the house waiting for them to wake up. I don't make a move until I know where the rest of the crowd is going. It's as if ever since you were a little girl, there's always been somebody or something that will take care of your life: your parents, or college, or falling in love, or having a child, or moving to a new house. Then you wake up one morning and there's nothing to look forward to.

A young wife in a Long Island development said:

I seem to sleep so much. I don't know why I should be so tired. This house isn't nearly so hard to clean as the cold-water flat we had when I was working. The children are at school all day. It's not the work. I just don't feel alive.

In 1960, the problem that has no name burst like a boil through the image of the happy American housewife. In the television commercials the pretty housewives still beamed over their foaming dishpans and *Time*'s cover story on 'The Suburban Wife, an American Phenomenon' protested: 'Having too good a time ... to believe that they should be un-happy.' But the actual unhappiness of the American housewife was suddenly being reported – from the *New York Times* and *Newsweek* to *Good Housekeeping* and C.B.S. Television ('The Trapped Housewife'), although almost everybody who talked about it found some superficial reason to dismiss it. Some said it was the old problem – education: more and more women had education, which naturally made them unhappy in their role as housewives. 'The road from Freud to Frigidaire, from Sophocles to Spock, has turned out to be a bumpy one,' reported the *New York Times* (28 June 1960).

Many young women – certainly not all – whose education plunged them into a world of ideas feel stifled in their homes. They find their routine lives out of joint with their training. Like shut-ins, they feel left out. In the last year, the problem of the educated housewife has provided the meat of dozens of speeches made by troubled presidents of women's colleges who maintain, in the face of complaints, that sixteen years of academic training is realistic preparation for wifehood and motherhood.

There was much sympathy for the educated housewife. ('Like a two-headed schizophrenic ... once she wrote a paper on the Graveyard poets; now she writes notes to the milkman. Once she determined the boiling point of sulphuric acid; now she determines her boiling point with the overdue repair-man. ... The housewife often is reduced to screams and tears. ... No one, it seems, is appreciative, least of all herself, of the kind of person she becomes in the process of turning from poetess into shrew.')

Home economists suggested more realistic preparation for housewives, such as high-school workshops in home ap-pliances. College educators suggested more discussion groups on home management and the family, to prepare women for the adjustment to domestic life. No month went by without a new book by a psychiatrist or sexologist offering technical advice on finding greater fulfilment through sex.

A male humorist joked in *Harper's Bazaar* (July 1960) that the problem could be solved by taking away woman's right to vote. ('In the pre-19th Amendment era, the American woman was placid, sheltered and sure of her role in American society. She left all the political decisions to her husband and he, in turn, left all the family decisions to her. Today a woman has to make both the family *and* the political decisions, and it's too much for her.')

A number of educators suggested seriously that women no longer be admitted to the four-year colleges and universities: in the growing college crisis, the education which girls could not use as housewives was more urgently needed than ever by boys to do the work of the atomic age.

The problem was also dismissed with drastic solutions no one could take seriously. (A woman writer proposed in *Harper's* that women be drafted for compulsory service as nurses' aides and baby-sitters.) And it was smoothed over with the age-old panaceas: 'love is their answer', 'the only answer is inner help', 'the secret of completeness – children', 'a private means of intellectual fulfilment', 'to cure this tooth-ache of the spirit – the simple formula of handing one's self and one's will over to God'.[1]

The problem was dismissed by telling the housewife she doesn't realize how lucky she is – her own boss, no time clock, no junior executive gunning for her job. What if she isn't happy – does she think men are happy in this world? Does she really, secretly, still want to be a man? Doesn't she know yet how lucky she is to be a woman?

The problem was also, and finally, dismissed by shrugging that there are no solutions: this is what being a woman means, and what is wrong with American women that they can't accept their role gracefully? As *Newsweek* put it (7 March 1960):

She is dissatisfied with a lot that women of other lands can only dream of. Her discontent is deep, pervasive, and impervious to the superficial remedies which are offered at every hand. ... An army of professional explorers have already charted the major sources of trouble. ... From the beginning of time, the female cycle has defined and confined woman's role. As Freud was credited with saying: 'Anatomy is destiny.' Though no group of women has ever pushed these natural restrictions as far as the American wife, it seems that she still cannot accept them with good grace. ... A young mother with a beautiful family, charm, talent and brains is apt to dismiss her role apologetically. 'What do I do?' you hear her say. 'Why nothing. I'm just a housewife.' A good education, it seems, has given this paragon among women an understanding of the value of everything except her own worth ...

And so she must accept the fact that 'American women's unhappiness is merely the most recently won of women's rights', and adjust and say with the happy housewife found by *Newsweek*:

We ought to salute the wonderful freedom we all have and be proud of our lives today. I have had college and I've worked, but being a housewife is the most rewarding and satisfying role.... My mother was never included in my father's business affairs ... she couldn't get out of the house and away from us children. But I am an equal to my husband; I can go along with him on business trips and to social business affairs.

The alternative offered was a choice that few women would contemplate. In the sympathetic words of the *New York Times*:

All admit to being deeply frustrated at times by the lack of privacy, the physical burden, the routine of family life, the confinement of it. However, none would give up her home and family if she had the choice to make again.

Redbook commented:

Few women would want to thumb their noses at husbands, children and community and go off on their own. Those who do may be talented individuals, but they rarely are successful women.

The year American women's discontent boiled over, it was also reported (*Look*) that the more than 21,000,000 American women who are single, widowed, or divorced do not cease even after fifty their frenzied, desperate search for a man. And the search begins early – for seventy per cent of all American women now marry before they are twenty-four. A pretty twenty-five-year-old secretary took thirty-five different jobs in six months in the futile hope of finding a husband. Women were moving from one political club to another, taking evening courses in accounting or sailing, learning to play golf or ski, joining a number of churches in succession, going to bars alone, in their ceaseless search for a man.

Of the growing thousands of women currently getting private psychiatric help in the United States, the married ones were reported dissatisfied with their marriages, the unmarried ones suffering from anxiety and, finally, depression. Strangely, a number of psychiatrists stated that, in their experience, unmarried women patients were happier than married ones. So the door of all those pretty suburban houses opened a crack to permit a glimpse of uncounted thousands of American housewives who suffered alone from a problem that suddenly everyone was talking about, and beginning to take for granted, as one of those unreal problems in American life that can never be solved – like the hydrogen bomb. By 1962 the plight of the trapped American housewife had become a national parlour game. Whole issues of magazines, newspaper columns, books learned and frivolous, educational conferences, and television panels were devoted to the problem.

Even so, most men, and some women, still did not know that this problem was real. A bitter laugh was beginning to be heard from American women. They got all kinds of advice from the growing armies of marriage and child-guidance counsellors, psychotherapists, and armchair psychologists, on how to adjust to their role as housewives. No other road to fulfilment was offered to them in the middle of the twentieth century. Most adjusted to their role and suffered or ignored the problem that has no name. It can be less painful, for a woman, not to hear the strange, dissatisfied voice stirring within her.

It is no longer possible to ignore that voice, to dismiss the desperation of so many American women. This is not what being a woman means, no matter what the experts say. For human suffering there is a reason; perhaps the reason has not been found because the right questions have not been asked, or pressed far enough. I do not accept the answer that there is no problem because American women have luxuries that women in other times and lands never dreamed of; part of the strange newness of the problem is that it cannot be understood in terms of the age-old material problems of man: poverty, sickness, hunger, cold. The women who suffer this problem have a hunger that food cannot fill. It persists in women whose husbands are struggling interns and law clerks, or prosperous doctors and lawyers; in wives of workers and executives who make $5,000 a year or $50,000. It is not caused by lack of material advantages; it may not even be felt by women preoccupied with desperate problems of hunger, poverty, or illness. And women who think it will be solved by more money, a bigger house, a second car, moving to a better suburb, often discover it gets worse.

It is no longer possible today to blame the problem on loss of femininity: to say that education and independence and equality with men have made American women unfeminine. I think, in fact, that this is the first clue to the mystery: the problem cannot be understood in the generally accepted terms by which scientists have studied women, doctors have treated them, counsellors have advised them, and writers have written about them. Women who suffer this problem have lived their whole lives in the pursuit of feminine fulfilment. They are not career women (although career women may have other problems); they are women whose greatest ambition has been marriage and children. For the oldest of these women, these daughters of the American middle class, no other dream was possible. The ones in their forties and fifties who once had other dreams gave them up and threw themselves joyously into life as housewives. For the youngest, the new wives and mothers, this was the only dream. They are the ones who quit high school and college to marry, or marked time in some job in which they had no real interest until they married.

Are the women who finished college, the women who once had dreams beyond housewifery, the ones who suffer the most? According to the experts they are, but listen to these four women:

My days are all busy, and dull, too. All I ever do is mess around. I get up at eight – I make breakfast, so I do the dishes, have lunch, do some more dishes and some laundry and cleaning in the afternoon. Then it's supper dishes and I get to sit down a few minutes before the children have to be sent to bed. .... That's all there is to my day. It's just like any other wife's day. Humdrum. The biggest time, I am chasing kids.

Ye Gods, what do I do with my time? Well, I get up at six. I get my son dressed and then give him breakfast. After that I wash dishes and bathe and feed the baby. Then I get lunch and while the children nap, I sew or mend or iron and do all the other things I can't get done before noon. Then I cook supper for the family and my husband watches TV while I do the dishes. After I get the children to bed, I set my hair and then I go to bed.

The problem is always being the children's mommy, or the minister's wife and never being myself.

A film made of any typical morning in my house would look like an old Marx Brothers' comedy. I wash the dishes, rush the older children off to school, dash out in the yard to cultivate the chrysanthemums, run back in to make a phone call about a committee meeting, help the youngest child build a blockhouse, spend fifteen minutes skimming the newspapers so I can be well-informed, then scamper down to the washing machines where my thrice-weekly laundry includes enough clothes to keep a primitive village going for an entire year. By noon I'm ready for a padded cell. Very little of what I've done has been really necessary or important. Outside pressures lash me through the day. Yet I look upon myself as one of the more relaxed housewives in the neighbourhood. Many of my friends are even more frantic. In the past sixty years we have come full circle and the American housewife is once again trapped in a squirrel cage. If the cage is now a modern plate-glass-and-broadloom ranch house or a convenient modern apartment, the situation is no less painful than when her grandmother sat over an embroidery hoop in her gilt-and-plush parlour and muttered angrily about women's rights.

The first two women never went to college. They live in developments in Levittown, New Jersey, and Tacoma, Washington, and were interviewed by a team of sociologists studying working-men's wives.[2] The third, a minister's wife, wrote on the fifteenth reunion questionnaire of her college that she never had any career ambitions, but wishes now she had.[3]

The fourth, who has a Ph.D. in anthropology, is today a Nebraska housewife with three children.⁴ Their words seem to indicate that housewives of all educational levels suffer the same feeling of desperation.

The fact is that no one today is muttering angrily about 'women's rights', even though more and more women have gone to college. In a recent study of all the classes that have graduated from Barnard College,⁵ a significant minority of earlier graduates blamed their education for making them want 'rights', later classes blamed their education for giving them career dreams, but recent graduates blamed the college for making them feel it was not enough simply to be a housewife and mother; they did not want to feel guilty if they did not read books or take part in community activities. But if education is not the cause of the problem, the fact that education somehow festers in these women may be a clue.

If the secret of feminine fulfilment is having children, never have so many women, with the freedom to choose, had so many children, in so few years, so willingly. If the answer is love, never have women searched for love with such determination. And yet there is a growing suspicion that the problem may not be sexual, though it must somehow be related to sex. I have heard from many doctors evidence of new sexual problems between man and wife – sexual hunger in wives so great their husbands cannot satisfy it. 'We have made woman a sex creature,' said a psychiatrist at the Margaret Sanger marriage counselling clinic. 'She has no identity except as a wife and mother. She does not know who she is herself. She waits all day for her husband to come home at night to make her feel alive. And now it is the husband who is not interested. It is terrible for the women, to lie there, night after night, waiting for her husband to make her feel alive.' Why is there such a market for books and articles offering sexual advice? The kind of sexual orgasm which Kinsey found in statistical plenitude in the recent generations of American women does not seem to make this problem go away.

On the contrary, new neuroses are being seen among women – and problems as yet unnamed as neuroses – which Freud and his followers did not predict, with physical symptoms, anxieties, and defence mechanisms equal to those caused by sexual repression. And strange new problems are being reported in the growing generations of children whose mothers were always there, driving them around, helping them with their homework – an inability to endure pain or discipline or pursue any self-sustained goal of any sort, a devastating boredom with life. Educators are increasingly uneasy about the dependence, the lack of self-reliance, of the boys and girls who are entering college today. 'We fight a continual battle to make our students assume manhood,' said a Columbia dean.

A White House conference was held on the physical and muscular deterioration of American children: were they being overnurtured? Sociologists noted the astounding organization of suburban children's lives: the lessons, parties, entertainments, play and study groups organized for them. A suburban housewife in Portland, Oregon, wondered why the children 'need' Brownies and Boy Scouts out here.

This is not the slums. The kids out here have the great outdoors. I think people are so bored, they organize the children, and then try to hook everyone else on it. And the poor kids have no time left just to lie on their beds and daydream.

When a woman tries to put the problem into words, she often merely describes the daily life she leads. What is there in this recital of comfortable domestic detail that could possibly cause such a feeling of desperation? Is she trapped simply by the enormous demands of her role as modern housewife: wife, mistress, mother, nurse, consumer, cook, chauffeur; expert on interior decoration, child care, appliance repair, furniture refinishing, nutrition, and education? Her day is fragmented; she can never spend more than fifteen minutes on any one thing; she has no time to read books, only magazines; even if she had time, she has lost the power to concentrate. At the end of the day, she is so terribly tired that sometimes her husband has to take over and put the children to bed.

This terrible tiredness took so many women to doctors in

the 1950s that one decided to investigate it. He found, sur-
prisingly, that his patients suffering from 'housewife's fatigue'
slept more than an adult needed to sleep – as much as ten
hours a day – and that the actual energy they expended on
housework did not tax their capacity. The real problem must
be something else, he decided – perhaps boredom. Some doctors told their women patients they must get out of the house
for a day, treat themselves to a movie in town. Others prescribed tranquillizers. Many suburban housewives were taking
tranquillizers like cough drops.

You wake up in the morning, and you feel as if there's no point
in going on another day like this. So you take a tranquillizer because
it makes you not care so much that it's pointless.

It is easy to see the concrete details that trap the suburban
housewife, the continual demands on her time. But the chains
that bind her in her trap are chains made up of mistaken ideas
and misinterpreted facts, of incomplete truths and unreal
choices. They are not easily seen and not easily shaken off.
I found many clues by talking to suburban doctors,
gynaecologists, obstetricians, child-guidance clinicians, pediatricians, high-school guidance counsellors, college professors,
marriage counsellors, psychiatrists, and ministers – questioning them not on their theories, but on their actual experience
in treating American women. I became aware of a growing
body of evidence, much of which has not been reported publicly because it does not fit current modes of thought about
women – evidence which throws into question the standards
of feminine normality, feminine adjustment, feminine fulfilment, and feminine maturity by which most women are still
trying to live.
I began to see in a strange new light the American return to
early marriage and the large families that are causing the
population explosion; the recent movement to natural childbirth and breastfeeding; suburban conformity, and the new
neuroses, character pathologies and sexual problems being
reported by the doctors. I began to see new dimensions to old
problems that have long been taken for granted among

women: menstrual difficulties, sexual frigidity, promiscuity, pregnancy fears, childbirth depression, the high incidence of emotional breakdown and suicide among women in their twenties and thirties, the menopause crises, the so-called passivity and immaturity of American men, the discrepancy between women's tested intellectual abilities in childhood and their adult achievement, the changing incidence of adult sexual orgasm in American women, and persistent problems in psychotherapy and in women's education.

If I am right, the problem that has no name stirring in the minds of so many American women today is not a matter of loss of feminity or too much education, or the demands of domesticity. It is far more important than anyone recognizes. It is the key to these other new and old problems which have been torturing women and their husbands and children, and puzzling their doctors and educators for years. It may well be the key to our future as a nation and a culture. We can no longer ignore that voice within women that says: 'I want something more than my husband and my children and my home.'

CHAPTER 2

The Happy Housewife Heroine

WHY have so many American wives suffered this nameless aching dissatisfaction for so many years, each one thinking she was alone? 'I've got tears in my eyes with sheer relief that my own inner turmoil is shared with other women,' a young Connecticut mother wrote me when I first began to put this problem into words.[1]

What need, what part of themselves, could so many women today be repressing? In this age after Freud, sex is immediately suspect. But this new stirring in women does not seem to be sex. Could there be another need, a part of themselves they have buried as deeply as the Victorian women buried sex?

The image of a good woman by which Victorian ladies lived simply left out sex. Does the image by which modern American women live also leave something out, the proud and public image of the high-school girl going steady, the college girl in love, the suburban housewife with an up-and-coming husband and a station wagon full of children? This image – created by the women's magazines, by advertisements, television, movies, novels, columns and books by experts on marriage and the family, child psychology, sexual adjustment, and by the popularizers of sociology and psychoanalysis – shapes women's lives today and mirrors their dreams. It may give a clue to the problem that has no name, as a dream gives a clue to a wish unnamed by the dreamer. In the mind's ear, a Geiger counter clicks when the image shows too sharp a discrepancy from reality. A Geiger counter clicked in my own inner ear when I could not fit the quiet desperation of so many women into the picture of the modern American housewife that I myself was helping to create, writing for the women's magazines.

In the early 1960s *McCall's* has been the fastest growing of the women's magazines. Its contents are a fairly accurate representation of the image of the American woman presented, and in part created, by the large-circulation magazines. Here are the complete editorial contents of a typical issue of *McCall's* (July 1960):

1. A lead article on 'increasing baldness in women', caused by too much brushing and dyeing.
2. A long poem in primer-size type about a child, called 'A Boy Is A Boy'.
3. A short story about how a teenager who doesn't go to college gets a man away from a bright college girl.
4. A short story about the minute sensations of a baby throwing his bottle out of the crib.
5. The first of a two-part intimate 'up-to-date' account by the Duke of Windsor on 'How the Duchess and I now live and spend our time. The influence of clothes on me and vice versa'.
6. A short story about a nineteen-year-old girl sent to a charm school to learn how to bat her eyelashes and lose at tennis. ('You're nineteen, and by normal American standards, I now am entitled to have you taken off my hands, legally and financially, by some beardless youth who will spirit you away to a one-and-a-half-room apartment in the Village while he learns the chicanery of selling bonds. And no beardless youth is going to do that as long as you volley to his backhand.')
7. The story of a honeymoon couple commuting between separate bedrooms after an argument over gambling at Las Vegas.
8. An article on 'how to overcome an inferiority complex'.
9. A story called 'Wedding Day'.
10. The story of a teenager's mother who learns how to dance rock-and-roll.
11. Six pages of glamorous pictures of models in maternity clothes.
12. Four glamorous pages on 'reduce the way the models do'.

13. An article on airline delays.
14. Patterns for home sewing.
15. Patterns with which to make 'Folding Screens – Bewitching Magic'.
16. An article called 'An Encyclopaedic Approach to Finding a Second Husband'.
17. A 'barbecue bonanza' dedicated 'to the Great American Mister who stands, chef's cap on head, fork in hand, on terrace or back porch, in patio or backyard anywhere in the land, watching his roast turning on the spit. And to his wife, without whom (sometimes) the barbecue could never be the smashing summer success it undoubtedly is . . .'

There were also the regular front-of-the-book 'service' columns on new drug and medicine developments, child-care facts, columns by Clare Luce and by Eleanor Roosevelt, and 'Pots and Pans', a column of readers' letters.

The image of woman that emerges from this big, pretty magazine is young and frivolous, almost childlike; fluffy and feminine; passive; gaily content in a world of bedroom and kitchen, sex, babies, and home. The magazine surely does not leave out sex; the only goal a woman is permitted is the pursuit of a man. It is crammed full of food, clothing, cosmetics, furniture, and the physical bodies of young women, but where is the world of thought and ideas, the life of the mind and spirit?

This was the year Castro led a revolution in Cuba and men were trained to travel into outer space; the year that the African continent brought forth new nations, and a plane whose speed is greater than the speed of sound broke up a Summit Conference; the year artists picketed a great museum in protest against the hegemony of abstract art; physicists explored the concept of anti-matter; astronomers, because of new radio telescopes, had to alter their concepts of the expanding universe; biologists made a breakthrough in the fundamental chemistry of life; and Negro youth in Southern schools forced the United States, for the first time since the Civil War,

32

to face a moment of democratic truth. But this magazine, published for over 5,000,000 American women, almost all of whom have been through high school and nearly half to college, contained almost no mention of the world beyond the home. And this was no anomaly of a single issue of a single women's magazine.

I sat one night at a meeting of magazine writers, mostly men, who work for all kinds of magazines, including women's magazines. The main speaker was a leader of the desegregation battle. Before he spoke, another man outlined the needs of the large women's magazine he edited:

Our readers are housewives, full time. They're not interested in the broad public issues of the day. They are not interested in national or international affairs. They are only interested in the family and the home. They aren't interested in politics, unless it's related to an immediate need in the home, like the price of coffee. Humour? Has to be gentle, they don't get satire. Travel? We have almost completely dropped it. Education? That's a problem. Their own education level is going up. They've generally all had a high-school education and many, college. They're tremendously interested in education for their children – fourth-grade arithmetic. You just can't write about ideas or broad issues of the day for women. That's why we're publishing 90 per cent service now and 10 per cent general interest.

At this point, the writers and editors spent an hour listening to Thurgood Marshall on the inside story of the desegregation battle, and its possible effect on the presidential election. 'Too bad I can't run that story,' one editor said. 'But you just can't link it to woman's world.'

As I listened to them, a German phrase echoed in my mind – 'Kinder, Küche, Kirche', the slogan by which the Nazis decreed that women must once again be confined to their biological role. But this was not Nazi Germany. This was America. The whole world lies open to American women. Why, then, does the image deny the world? Not long ago, women dreamed and fought for equality, their own place in the world. What happened to their dreams; when did women decide to give up the world and go back home?

A geologist brings up a core of mud from the bottom of the ocean and sees layers of sediment as sharp as a razor blade deposited over the years – clues to changes in the geological evolution of the earth so vast that they would go unnoticed during the lifespan of a single man. I sat for many days in the New York Public Library, going back through bound volumes of American women's magazines for the last twenty years. I found a change in the image of the American woman, and in the boundaries of the woman's world, as sharp and puzzling as the changes revealed in cores of ocean sediment.

In 1939, the heroines of women's magazine stories were not always young, but in a certain sense they were younger than their fictional counterparts today. They were New Women, creating with a gay determined spirit a new identity for women – a life of their own. There was an aura about them of becoming, of moving into a future that was going to be different from the past. The majority of heroines in the four major women's magazines (then *Ladies' Home Journal*, *McCall's*, *Good Housekeeping*, *Woman's Home Companion*) were career women – happily, proudly, adventurously, attractively career women – who loved and were loved by men. And the spirit, courage, independence, determination – the strength of character they showed in their work as nurses, teachers, artists, actresses, copywriters, saleswomen – were part of their charm. There was a definite aura that their individuality was something to be admired, not unattractive to men, that men were drawn to them as much for their spirit and character as for their looks.

These were the mass women's magazines – in their heyday. The stories were conventional: girl-meets-boy or girl-gets-boy. But very often this was not the major theme of the story. These heroines were usually marching towards some goal or vision of their own, struggling with some problem of work or the world, when they found their man. And this New Woman, less fluffily feminine, so independent and determined to find a new life of her own, was the heroine of a different kind of love story. She was less aggressive in pursuit of a man. Her passionate involvement with the world, her own sense of herself as an individual, her self-reliance, gave a different flavour to her relationship with the man. The heroine and hero of one of these stories meet and fall in love at an ad agency where they both work. 'I don't want to put you in a garden behind a wall,' the hero says. 'I want you to walk with me hand in hand, and together we could accomplish whatever we wanted to' ('A Dream to Share', *Redbook*, January, 1939).

These New Women were almost never housewives; in fact, the stories usually ended before they had children. They were young because the future was open. But they seemed, in another sense, much older, more mature than the childlike, kittenish young housewife heroines today.

It is like remembering a long-forgotten dream, to recapture the memory of what a career meant to women before 'career woman' became a dirty word in America. Jobs meant money, of course, at the end of the depression. But the readers of these magazines were not the women who got the jobs: career meant more than job. It seemed to mean doing something, being somebody yourself, not just existing in and through others.

I found the last clear note of the passionate search for individual identity that a career seems to have symbolized in the pre-1950 decades in a story called 'Sarah and the Seaplane' (*Ladies' Home Journal*, February 1949). Sarah, who for nineteen years has played the part of docile daughter, is secretly learning to fly. She misses her flying lesson to accompany her mother on a round of social calls. An elderly doctor houseguest says: 'My dear Sarah, every day, all the time, you are committing suicide. It's a greater crime than not pleasing others, not doing justice to yourself.' Sensing some secret, he asks if she is in love.

She found it difficult to answer. In love? In love with the good-natured, the beautiful Henry [the flying teacher]? In love with the flashing water and the lift of wings at the instant of freedom, and the vision of the smiling, limitless world? 'Yes,' she answered, 'I think I am.'

The next morning, Sarah solos. Henry

stepped away, slamming the cabin door shut, and swung the ship about for her. She was alone. There was a heady moment when everything she had learned left her, when she had to adjust herself to be alone, entirely alone in the familiar cabin. Then she drew a deep breath and suddenly a wonderful sense of competence made her sit erect and smiling. She was alone! She was answerable to herself alone, and she was sufficient.

'I can do it!' she told herself aloud. ... The wind flew back from the floats in glittering streaks, and then effortlessly the ship lifted itself free and soared.

Even her mother can't stop her now from getting her flying licence. She is not 'afraid of discovering my own way of life.' In bed that night she smiles sleepily, remembering how Henry had said, 'You're my girl.'

Henry's girl! She smiled. No, she was not Henry's girl. She was Sarah. And that was sufficient. And with such a late start it would be some time before she got to know herself. Half in a dream now, she wondered if at the end of that time she would need someone else and who it would be.

And then suddenly the image blurs. The New Woman, soaring free, hesitates in midflight, shivers in all that blue sunlight, and rushes back to the cosy walls of home. In the same year that Sarah soloed, the *Ladies' Home Journal* printed the prototype of the innumerable paeans to 'Occupation: Housewife' that started to appear in the women's magazines, paeans that resounded throughout the fifties. They usually begin with a woman complaining that when she has to write 'Housewife' on the census blank, she gets an inferiority complex. Then the author of the paean, who somehow never is a housewife (in this case, Dorothy Thompson, newspaper woman, foreign correspondent, famous columnist, in *Ladies' Home Journal*, March 1949), roars with laughter. The trouble with you, she scolds, is you don't realize you are expert in a dozen careers, simultaneously.

You might write: business manager, cook, nurse, chauffeur, dressmaker, interior decorator, accountant, caterer, teacher, private secretary – or just put down philanthropist. ... All your life you have been giving away your energies, your skills, your talents, your services, for love.

But still, the housewife complains, I'm nearly fifty and I've never done what I hoped to do in my youth – music – I've wasted my college education.

'Ho-ho,' laughs Miss Thompson, 'aren't your children musical because of you, and all those struggling years while your husband was finishing his great work, didn't you keep a charming home on $3,000 a year, and make all your children's clothes and your own, and paper the living-room yourself, and watch the markets like a hawk for bargains? And in time off, didn't you type and proofread your husband's manuscripts, plan festivals to make up the church deficit, play piano duets with the children to make practising more fun, read their books in high school to follow their study?' 'But all this vicarious living – through others,' the housewife sighs. 'As vicarious as Napoleon Bonaparte,' Miss Thompson scoffs, 'or a Queen. I simply refuse to share your self-pity. You are one of the most successful women I know.'

As for woman's spirit being broken by the boredom of household tasks, maybe the genius of some women has been thwarted, but 'a world full of feminine genius, but poor in children, would come rapidly to an end. ... Great men have great mothers.'

And the American housewife is reminded that Catholic countries in the Middle Ages 'elevated the gentle and inconspicuous Mary into the Queen of Heaven, and built their loveliest cathedrals to "Notre Dame – Our Lady".'

In 1949, the *Ladies' Home Journal* also ran Margaret Mead's *Male and Female*. All the magazines were echoing Farnham and Lundberg's *Modern Woman: The Lost Sex*, which came out in 1942, with its warning that careers and higher education were leading to the 'masculinization of women with enormously dangerous consequences to the home, the children dependent on it and to the ability of the woman, as well as her husband, to obtain sexual gratification.'

And so the feminine mystique began to spread through the land, grafted on to old prejudices and comfortable conventions which so easily give the past a stranglehold on the future. Behind the new mystique were concepts and theories deceptive in their sophistication and their assumption of accepted truth.

These theories were supposedly so complex that they were inaccessible to all but a few initiates, and therefore irrefutable. It will be necessary to break through this wall of mystery to understand fully what has happened to American women.

The feminine mystique says that the highest value and the only commitment for women is the fulfilment of their own femininity. It says that the great mistake of Western culture, through most of its history, has been the undervaluation of this femininity. It says this femininity is so mysterious and intuitive and close to the creation and origin of life that man-made science may never be able to understand it. But however special and different, it is in no way inferior to the nature of man; it may even in certain respects be superior. The mistake, says the mystique, the root of women's troubles in the past is that women envied men, women tried to be like men, instead of accepting their own nature, which can find fulfilment only in sexual passivity, male domination, and nurturing maternal love.

But the new image this mystique gives to American women is the old image: 'Occupation: housewife'. Beneath the sophisticated trappings, it simply makes certain concrete, finite, domestic aspects of feminine existence – as it was lived by women whose lives were confined, by necessity, to cooking, cleaning, washing, bearing children – into a religion, a pattern by which all women must now live or deny their femininity.

The transformation, reflected in the pages of the women's magazines, was sharply visible in 1949 and progressive through the fifties. 'Femininity Begins at Home', 'It's a Man's World Maybe', 'Have Babies While You're Young', 'How to Snare a Male', 'Should I stop Work When We Marry?', 'Are You Training Your Daughter to be a Wife?', 'Careers at Home', 'Do Women Have to Talk So Much?', 'Why GIs Prefer Those German Girls', 'What Women Can Learn from Mother Eve', 'Really a Man's World, Politics', 'How to Hold On to a Happy Marriage', 'Don't Be Afraid to Marry Young', 'The Doctor Talks about Breast-Feeding', 'Our Baby was Born at Home', 'Cooking to Me is Poetry', 'The Business of Running a Home'.

By the end of 1949, only one out of three heroines in the women's magazines was a career woman – and she was shown in the act of renouncing her career and discovering that what she really wanted to be was a housewife. In 1958, and again in 1959, I went through issue after issue of the three major women's magazines (the fourth, *Woman's Home Companion*, had died) without finding a single heroine who had a career, a commitment to any work, art, profession, or mission in the world, other than 'Occupation: housewife'. Only one in a hundred heroines had a job; even the young unmarried heroines no longer worked except at snaring a husband.[2]

These new happy housewife heroines seem to get younger all the time – in looks, and a childlike kind of dependence. The only active growing figure in their world is the child. The housewife heroines are for ever young, because their own image *ends* in childbirth. Like Peter Pan, they must remain young, while their children grow up with the world. They must keep on having babies, because the feminine mystique says there is no other way for a woman to be a heroine. Here is a typical specimen from a story called 'The Sandwich Maker' (*Ladies' Home Journal*, April 1959). She took home economics in college, learned how to cook, never held a job, and still plays the child bride, though she now has three children of her own. Her problem is money. 'Oh, nothing boring, like taxes or reciprocal trade agreements, or foreign-aid programmes. I leave all that economic jazz to my con-stitutionally elected representative in Washington, heaven help him.'

The problem is her $42.10 allowance. She hates having to ask her husband for money every time she needs a pair of shoes, but he won't trust her with a charge account. 'Oh, how I yearned for a little money of my own! Not much, really. A few hundred a year would have done it. Just enough to meet a friend for lunch occasionally, to indulge in extravagantly coloured stockings, a few small items, without having to ap-peal to Charley. But, alas, Charley was right. I had never earned a dollar in my life, and had no idea of how money was made. So all I did for a long time was brood, as I continued with my cooking, cleaning, cooking, washing, ironing, cooking.'

At last the solution comes – she will take orders for sandwiches from other men at her husband's plant. She earns $52.50 a week, except that she forgets to count costs, and she doesn't remember what a gross is so she has to hide 8,640 sandwich bags behind the furnace. Charley says she's making the sandwiches too fancy. She explains: 'If it's only ham on rye, then I'm just a sandwich maker, and I'm not interested. But the extras, the special touches – well, they make it sort of creative.' So she chops, wraps, peels, seals, spreads bread, starting at dawn and never finished, for $9.00 net, until she is disgusted by the smell of food, and finally staggers downstairs after a sleepless night to slice a salami for the eight gaping lunch boxes. 'It was too much. Charley came down just then, and after one quick look at me, ran for a glass of water.' She realizes that she is going to have another baby.

'Charley's first coherent words were "I'll cancel your lunch orders. You're a mother. That's your job. You don't have to earn money, too." It was all so beautifully simple! "Yes, boss," I murmured obediently, frankly relieved.' That night he brings her home a chequebook; he will trust her with a joint account. So she decides just to keep quiet about the 8,640 sandwich bags. Anyhow, she'll have used them up, making sandwiches for four children to take to school, by the time the youngest is ready for college.

The road from Sarah and the seaplane to the sandwich maker was travelled in only ten years. In those ten years, the image of American woman seems to have suffered a schizophrenic split. And the split in the image goes much further than the savage obliteration of career from women's dreams.

In an earlier time, the image of woman was also split in two – the good, pure woman on the pedestal, and the whore of the desires of the flesh. The split in the new image opens a different fissure – the feminine woman, whose goodness includes the desires of the flesh, and the career woman, whose evil includes every desire of the separate self. The new feminine morality

story is the exorcising of the forbidden career dream, the heroine's victory over Mephistopheles: the devil, first in the form of a career woman, who threatens to take away the heroine's husband or child, and finally, the devil inside the heroine herself, the dream of independence, the discontent of spirit, and even the feeling of a separate identity that must be exorcised to win or keep the love of husband and child.

With the career woman out of the way, the housewife with interests in the community becomes the devil to be exorcised. Even P.T.A. takes on a suspect connotation, not to mention interest in some international cause (see 'Almost a Love Affair', *McCall's*, November 1955). The housewife who simply has a mind of her own is the next to go. The heroine of 'I Didn't Want to Tell You' (*McCall's*, January 1958) is shown balancing the chequebook by herself and arguing with her husband about a small domestic detail. It develops that she is losing her husband to a 'helpless little widow' whose main appeal is that she can't 'think straight' about an insurance policy or mortgage. The betrayed wife says: 'She must have sex appeal and what weapon has a wife against that?' But her best friend tells her: 'You're making this too simple. You're forgetting how helpless Tania can be, and how grateful to the man who helps her ...'

'I couldn't be a clinging vine if I tried,' the wife says. 'I had a better than average job after I left college and I was always a pretty independent person. I'm not a helpless little woman and I can't pretend to be.' But she learns, that night. She hears a noise that might be a burglar; even though she knows it's only a mouse, she calls helplessly to her husband, and wins him back. As he comforts her pretended panic, she murmurs that, of course, he was right in their argument that morning. 'She lay still in the soft bed, smiling in sweet, secret satisfaction, scarcely touched with guilt.'

The end of the road, in an almost literal sense, is the disappearance of the heroine altogether, as a separate self and the subject of her own story. The end of the road is togetherness, where the woman has no independent self to hide even in

guilt; she exists only for and through her husband and children.

Coined by the publishers of *McCall's* in 1954, the concept 'togetherness' was seized upon avidly as a movement of spiritual significance by advertisers, ministers, newspaper editors. For a time, it was elevated into virtually a national purpose. But very quickly there was sharp social criticism, and bitter jokes about 'togetherness' as a substitute for larger human goals – for men. Women were taken to task for making their husbands do housework, instead of letting them pioneer in the nation and the world. Why, it was asked, should men with the capacities of statesmen, anthropologists, physicists, poets, have to wash dishes and diaper babies on weekday evenings or Saturday mornings when they might use those extra hours to fulfil larger commitments to their society?

Significantly, critics resented only that men were being asked to share 'woman's world'. Few questioned the boundaries of this world for women. No one seemed to remember that women were once thought to have the capacity and vision of statesmen, poets, and physicists. Few saw the big lie of togetherness for women.

Consider the Easter 1954 issue of *McCall's* which announced the new era of togetherness, sounding the requiem for the days when women fought for and won political equality, and the women's magazines 'helped you to carve out large areas of living formerly forbidden to your sex'. The new way of life in which 'men and women in ever-increasing numbers are marrying at an earlier age, having children at an earlier age, rearing larger families and gaining their deepest satisfaction' from their own homes, is one which 'men, women and children are achieving together ... not as women alone, or men alone, isolated from one another, but as a family, sharing a common experience'.

The picture essay detailing that way of life is called 'a man's place is in the home'. It describes, as the new image and ideal, a New Jersey couple with three children in a grey-shingle split-level house. Ed and Carol have 'centred their lives almost completely around their children and their home'. They are

shown shopping at the supermarket, carpentering, dressing the children, making breakfast together. 'Then Ed joins the members of his car pool and heads for the office.'

Ed, the husband, chooses the colour scheme for the house and makes the major decorating decisions. The chores Ed likes are listed: putter around the house, make things, paint, select furniture, rugs, and draperies, dry dishes, read to the children and put them to bed, work in the garden, feed and dress and bathe the children, attend P.T.A. meetings, cook, buy clothes for his wife, buy groceries.

Ed doesn't like these chores: dusting, vacuuming, finishing jobs he's started, hanging draperies, washing pots and pans and dishes, picking up after the children, shovelling snow or mowing the lawn, changing diapers, taking the baby-sitter home, doing the laundry, ironing. Ed, of course, does not do these chores.

For the sake of every member of the family, the family needs a head. This means Father, not Mother. ... Children of both sexes need to learn, recognize and respect the abilities and functions of each sex. ... He is not just a substitute mother, even though he's ready and willing to do his share of bathing, feeding, comforting, playing. He is a link with the outside world he works in. If in that world he is interested, courageous, tolerant, constructive, he will pass on these values to his children.

There were many agonized editorial sessions, in those days at *McCall's*. 'Suddenly, everybody was looking for this spiritual significance in togetherness, expecting us to make some mysterious religious movement out of the life everyone had been leading for the last five years – crawling into the home, turning their backs on the world – but we never could find a way of showing it that wasn't a monstrosity of dullness,' a former *McCall's* editor reminisces.

It always boiled down to, goody, goody, goody, Daddy is out there in the garden barbecuing. We put men in the fashion pictures and the food pictures, and even the perfume pictures. But we were stifled by it editorially.

We had articles by psychiatrists that we couldn't use because they would have blown it wide open: all those couples propping their whole weight on their kids. But what else could you do with togetherness but child care? We were pathetically grateful to find anything else where we could show father photographed with mother. Sometimes, we used to wonder what would happen to women, with men taking over the decorating, child care, cooking, all the things that used to be hers alone. But we couldn't show women getting out of the home and having a career. The irony is, what we meant to do was to stop editing for women as women, and edit for the men and women together. We wanted to edit for people, not women.

But forbidden to join men in the world, can women be people? Forbidden independence, they finally are swallowed in an image of such passive dependence that they want men to make the decisions, even in the home. The frantic illusion that togetherness can impart a spiritual content to the dullness of domestic routine, the need for a religious movement to make up for the lack of identity, betrays the measure of women's loss and the emptiness of the image. Could making men share the housework compensate women for their loss of the world? Could vacuuming the living-room floor together give the housewife some mysterious new purpose in life?

In 1956, at the peak of togetherness, the bored editors of *McCall's* ran a little article called 'The Mother Who Ran Away'. To their amazement, it brought the highest readership of any article they had ever run. 'It was our moment of truth,' said a former editor. 'We suddenly realized that all those women at home with their three and a half children were miserably unhappy.'

But by then the new image of American woman, 'Occupation: housewife', had hardened into a mystique, unquestioned and permitting no questions, shaping the very reality it distorted.

Politics, for women, became Mamie's clothes and the Nixons' home life. Out of conscience, a sense of duty, the *Ladies' Home Journal* might run a series like 'Political Pilgrim's Progress' showing women trying to improve their children's schools and playgrounds. But even approaching politics through mother-love did not really interest women, it was thought in the trade. Everyone knew those readership percentages. An editor of *Redbook* ingeniously tried to bring the bomb down to the feminine level by showing the emotions of a wife whose husband sailed into a contaminated area.

In 1960, a perceptive social psychologist showed me some sad statistics which seemed to prove unmistakably that American women under thirty-five are not interested in politics. 'They may have the vote, but they don't dream about running for office,' he told me. 'If you write a political piece, they won't read it. You have to translate it into issues they can understand – romance, pregnancy, nursing, home furnishings, clothes. Run an article on the economy, or the race question, civil rights, and you'd think that women had never heard of them.'

Maybe they hadn't heard of them. Ideas are not like instincts of the blood that spring into the mind intact. They are communicated by education, by the printed word. The new young housewives, who leave high school or college to marry, do not read books, the psychological surveys say. They only read magazines. Magazines today assume women are not interested in ideas. But going back to the bound volumes in the library, I found in the thirties and forties that the mass-circulation magazines like *Ladies' Home Journal* carried hundreds of articles about the world outside the home. 'The first inside story of American diplomatic relations preceding declared war'; 'Can the U.S. Have Peace After This War?' by Walter Lippman; 'Stalin at Midnight', by Harold Stassen; 'General Stilwell Reports on China'; articles about the last days of Czechoslovakia by Vincent Sheean; the persecution of Jews in Germany; the New Deal; Carl Sandburg's account of Lincoln's assassination; Faulkner's stories of Mississippi, and Margaret Sanger's battle for birth control.

In the 1950s they printed virtually no articles except those that serviced women as housewives, or described women as housewives, or permitted a purely feminine identification like the Duchess of Windsor or Princess Margaret. 'If we get an article about a woman who does anything adventurous, out of the way, something by herself, you know, we figure she must be terribly aggressive, neurotic,' a *Ladies' Home Journal* editor told me. Margaret Sanger would never get in today.

In 1960, I saw statistics that showed that women under thirty-five could not identify with a spirited heroine of a story who worked in an ad agency and persuaded the boy to stay and fight for his principles in the big city instead of running home to the security of a family business. Nor could these new young housewives identify with a young minister, acting on his belief in defiance of convention. But they had no trouble at all identifying with a young man paralysed at eighteen. ('I regained consciousness to discover that I could not move or even speak. I could wiggle only one finger of one hand.' With help from faith and a psychiatrist, 'I am now finding reasons to live as fully as possible.')

Writing for these magazines, I was continually reminded by editors that 'women *have* to identify'. Once I wanted to write an article about an artist. So I wrote about her cooking and marketing and falling in love with her husband, and painting a crib for her baby. I had to leave out the hours she spent painting pictures, her serious work – and the way she felt about it. You could sometimes get away with writing about a woman who was not really a housewife, if you made her *sound* like a housewife, if you left out her commitment to the world outside the home, or the private vision of mind or spirit that she pursued. In February 1949, the *Ladies' Home Journal* ran a feature, 'Poet's Kitchen', showing Edna St Vincent Millay cooking. 'Now I expect to hear no more about housework's being beneath anyone, for if one of the greatest poets of our day, and any day, can find beauty in simple household tasks, this is the end of the old controversy.'

The one 'career woman' who was always welcome in the pages of the women's magazines was the actress. But her image also underwent a remarkable change: from a complex individual of fiery temper, inner depth, and a mysterious blend of spirit and sexuality, to a sexual object, a babyface bride, or a housewife. Think of Greta Garbo, for instance, and Marlene Dietrich, Bette Davis, Rosalind Russell, Katherine Hepburn.

Then think of Marilyn Monroe, Debbie Reynolds, Brigitte Bardot, and 'I love Lucy'.

When you wrote about an actress for a women's magazine, you wrote about her as a housewife. You never showed her doing or enjoying her work as an actress, unless she eventually paid for it by losing her husband or her child, or otherwise admitting failure as a woman. A *Redbook* profile of Judy Holliday (June 1957) described how 'a brilliant woman begins to find in her work the joy she never found in life'. On the screen, we are told, she plays 'with warmth and conviction the part of a mature, intelligent wife and expectant mother, a role unlike anything she had previously attempted'. She must find fulfilment in her career because she is divorced from her husband, has 'strong feelings of inadequacy as a woman. ... It is a frustrating irony of Judy's life, that as an actress she has succeeded almost without trying, although, as a woman, she has failed ...'

Strangely enough, as the feminine mystique spread, denying women careers or any commitment outside the home, the proportion of American women working outside the home increased to one out of three. True, two out of three were still housewives, but why, at the moment when the doors of the world were finally open to all women, should the mystique deny the very dreams that had stirred women for a century?

I found a clue one morning, sitting in the office of a women's magazine editor – a woman who, older than I, remembers the days when the old image was being created, and who had watched it being displaced. The old image of the spirited career girl was largely created by writers and editors who were women, she told me. The newi mage of woman as housewife-mother has been largely created by writers and editors who are men.

'Most of the material used to come from women writers,' she said, almost nostalgically. 'As the young men returned from the war, a great many women writers dropped out of the field. The young women started having a lot of children, and stopped writing. The new writers were all men, back from the war, who had been dreaming about home, and a cosy domestic

47

life.' One by one, the creators of the gay 'career girl' heroines of the thirties began to retire. By the end of the forties, the writers who couldn't get the knack of writing in the new housewife image had left the women's magazine field. The new magazine pros were men, and a few women who could write comfortably according to the housewife formula. Other people began to assemble backstage at the women's magazines: there was a new kind of woman writer who lived in the house-wife image, or pretended to; and there was a new kind of women's editor or publisher, less interested in ideas to reach women's minds and hearts than in selling them the things that interest advertisers – appliances, detergents, lipstick. Today, the deciding voice on most of these magazines is cast by men. Women often carry out the formulas, women edit the house-wife 'service' departments, but the formulas themselves, which have dictated the new housewife image, are the product of men's minds.

Also during the forties and fifties, serious fiction writers of either sex disappeared from the mass-circulation women's magazines. In fact, fiction of any quality was almost completely replaced by a different kind of article, the new 'service' feature. Sometimes these articles lavished the artistry of a poet and the honesty of a crusading reporter on baking chiffon pies, or buying washing machines, or the miracles paint can do for a living-room, or diets, drugs, clothes, and cosmetics to make the body into a vision of physical beauty. Sometimes they dealt with very sophisticated ideas: new developments in psychiatry, child psychology, sex and marriage, medicine. It was assumed that women readers could take these ideas, which appealed to their needs as wives and mothers, but only if they were boiled down to concrete physical details, spelled out in terms of the daily life of an average housewife with concrete dos and don'ts: how to keep your husband happy; how to solve your child's bedwetting; how to keep death out of your medicine cabinet . . .

But here is a curious thing. Within their narrow range, these women's magazine articles, whether straight service to the housewife or a documentary report about the housewife, were almost always superior in quality to women's magazine fiction. They were better written, more honest, more sophisticated. This observation was made over and over again by intelligent readers and puzzled editors, and by writers themselves. 'The serious fiction writers have become too internal. They're inaccessible to our readers, so we're left with the formula writers,' an editor of *Redbook* said. And yet, in the old days, serious writers like Nancy Hale, even William Faulkner, wrote for the women's magazines and were not considered inaccessible. Perhaps the new image of woman did not permit the internal honesty, the depth of perception, and the human truth essential to good fiction.

At the very least, fiction requires a hero or, understandably for women's magazines, a heroine, who is an 'I' in pursuit of some human goal or dream. There is a limit to the number of stories that can be written about a girl in pursuit of a boy, or a housewife in pursuit of a ball of dust under the sofa. Thus the service article takes over, replacing the internal honesty and truth needed in fiction with a richness of honest, objective, concrete, realistic domestic detail – the colour of walls or lipstick, the exact temperature of the oven.

Judging from the women's magazines today, it would seem that the concrete details of women's lives are more interesting than their thoughts, their ideas, their dreams. Or does the richness and realism of the detail, the careful description of small events, mask the lack of dreams, the vacuum of ideas, the terrible boredom that has settled over the American housewife?

I sat in the office of another old-timer, one of the few women editors left in the women's magazine world, now so largely dominated by men. She explained her share in creating the feminine mystique. 'Many of us were psychoanalysed,' she recalled. 'And we began to feel embarrassed about being career women ourselves. There was this terrible fear that we were losing our femininity. We kept looking for ways to help women accept their feminine role.'

If the real women editors were not, somehow, able to give

up their own careers, all the more reason to 'help' other women fulfil themselves as wives and mothers. The few women who still sit in editorial conferences do not bow to the feminine mystique in their own lives. But such is the power of the image they have helped create that many of them feel guilty. And if they have missed out somewhere on love or children, they wonder if their careers were to blame.

Behind her cluttered desk, a *Mademoiselle* editor said uneasily:

The girls we bring in now as college guest editors seem almost to pity us. Because we are career women, I suppose. At a luncheon session with the last bunch, we asked them to go round the table, telling us their own career plans. Not one of the twenty raised her hand. When I remember how I worked to learn this job and loved it – were we all crazy then?

Coupled with the women editors who sold themselves their own bill of goods, a new breed of women writers began to write about themselves as if they were 'just housewives', revelling in a comic world of children's pranks and eccentric washing machines and Parents' Night at the P.T.A. 'After making the bed of a twelve-year-old boy week after week, climbing Mount Everest would seem a laughable anticlimax,' writes Shirley Jackson (*McCall's*, April 1956). When Shirley Jackson, who all her adult life has been an extremely capable writer, pursuing a craft far more demanding than bedmaking, and Jean Kerr, who is a playwright, and Phyllis McGinley, who is a poet, picture themselves as housewives, they may or may not overlook the housekeeper or maid who really makes the beds. But they implicitly deny the vision, and the satisfying hard work involved in their stories, poems, and plays. They deny the lives they lead, not as housewives, but as individuals.

They are good craftsmen, the best of these Housewife Writers. And some of their work is funny. But there is something about Housewife Writers that isn't funny – like Uncle Tom, or Amos and Andy. 'Laugh,' the Housewife Writers tell the real housewife, 'if you are feeling desperate, empty, bored, trapped in the bedmaking, chauffeuring, and dishwashing details. Isn't it funny? We're all in the same trap.' Do real housewives then dissipate in laughter their dreams and their sense of desperation? Do they think their frustrated abilities and their limited lives are a joke? Shirley Jackson makes the beds, loves and laughs at her son – and writes another book. Jean Kerr's plays are produced on Broadway. The joke is not on *them*.

Some of the new Housewife Writers *live* the image; *Redbook* tells us that the author of an article on 'Breast-Feeding', a woman named Betty Ann Countrywoman, 'had planned to be a doctor. But just before her graduation from Radcliffe *cum laude*, she shrank from the thought that such a dedication might shut her off from what she really wanted, which was to marry and have a large family. She enrolled in the Yale University School of Nursing and then became engaged to a young psychiatrist on their first date. Now they have six children, ranging in age from 2 to 13, and Mrs Country-woman is instructor in breast-feeding at the Maternity League of Indianapolis' (*Redbook*, June 1960). She says:

> For the mother, breast-feeding becomes a complement to the act of creation. It gives her a heightened sense of fulfilment and allows her to participate in a relationship as close to perfection as any that a woman can hope to achieve. ... The simple fact of giving birth, however, does not of itself fulfil this need and longing. ... Mother-liness is a way of life. It enables a woman to express her total self with the tender feelings, the protective attitudes, the encompassing love of the motherly woman.

When motherhood, a fulfilment held sacred down the ages, is defined as a total way of life, must women themselves deny the world and the future open to them? Or does the denial of that world *force* them to make motherhood a total way of life? The line between mystique and reality dissolves; real women embody the split in the image. In the spectacular Christmas 1956 issue of *Life*, devoted in full to the 'new' American woman, we see, not as women's magazine villain, but as documentary fact, the typical 'career woman – that fatal error that feminism propagated' – seeking 'help' from a psychia-trist. She is bright, well-educated, ambitious, attractive; she makes about the same money as her husband; but she is pictured here as 'frustrated', so 'masculinized' by her career that her castrated, impotent, passive husband is indifferent to her sexually. He refuses to take responsibility and drowns his destroyed masculinity in alcoholism.

Then there is the discontented suburban wife who raises hell at the P.T.A.; morbidly depressed, she destroys her children and dominates her husband, whom she envies for going out into the business world.

The wife, having worked before marriage, or at least having been educated for some kind of intellectual work, finds herself in the lamentable position of being 'just a housewife'. ... In her disgruntlement she can work as much damage on the lives of her husband and children (and her own life) as if she were a career woman, and indeed, sometimes more.

And finally, in bright and smiling contrast, are the new housewife-mothers, who cherish their 'differentness', their 'unique femininity', the 'receptivity and passivity implicit in their sexual nature'. Devoted to their own beauty and their ability to bear and nurture children, they are 'feminine women, with truly feminine attitudes, admired by men for their miraculous, God-given, sensationally unique ability to wear skirts, with all the implications of that fact'. Rejoicing in 'the reappearance of the old-fashioned three-to-five child family in an astonishing quarter, the upper- and upper-middle class suburbs', *Life* says:

Here, among women who might be best qualified for 'careers', there is an increasing emphasis on the nurturing and homemaking values. One might guess ... that because these women are better informed and more mature than the average, they have been the first to comprehend the penalties of 'feminism' and to react against them. ... Styles in ideas as well as in dress and decoration tend to seep down from such places to the broader population. ... This is the countertrend which may eventually demolish the dominant and disruptive trend and make marriage what it should be: a true partnership in which ... men are men, women are women, and both are quietly, pleasantly, securely confident of which they are – and absolutely delighted to find themselves married to someone of the opposite sex.

Look glowed at about the same time (16 October 1956):

The American woman is winning the battle of the sexes. Like a teenager, she is growing up and confounding her critics. ... No longer a psychological immigrant to man's world, she works, rather casually, as a third of the U.S. labour force, less towards a 'big career' than as a way of filling a hope chest or buying a new home freezer. She gracefully concedes the top jobs to men. This wondrous creature also marries younger than ever, bears more babies and looks and acts far more feminine than the 'emancipated' girl of the 1920s or even 30s. Steelworker's wife and Junior Leaguer alike do their own housework. ... Today, if she makes an old-fashioned choice and lovingly tends a garden and a bumper crop of children, she rates louder hosannas than ever before.

In the new America, fact is more important than fiction. The documentary *Life* and *Look* images of real women who devote their lives to children and home are played back as the ideal, the way women should be: this is powerful stuff, not to be shrugged off like the heroines of women's magazine fiction. When a mystique is strong, it makes its own fiction of fact. It feeds on the very facts which might contradict it, and seeps into every corner of the culture, bemusing even the social critics.

Adlai Stevenson, in a commencement address at Smith College in 1955, reprinted in *Woman's Home Companion* (September 1955), dismissed the desire of educated women to play their own political part in 'the crises of the age'. Modern woman's participation in politics is through her role as wife and mother, said the spokesman of democratic liberalism: 'Women, especially educated women, have a unique opportunity to influence us, man and boy.' The only problem is woman's failure to appreciate that her true part in the political crisis is as wife and mother.

Once immersed in the very pressing and particular problems of domesticity, many women feel frustrated and far apart from the great issues and stirring debate for which their education has given them understanding and relish. Once they wrote poetry. Now it's the laundry list. Once they discussed art and philosophy until late in the night. Now they are so tired they fall asleep as soon as the dishes are finished. There is, often, a sense of contraction, of closing horizons and lost opportunities. They had hoped to play their part in the crises of the age. But what they do is wash the diapers.

The point is that whether we talk of Africa, Islam or Asia, women 'never had it so good' as you. In short, far from the vocation of marriage and motherhood leading you away from the great issues of our day, it brings you back to their very centre and places upon you an infinitely deeper and more intimate responsibility than that borne by the majority of those who hit the headlines and make the news and live in such a turmoil of great issues that they end by being totally unable to distinguish which issues are really great.

Woman's political job is to 'inspire in her home a vision of the meaning of life and freedom ... to help her husband find values that will give purpose to his specialized daily chores ... to teach her children the uniqueness of each individual human being.'

This assignment for you, as wives and mother, you can do in the living-room with a baby in your lap or in the kitchen with a can opener in your hand. If you're clever, maybe you can even practise your saving arts on that unsuspecting man while he's watching television. I think there is much you can do about our crisis in the humble role of housewife. I could wish you no better vocation than that.

Thus the logic of the feminine mystique re-defined the very nature of woman's problem. When a woman was seen as a human being of limitless human potential, equal to man, anything that kept her from realizing her full potential was a problem to be solved: barriers to higher education and political participation, discrimination or prejudice in law or morality. But now that woman is seen only in terms of her sexual role, the barriers to the realization of her full potential, the prejudices which deny her full participation in the world, are no longer problems. The only problems now are those that might disturb her adjustment as a housewife. So career is a problem, education is a problem, political interest, even the very admission of women's intelligence and individuality, is a problem. And finally there is the problem that has no name, a vague undefined wish for 'something more' than washing dishes, ironing, punishing and praising the children. In the women's magazines, it is solved either by dyeing one's hair blonde or by having another baby. 'Remember, when we were all children, how we all planned to "be something"?' says a young housewife in the *Ladies' Home Journal* (February 1960). Boasting that she has worn out six copies of Dr Spock's baby-care book in seven years, she cries, 'I'm lucky! Lucky! I'M SO GLAD TO BE A WOMAN!'

When the young housewife in 'The Man Next to Me' (*Redbook*, November 1948) discovers that her elaborate dinner party didn't help her husband get a raise after all, she is in despair. ('You should say I helped. You should say I'm good for something ... Life was like a puzzle with a piece missing, and the piece was me, and I couldn't figure my place in it at all.') So she dyes her hair blonde, and when her husband reacts satisfactorily in bed to the new 'blonde me', she 'felt a new sense of peace, as if I'd answered the question within myself'.

Over and over again, stories in women's magazines insist that woman can know fulfilment only at the moment of giving birth to a child. They deny the years when she can no longer look forward to giving birth, even if she repeats that act over and over again. In the feminine mystique, there is no other way for a woman to dream of creation or of the future. There is no way she can even dream about herself, except as her children's mother, her husband's wife. And the documentary articles play back new young housewives, grown up under the mystique, who do not have even that 'question within myself'. Says one, described in 'How America Lives' (*Ladies' Home Journal*, June 1959): 'If he doesn't want me to wear a certain colour or a certain kind of dress, then I truly don't want to, either. The thing is, whatever he has wanted is what I also want. ... I don't believe in fifty-fifty marriages.' Giving up college and job to marry at eighteen, with no regrets, she 'never tried to enter into the discussion when the men were talking. She never disputed her husband in anything. ... She spent a great deal of time looking out the window at the snow, the rain, and the gradual emergence of the first crocuses. One great time-passer and consolation was ... embroidery: tiny stitches in gold-metal or silken thread which require infinite concentration.'

There is no problem, in the logic of the feminine mystique, for such a woman who has no wishes of her own, who defines herself only as wife and mother. The problem, if there is one, can only be her children's, or her husband's. It is the husband who complains to the marriage counsellor (*Redbook*, June 1955): 'The way I see it, marriage takes two people, each living his own life and then putting them together. Mary seems to think we both ought to live one life: mine.' Mary insists on going with him to buy shirts and socks, tells the clerk his size and colour. When he comes home at night, she asks with whom he ate lunch, where, what did he talk about? When he protests, she says, 'But darling, I want to share your life, be part of all you do, that's all. ... I want us to be one, the way it says in the marriage service ...' It doesn't seem reasonable to the husband that

... two people can ever be one the way Mary means it. It's just plain ridiculous on the face of it. Besides, I wouldn't like it. I don't want to be so bound to another person that I can't have a thought or an action that's strictly my own.

The answer to 'Pete's problem', says Dr Emily Mudd, the famous marriage counsellor, is to make Mary *feel* she is living his life: invite her to town to lunch with the people in his office once in a while, order his favourite veal dish for her and maybe find her some 'healthy physical activity', like swimming, to drain off her excess energy. It is not Mary's problem that she has no life of her own.

The ultimate, in housewife happiness, is finally achieved by the Texas housewife, described in 'How America Lives' (*Ladies' Home Journal*, October 1960), who

... sits on a pale aqua satin sofa gazing out her picture window at the street. Even at this hour of the morning (it is barely nine o'clock), she is wearing rouge, powder and lipstick, and her cotton dress is immaculately fresh.

She says proudly:

By 8.30 a.m., when my youngest goes to school, my whole house is clean and neat and I am dressed for the day. I am free to play bridge, attend club meetings, or stay home and read, listen to Beethoven, and just plain loaf.

Sometimes, she washes and dries her hair before sitting down at a bridge table at 1.30. Mornings she is having bridge at her house are the busiest, for then she must get out the tables, cards, tallies, prepare fresh coffee and organize lunch. ... During the winter months, she may play as often as four days a week from 9.30 to 3 p.m. ... Janice is careful to be home, before her sons return from school at 4 p.m.

She is not frustrated, this new young housewife. An honour student at high school, married at eighteen, remarried and pregnant at twenty, she has the house she spent seven years dreaming and planning in detail. She is proud of her efficiency as a housewife, getting it all done by 8.30. She does the major housecleaning on Saturday, when her husband fishes and her sons are busy with Boy Scouts. ('There's nothing else to do. No bridge games. It's a long day for me.')

'I love my home,' she says. ... The pale gray paint in her L-shaped living and dining room is five years old, but still in perfect condition. ... The pale peach and yellow and aqua damask upholstery looks spotless after eight years' wear. 'Sometimes, I feel I'm too passive, too content,' remarks Janice, fondly, regarding the wristband of large family diamonds she wears even when the watch itself is being repaired. ... Her favourite possession is her four-poster spool bed with a pink taffeta canopy. 'I feel just like Queen Elizabeth sleeping in that bed,' she says happily. (Her husband sleeps in another room, since he snores.)

'I'm so grateful for my blessings,' she says. 'Wonderful husband, handsome sons with dispositions to match, big comfortable house. ... I'm thankful for my good health and faith in God and such material possessions as two cars, two TVs and two fireplaces.'

Staring uneasily at this image, I wonder if a few problems are not somehow better than this smiling empty passivity. If they are happy, these young women who live the feminine mystique, then is this the end of the road? Or are the seeds of something worse than frustration inherent in this image? Is there a growing divergence between this image of woman and human reality?

Consider, as a symptom, the increasing emphasis on glamour in the women's magazines: the housewife wearing eye make-up as she vacuums the floor – 'The Honour of Being a Woman'. Why does 'Occupation: housewife' require such insistent glamorizing year after year?

The image of woman in another era required increasing prudishness to keep denying sex. This new image seems to require increasing mindlessness, increasing emphasis on things: two cars, two TV's, two fireplaces. Whole pages of women's magazines are filled with gargantuan vegetables: beets, cucumbers, green peppers, potatoes, described like a love affair. The very size of their print is raised until it looks like a first-grade primer. The new *McCall's* frankly assumes women are brainless, fluffy kittens; the *Ladies' Home Journal*, feverishly competing, procures rock-and-roller Pat Boone as a counsellor to teenagers; *Redbook* and the others enlarge their own type size. Does the size of the print mean that the new young women, whom all the magazines are courting, have only first-grade minds? Or does it try to hide the triviality of the content? Within the confines of what is now accepted as woman's world, an editor may no longer be able to think of anything big to do except blow up a baked potato, or describe a kitchen as if it were the Hall of Mirrors; he is, after all, forbidden by the mystique to deal with a big idea. But does it not occur to any of the men who run the women's magazines that their troubles may stem from the smallness of the image with which they are truncating women's minds?

During the years in which that image has narrowed woman's world down to the home, cut her role back to housewife, five of the mass-circulation magazines geared to women have ceased publication; others are on the brink.

The growing boredom of women with the empty, narrow image of the women's magazines may be the most hopeful sign of the image's divorce from reality. But there are more

violent symptoms on the part of women who are committed
to that image. In 1960, the editors of a magazine specifically
geared to the happy young housewife – or rather to the new
young couples (the wives are not considered separate from
their husbands and children) – ran an article asking, 'Why
Young Mothers Feel Trapped' (*Redbook*, September 1960).
As a promotion stunt, they invited young mothers with such a
problem to write in the details, for $500. The editors were
shocked to receive 24,000 replies. Can an image of woman be
cut down to the point where it becomes itself a trap?

I helped create this image. I have watched American women
for fifteen years try to conform to it. But I can no longer deny
my own knowledge of its terrible implications. It is not a
harmless image. There may be no psychological terms for the
harm it is doing. But what happens when women try to live
according to an image that makes them deny their minds?
What happens when women grow up in an image that makes
them deny the reality of the changing world?

The material details of life, the daily burden of cooking and
cleaning, of taking care of the physical needs of husband and
children – these did indeed define a woman's world a century
ago when Americans were pioneers, and the American frontier
lay in conquering the land. But the women who went west
with the wagon trains also shared the pioneering purpose.
Now the American frontiers are of the mind, and of the
spirit. Love and children and home are good, but they are not
the whole world, even if most of the words now written for
women pretend they are.

Down through the ages man has known that he was set
apart from other animals by his mind's power to have an idea,
a vision, and shape the future to it. He shares a need for food
and sex with other animals, but when he loves, he loves as a
man, and when he discovers and creates and shapes a future
different from his past, he is a man, a human being.

This is the real mystery: why did so many American women,
with the ability and education to discover and create, go back
home again, to look for 'something more' in housework and
rearing children? For, paradoxically, in the same fifteen years

in which the spirited New Woman was replaced by the Happy Housewife, the boundaries of the human world have widened, the pace of world change has quickened, and the very nature of human reality has become increasingly free from biological and material necessity.

It is more than a strange paradox that as all professions are finally open to women in America, 'career woman' has become a dirty word; that as higher education becomes available to any woman with the capacity for it, education for women has become so suspect that more and more drop out of high school and college to marry and have babies; that as so many roles in modern society become theirs for the taking, women so insistently confine themselves to one role. Why, with the removal of all the legal, political, economic, and educational barriers that once kept woman from being man's equal, a person in her own right, an individual free to develop her own potential, should she accept this new image which insists she is not a person but a 'woman', by definition barred from the freedom of human existence and a voice in human destiny?

The feminine mystique is so powerful that women grow up no longer knowing that they have the desires and capacities the mystique forbids. But such a mystique does not fasten itself on a whole nation in a few short years, reversing the trends of a century, without cause. What gives the mystique its power? Why did women go home again?

CHAPTER 3

The Crisis in Woman's Identity

I DISCOVERED a strange thing, interviewing women of my
own generation over the past ten years. When we were growing up, many of us could not see ourselves beyond the age of
twenty-one. We had no image of our own future, of ourselves
as women.

I remember the stillness of a spring afternoon on the Smith
campus in 1942, when I came to a frightening dead end in my
own vision of the future. A few days earlier, I had received a
notice that I had won a graduate fellowship. During the con-
gratulations, underneath my excitement, I felt a strange uneasiness; there was a question that I did not want to think
about.

'Is this really what I want to be?' The question shut me off,
cold and alone, from the girls talking and studying on the
sunny hillside behind the college house. I thought I was going
to be a psychologist. But if I wasn't sure, what did I want to
be? I felt the future closing in – and I could not see myself in it
at all. I had come at seventeen from a Midwestern town, an
unsure girl; the wide horizons of the world and the life of
the mind had been opened to me. I had begun to know who I
was and what I wanted to do. I could not go back now. But
the time had come to make my own future, to take the deciding step, and I suddenly did not know what I wanted to
be.

I took the fellowship, but the next spring, under the alien
California sun of another campus, the question came again,
and I could not put it out of my mind. I had won another
fellowship that would have committed me to research for my
doctorate, to a career as professional psychologist. 'Is this
really what I want to be?' The decision now truly terrified

me. I lived in a terror of indecision for days, unable to think of anything else.

The question was not important, I told myself. No question was important to me that year but love. We walked in the Berkeley hills and a boy said: 'Nothing can come of this, between us. I'll never win a fellowship like yours.' Did I think I would be choosing, irrevocably, the cold loneliness of that afternoon if I went on? I gave up the fellowship, in relief. But for years afterwards I could not read a word of the science that once I had thought of as my future life's work; the reminder of its loss was too painful.

I never could explain, hardly knew myself, why I gave up this career. I lived in the present, working on newspapers with no particular plan. I married, had children, lived according to the feminine mystique as a suburban housewife. But still the question haunted me. I could sense no purpose in my life, I could find no peace, until I finally faced it and worked out my own answer.

I discovered, talking to Smith seniors in 1959, that the question is no less terrifying to girls today. Only they answer it now in a way that my generation found, after half a lifetime, not to be an answer at all. These girls, mostly seniors, were sitting in the living-room of the college house, having coffee. It was not too different from such an evening when I was a senior, except that many more of the girls wore rings on their left hands. I asked the ones around me what they planned to be. The engaged ones spoke of weddings, apartments, getting a job as a secretary while husband finished school. The others, after a hostile silence, gave vague answers about this job or that, graduate study, but no one had any real plans. A blonde with a ponytail asked me the next day if I had believed the things they had said. 'None of it was true,' she told me. 'We don't like to be asked what we want to do. None of us know. None of us even like to think about it. The ones who are going to be married right away are the lucky ones. They don't have to think about it.'

But I noticed that night that many of the engaged girls, sitting silently around the fire while I asked the others about jobs, had also seemed angry about something. 'They don't want to think about not going on,' my pony-tailed informant said. 'They know they're not going to use their education. They'll be wives and mothers. You can say you're going to keep on reading and be interested in the community. But that's not the same. You won't really go on. It's a disappointment to know you're going to stop now, and not go on and use it.'

In counterpoint, I heard the words of a woman, fifteen years after she left college, a doctor's wife, mother of three, who said over coffee in her New England kitchen:

The tragedy was, nobody ever looked us in the eye and said you have to decide what you want to do with your life, besides being your husband's wife and children's mother. I never thought it through until I was thirty-six, and my husband was so busy with his practice that he couldn't entertain me every night. The three boys were in school all day. I kept on trying to have babies despite an Rh discrepancy. After two miscarriages, they said I must stop. I thought that my own growth and evolution were over. I always knew as a child that I was going to grow up and go to college, and then get married, and that's as far as a girl has to think. After that, your husband determines and fills your life. It wasn't until I got so lonely as the doctor's wife and kept screaming at the kids because they didn't fill my life that I realized I had to make my own life. I still had to decide what I wanted to be. I hadn't finished evolving at all. But it took me ten years to think it through.

The feminine mystique permits, even encourages, women to ignore the question of their identity. The mystique says they can answer the question 'Who am I?' by saying 'Tom's wife ... Mary's mother'. But I don't think the mystique would have such power over American women if they did not fear to face this terrifying blank which makes them unable to see themselves after twenty-one. The truth is – and how long it has been true, I'm not sure, but it was true in my generation and it is true of girls growing up today – an American woman no longer has a private image to tell her who she is, or can be, or wants to be.

The public image, in the magazines and television commercials, is designed to sell washing machines, cake mixes, deodorants, detergents, rejuvenating face-creams, hair tints. But the power of that image, on which companies spend millions of dollars for television time and ad space, comes from this: American women no longer know who they are. They are sorely in need of a new image to help them find their identity. As the motivational researchers keep telling the advertisers, American women are so unsure of who they should be that they look to this glossy public image to decide every detail of their lives. They look for the image they will no longer take from their mothers.

In my generation, many of us knew that we did not want to be like our mothers, even when we loved them. We could not help but see their disappointment. Did we understand, or only resent, the sadness, the emptiness, that made them hold too fast to us, try to live our lives, run our fathers' lives, spend their days shopping or yearning for things that never seemed to satisfy them, no matter how much money they cost? Strangely, many mothers who loved their daughters – and mine was one – did not want their daughters to grow up like them either. They knew we needed something more.

But even if they urged, insisted, fought to help us educate ourselves, even if they talked with yearning of careers that were not open to them, they could not give us an image of what we could be. They could only tell us that their lives were too empty, tied to home; that children, cooking, clothes, bridge, and charities were not enough. A mother might tell her daughter, spell it out, 'Don't be just a housewife like me.' But that daughter, sensing that her mother was too frustrated to savour the love of her husband and children, might feel: 'I will succeed where my mother failed, I will fulfil myself as a woman,' and never read the lesson of her mother's life.

Recently, interviewing high-school girls who had started out full of promise and talent, but suddenly stopped their education, I began to see new dimensions to the problem of feminine conformity. These girls, it seemed at first, were merely following the typical curve of feminine adjustment. Earlier interested in geology or poetry, they now were interested only in being popular; to get boys to like them, they had concluded, it was better to be like all the other girls. On closer examination, I found that these girls were so terrified of becoming like their mothers that they could not see themselves at all. They were afraid to grow up. They had to copy in identical detail the composite image of the popular girl – denying what was best in themselves out of fear of femininity as they saw it in their mothers. One of these girls, seventeen years old, told me:

I want so badly to feel like the other girls. I never get over this feeling of being a neophyte, not initiated. When I get up and have to cross a room, it's like I'm a beginner, or have some terrible affliction, and I'll never learn. I go to the local hangout after school and sit there for hours talking about clothes and hairdos and the twist, and I'm not that interested, so it's an effort. But I found out I could make them like me – just do what they do, dress like them, talk like them, not do things that are different. I guess I even started to make myself not different inside.

I used to write poetry. The guidance office says I have this creative ability and I should be at the top of the class and have a great future. But things like that aren't what you need to be popular. The important thing for a girl is to be popular.

Now I go out with boy after boy, and it's such an effort because I'm not myself with them. It makes you feel even more alone. And besides, I'm afraid of where it's going to lead. Pretty soon, all my differences will be smoothed out, and I'll be the kind of girl that could be a housewife.

I don't want to think of growing up. If I had children, I'd want them to stay the same age. If I had to watch them grow up, I'd see myself growing older, and I wouldn't want to. My mother says she can't sleep at night, she's sick with worry over what I might do. When I was little, she wouldn't let me cross the street alone, long after the other kids did.

I can't see myself as being married and having children. It's as if I wouldn't have any personality myself. My mother's like a rock that's been smoothed by the waves, like a void. She's put so much into her family that there's nothing left, and she resents us because she doesn't get enough in return. But sometimes it seems like there's nothing there. My mother doesn't serve any purpose except cleaning the house. She isn't happy, and she doesn't make my father happy. If she didn't care about us children at all, it would have the same effect as caring too much. It makes you want to do the opposite. I don't think it's really love. When I was little and I ran in all excited to tell her I'd learned how to stand on my head, she was never listening.

Lately, I look into the mirror, and I'm so afraid I'm going to look like my mother. It frightens me, to catch myself being like her in gestures or speech or anything. I'm not like her in so many ways, but if I'm like her in this one way, perhaps I'll turn out like my mother after all. And that terrifies me.

And so the seventeen-year-old was so afraid of being a woman like her mother that she turned her back on all the things in herself and all the opportunities that would have made her a different woman, to copy from the outside the 'popular' girls. And finally, in panic at losing herself, she turned her back on her own popularity and defied the conventional good behaviour that would have won her a college scholarship. For lack of an image that would help her grow up as a woman true to herself, she retreated into the beatnik vacuum.

Another girl, a college junior from South Carolina told me:

I don't want to be interested in a career I'll have to give up.

My mother wanted to be a newspaper reporter from the time she was twelve, and I've seen her frustration for twenty years. I don't want to be interested in world affairs. I don't want to be interested in anything beside my home and being a wonderful wife and mother. Maybe education is a liability. Even the brightest boys at home want just a sweet, pretty girl. Only sometimes I wonder how it would feel to be able to stretch and stretch and stretch, and learn all you want, and not have to hold yourself back.

Her mother, almost all our mothers, were housewives, though many had started or yearned for or regretted giving up careers. We did not want to be like them, and yet what other model did we have?

The only other kind of women I knew, growing up, were the old-maid high-school teachers; the librarian; the one woman doctor in our town, who cut her hair like a man; and a few of my college professors. None of these women lived in the warm centre of life as I had known it at home. Many had not married or had children. I dreaded being like them, even the ones who taught me truly to respect my own mind and use it, to feel that I had a part in the world. I never knew a woman, when I was growing up, who used her mind, played her own part in the world, and also loved, and had children.

The strange, terrifying jumping-off point that American women reach – at eighteen, twenty-one, twenty-five, forty-one – has been noticed for many years by sociologists, psychologists, analysts, educators. But I think it has not been understood for what it is. It has been called a 'discontinuity' in cultural conditioning; it has been called woman's 'role crisis'. It has been blamed on the education which made American girls grow up feeling free and equal to boys – playing baseball, riding bicycles, conquering geometry and college boards, going away to college, going out in the world to get a job, living alone in an apartment in New York or Chicago or San Francisco, testing and discovering their own powers in the world. All this gave girls the feeling they could be and do whatever they wanted to, with the same freedom as boys, the critics said. It did not prepare them for their role as women. The crisis comes when they are forced to adjust to this role. Today's high rate of emotional distress and breakdown among women in their twenties and thirties is usually attributed to this 'role crisis'. If girls were educated for their role as women, they would not suffer this crisis, the adjusters say.

But I think they have seen only half the truth.

What if the terror a girl faces at twenty-one is the terror of freedom to decide her own life, with no one to order which path she will take? What if those who choose the path of 'feminine adjustment' – evading this terror by marrying at eighteen, losing themselves in having babies and the details of housekeeping – are simply refusing to grow up, to face the question of their own identity?

Mine was the first college generation to run head-on into the new mystique of feminine fulfilment. Before then, while most women did indeed end up as housewives and mothers, the point of education was to discover the life of the mind, to pursue truth, and to take a place in the world. There was a sense, already dulling when I went to college, that we would be New Women. Our world would be much larger than home. Forty per cent of my college class at Smith had career plans. But I remember how, even then, some of the seniors, suffering the pangs of that bleak fear of the future, envied the few who escaped it by getting married right away.

The ones we envied then are suffering that terror now at forty. 'Never have decided what kind of woman I am. Too much personal life in college. Wish I'd studied more science, history, government, gone deeper into philosophy,' one wrote on an alumnae questionnaire, fifteen years later. 'Still trying to find the rock to build on. Wish I had finished college. I got married instead.' 'Wish I'd developed a deeper and more creative life of my own and that I hadn't become engaged and married at nineteen. Having expected the ideal in marriage, including a hundred-per-cent devoted husband, it was a shock to find this isn't the way it is,' wrote a mother of six.

Many of the younger generation of wives who marry early have never suffered this lonely terror. They thought they did not have to choose, to look into the future and plan what they wanted to do with their lives. They slid easily into their sexual role as women before they knew who they were themselves. It is these women who suffer most the problem that has no name.

It is my thesis that the core of the problem for women today is not sexual but a problem of identity – a stunting or evasion of growth that is perpetuated by the feminine mystique. It is my thesis that as the Victorian culture did not permit women to accept or gratify their basic sexual needs, our culture does not permit women to accept or gratify their basic need to grow and fulfil their potentialities as human beings, a need which is not solely defined by their sexual role.

There have been identity crises for man at all the crucial turning points in human history, though those who lived through them did not give them that name. It is only in recent years that the theorists of psychology, sociology, and theology have isolated this problem, and given it a name. But it is considered a man's problem. It is defined, for men, as the crisis of growing up, of choosing his identity, 'the decision as to what one is and is going to be,' in the words of the brilliant psychoanalyst Erik H. Erikson:

I have called the major crisis of adolescence the identity crisis; it occurs in that period of the life cycle when each youth must forge for himself some central perspective and direction, some working unity, out of the effective remnants of his childhood and the hopes of his anticipated adulthood; he must detect some meaningful resemblance between what he has come to see in himself and what his sharpened awareness tells him others judge and expect him to be. ... In some people, in some classes, at some periods in history, the crisis will be minimal; in other people, classes and periods, the crisis will be clearly marked off as a critical period, a kind of 'second birth', apt to be aggravated either by widespread neurotic-isms or by pervasive ideological unrest.[1]

Even today a young man learns soon enough that he must decide who he wants to be. If he does not decide in junior high, in high school, in college, he must somehow come to terms with it by twenty-five or thirty, or he is lost. But this search for identity is seen as a greater problem now because more and more boys cannot find images in our culture – from their fathers or other men – to help them in their search. The old frontiers have been conquered, and the boundaries of the new are not so clearly marked. More and more young men in America today suffer an identity crisis for want of any image of man worth pursuing, for want of a purpose that truly realizes their human abilities.

But why have theorists not recognized this same identity crisis in women? In terms of the old conventions and the new feminine mystique women are not expected to grow up to find out who they are, to choose their human identity. Anatomy is woman's destiny, say the theorists of femininity; the identity of women is determined by her biology.

But is it? For the first time in their history, women are becoming aware of an identity crisis in their own lives, a crisis which began many generations ago, has grown worse with each succeeding generation, and will not end until they, or their daughters, turn an unknown corner and make of themselves and their lives the new image that so many women now so desperately need.

In a sense that goes beyond any one woman's life, I think this is the crisis of women growing up – a turning point from an immaturity that has been called femininity to full human identity. I think women had to suffer this crisis of identity, which began a hundred years ago, and have to suffer it still today, simply to become fully human.

CHAPTER 4

The Passionate Journey

IT was the need for a new identity that started women, a century ago, on that passionate journey, that vilified, misinterpreted journey away from home.

It has been popular in recent years to laugh at feminism as one of history's dirty jokes: to pity, sniggering, those old-fashioned feminists who fought for women's rights to higher education, careers, the vote. They were neurotic victims of penis envy who wanted to be men, it is said now. In battling for women's freedom to participate in the major work and decisions of society as the equals of men, they denied their very nature as women, which fulfils itself only through sexual passivity, acceptance of male domination, and nurturing motherhood.

But if I am not mistaken, it is this first journey which holds the clue to much that has happened to women since. It is one of the strange blind spots of contemporary psychology not to recognize the reality of the passion that moved these women to leave home in search of new identity, or, staying home, to yearn bitterly for something more. Theirs was an act of rebellion, a violent denial of the identity of women as it was then defined. It was the need for a new identity that led those passionate feminists to forge new trails for women. Some of those trails were unexpectedly rough, some were dead ends, and some may have been false, but the need for women to find new trails was real.

Changeless woman, childish woman, a woman's place is in the home, the feminists were told. But man was changing; his place was in the world and his world was widening. Woman was being left behind. Anatomy was her destiny; she might die giving birth to one baby, or live to be thirty-five, giving

71

birth to twelve, while man controlled his destiny with that part of his anatomy which no other animal had: his mind.

Women also had minds. They also had the human need to grow. But the work that fed life and moved it forward was no longer done at home, and women were not trained to understand and work in the world. Confined to the home, a child among her children, passive, no part of her existence under her own control, a woman could only exist by pleasing man. She was wholly dependent on his protection in a world that she had no share in making: man's world. She could never grow up to ask the simple human question, 'Who am I? What do I want?'

Even if man loved her as a child, a doll, a decoration; even if he gave her rubies, satin, velvets; even if she was warm in her house, safe with her children, would she not yearn for something more? She was, at that time, so completely defined as object by man, never herself as subject, 'I', that she was not even expected to enjoy or participate in the act of sex. 'He took his pleasure with her ... he had his way with her,' as the sayings went. Is it so hard to understand that emancipation, the right to full humanity, was important enough to generations of women, still alive or only recently dead, that some fought with their fists, and went to jail and even died for it? And for the right to human growth, some women denied their own sex, the desire to love and be loved by a man, and to bear children.

It is a strangely unquestioned perversion of history that the passion and fire of the feminist movement came from man-hating, embittered, sex-starved spinsters, from castrating, unsexed non-women who burned with such envy for the male organ that they wanted to take it away from all men, or destroy them, demanding rights only because they lacked the power to love as women. Mary Wollstonecraft, Angelina Grimké, Ernestine Rose, Margaret Fuller, Elizabeth Cady Stanton, Julia Ward Howe, Margaret Sanger all loved, were loved, and married; many seem to have been as passionate in their relations with lover and husband, in an age when passion in woman was as forbidden as intelligence, as they were in their battle for woman's chance to grow to full human stature. But if they, and those like Susan Anthony, whom fortune or bitter experience turned away from marriage, fought for a chance for woman to fulfil herself, not in relation to man, but as an individual, it was from a need as real and burning as the need for love. ('What woman needs,' said Margaret Fuller, 'is not as a woman to act or rule, but as a nature to grow, as an intellect to discern, as a soul to live freely, and unimpeded to unfold such powers as were given her.')

The feminists had only one model, one image, one vision, of a full and free human being: man. For until very recently, only men (though not all men) had the freedom and the education necessary to realize their full abilities, to pioneer and create and discover, and map new trails for future generations. Only men had the vote: the freedom to shape the major decisions of society. Only men had the freedom to love, and enjoy love, and decide for themselves in the eyes of their God the problems of right and wrong. Did women want these freedoms because they wanted to be men? Or did they want them because they also were human?

That this is what feminism was all about was seen symbolically by Henrik Ibsen. When he said in the play *A Doll's House*, in 1879, that a woman was simply a human being, he struck a new note in literature. Thousands of women in middle-class Europe and America, in that Victorian time, saw themselves in Nora. And in 1960, almost a century later, millions of American housewives, who watched the play on television, also saw themselves as they heard Nora say:

You have always been so kind to me. But our home has been nothing but a playroom. I have been your doll wife, just as at home I was Papa's doll child; and here the children have been my dolls. I thought it great fun when you played with me, just as they thought it fun when I played with them. That is what our marriage has been, Torvald. . . .

How am I fitted to bring up the children? . . . There is another task I must undertake first. I must try and educate myself – you

73

are not the man to help me in that. I must do that for myself. And that is why I am going to leave you now. . . . I must stand quite alone if I am to understand myself and everything about me. It is for that reason that I cannot remain with you any longer. . . .

Her shocked husband reminds Nora that woman's 'most sacred duties' are her duties to her husband and children. 'Before all else, you are a wife and mother,' he says. And Nora answers:

I believe that before all else I am a reasonable human being, just as you are – or, at all events, that I must try and become one. I know quite well, Torvald, that most people would think you right, and that views of that kind are to be found in books; but I can no longer content myself with what most people say or with what is found in books. I must think over things for myself and get to understand them. . . .

Not very many women then, or even now, dared to leave the only security they knew – dared to turn their backs on their homes and husbands to begin Nora's search. But a great many, then as now, must have found their existence as house-wives so empty that they could no longer savour the love of husband and children.

Some of them – and even a few men who realized that half the human race was denied the right to become fully human – set out to change the conditions that held women in bondage. Those conditions were summed up by the first Woman's Rights Convention in Seneca Falls, New York, in 1848, as woman's grievances against man:

He has compelled her to submit to laws in the formation of which she has no voice. . . . He has made her, if married, in the eyes of the law, civilly dead. He has taken from her all right to property, even to the wages she earns. . . . In the covenant of marriage, she is compelled to promise obedience to her husband, he becoming to all intents and purposes her master – the law giving him power to deprive her of her liberty, and to administer chastisement. . . . He closes against her all the avenues of wealth and distinction which he considers most honourable to himself. As a teacher of theology, medicine or law, she is not known. He has denied her the facilities for obtaining a thorough education, all colleges being closed

74

against her. ... He has created a false public sentiment by giving to the world a different code of morals for men and women by which moral delinquencies which exclude women from society are not only tolerated, but deemed of little account to man. He has usurped the prerogative of Jehovah himself, claiming it as his right to assign for her a sphere of action, when that belongs to her conscience and to her God. He has endeavoured in every way that he could to destroy her confidence in her own powers, to lessen her self-respect, and to make her willing to lead a dependent and abject life.

It is hardly a coincidence that the struggle to free woman began in America on the heels of the Revolutionary War, and grew strong with the movement to free the slaves.[1] Thomas Paine, the spokesman for the Revolution, was among the first to condemn in 1775 the position of women 'even in countries where they may be esteemed the most happy, constrained in their desires in the disposal of their goods, robbed of freedom and will by the laws, the slaves of opinion ...' During the Revolution, some ten years before Mary Wollstonecraft spearheaded the feminist movement in England, an American woman, Judith Sargent Murray, said woman needed knowledge to envision new goals and grow by reaching for them. In 1837, the year Mount Holyoke opened its doors to give women their first chance at education equal to men's, American women were also holding their first national anti-slavery convention in New York. The women who formally launched the women's rights movement at Seneca Falls met each other when they were refused seats at an anti-slavery convention in London. Shut off behind a curtain in the gallery, Elizabeth Stanton, on her honeymoon, and Lucretia Mott, demure mother of five, decided that it was not only the slaves who needed to be liberated.

Whenever, wherever in the world there has been an upsurge of human freedom, women have won a share of it for themselves. Sex did not fight the French Revolution, free the slaves in America, overthrow the Russian Tsar, drive the British out of India; but when the idea of human freedom moves the minds of men, it also moves the minds of women. The cadences of the Seneca Falls Declaration came straight from the Declaration of Independence:

> When, in the course of human events, it becomes necessary for one portion of the family of man to assume among the people of the earth a position different from that they have hitherto occupied. ... We hold these truths to be self-evident: that all men and women are created equal.

Feminism was not a dirty joke. The feminist revolution had to be fought because women quite simply were stopped at a stage of evolution far short of their human capacity. 'The domestic function of woman does not exhaust her powers,' the Rev. Theodore Parker preached in Boston in 1853. 'To make one half the human race consume its energies in the functions of housekeeper, wife and mother is a monstrous waste of the most precious material God ever made.' And running like a bright and sometimes dangerous thread through the history of the feminist movement was also the idea that equality for woman was necessary to free both man and woman for true sexual fulfilment.[2] For the degradation of woman also degraded marriage, love, all relations between man and woman. After the sexual revolution, said Robert Dale Owen, 'then will the monopoly of sex perish with other unjust monopolies; and women will not be restricted to one virtue, and one passion, and one occupation.'[3]

The women and men who started that revolution anticipated 'no small amount of misconception, misrepresentation, and ridicule'. And they got it. The first to speak out in public for women's rights in America – Fanny Wright, daughter of a Scotch nobleman, and Ernestine Rose, daughter of a rabbi – were called, respectively, 'red harlot of infidelity' and 'woman a thousand times below a prostitute'. The declaration at Seneca Falls brought such an outcry of 'Revolution', 'Insurrection Among Women', 'The Reign of Petticoats', 'Blasphemy', from newspapers and clergymen that the faint-hearted withdrew their signatures. Lurid reports of 'free love' and 'legalized adultery' competed with fantasies of court sessions, church sermons, and surgical operations interrupted while a lady lawyer or minister or doctor hastily presented her husband with a baby.

At every step of the way, the feminists had to fight the conception that they were violating the God-given nature of woman. Clergymen interrupted women's-rights conventions, waving Bibles and quoting from the Scriptures: 'Saint Paul said: ... and the head of every woman is man'...'Let your women be silent in the churches, for it is not permitted unto them to speak' ... 'And if they will learn anything, let them ask their husbands at home; for it is a shame for women to speak in the church' ... 'But I suffer not a woman to teach, nor to usurp authority over the man, but to be in silence; for Adam was first formed, then Eve' ... 'Saint Peter said: Likewise, ye wives, be in subjection to your own husbands' ...

To give women equal rights would destroy that 'milder, gentler nature, which not only makes them shrink from, but disqualifies them for the turmoil and battle of public life,' a Senator from New Jersey intoned piously in 1866.

They have a higher and a holier mission. It is in retiracy to make the character of coming men. Their mission is at home, by their blandishments, and their love, to assuage the passions of men as they come in from the battle of life, and not themselves by joining in the contest to add fuel to the very flames.

'They do not appear to be satisfied with having unsexed themselves, but they desire to unsex every female in the land,' said a New York assemblyman who opposed one of the first petitions for a married woman's right to property and earnings. Since 'God created man as the representative of the race,' then 'took from his side the material for woman's creation' and returned her to his side in matrimony as 'one flesh, one being', the assembly smugly denied the petition: 'A higher power than that from which emanates legislative enactments has given forth the mandate that man and woman shall not be equal.'[4]

The myth that these women were 'unnatural monsters' was based on the belief that to destroy the God-given subservience of women would destroy the home and make slaves of men.

Such myths arise in every kind of revolution that advances a new portion of the family of man to equality.

The name of Lucy Stone today brings to mind a man-eating fury, wearing pants, brandishing an umbrella. It took a long time for the man who loved her to persuade her to marry him, and though she loved him and kept his love throughout her long life, she never took his name. When she was born, her gentle mother cried: 'Oh, dear! I am sorry it is a girl. A woman's life is so hard.' A few hours before the baby came, this mother, on a farm in western Massachusetts in 1818, milked eight cows because a sudden thunderstorm had called all hands into the field: it was more important to save the hay crop than to safeguard a mother on the verge of childbirth. Though this gentle, tired mother carried the endless work of farmhouse and bore nine children, Lucy Stone grew up with the knowledge that 'There was only one will in our house, and that was my father's.'

She rebelled at being born a girl if that meant being as lowly as the Bible said, as her mother said. She rebelled when she raised her hand at church meeting and, time and again, it was not counted. At a church sewing circle, where she was making a shirt to help a young man through theological seminary, she heard Mary Lyon talk of education for women. She left the shirt unfinished, and at sixteen started teaching school for $1 a week, saving her earnings for nine years, until she had enough to go to college herself. She wanted to train herself 'to plead not only for the slave, but for suffering humanity everywhere. Especially do I mean to labour for the elevation of my own sex.' But at Oberlin, where she was one of the first women to graduate from the 'regular course', she had to practise public speaking secretly in the woods. Even at Oberlin, the girls were forbidden to speak in public.

Washing the men's clothes, caring for their rooms, serving them at table, listening to their orations, but themselves remaining respectfully silent in public assemblages, the Oberlin 'co-eds' were being prepared for intelligent motherhood and a properly subservient wifehood.[5]

In appearance, Lucy Stone was a little woman, with a gentle, silvery voice which could quiet a violent mob. She lectured on abolition Saturdays and Sundays, as an agent for the Anti-Slavery Society, and for women's rights the rest of the week on her own – facing down and winning over men who threatened her with clubs, threw prayer books and eggs at her head, and once in mid-winter shoved a hose through a window and turned icy water on her.

In one town, the usual report was circulated that a big masculine woman, wearing boots, smoking a cigar, swearing like a trooper, had arrived to lecture. The ladies who came to hear this freak expressed their amazement to find Lucy Stone, small and dainty, dressed in a black satin gown with a white lace frill at the neck, 'a prototype of womanly grace ... fresh and fair as the morning'.[6]

Her voice so rankled pro-slavery forces that the *Boston Post* published a rude poem promising 'fame's loud trumpet shall be blown' for the man who 'with a wedding kiss shuts up the mouth of Lucy Stone'. Lucy Stone felt that 'marriage is to a woman a state of slavery'. Even after Henry Blackwell had pursued her from Cincinnati to Massachusetts ('She was born locomotive,' he complained), and vowed to 'repudiate the supremacy of either woman or man in marriage', and wrote her: 'I met you at Niagara and sat at your feet by the whirlpool looking down into the dark waters with a passionate and unshared and unsatisfied yearning in my heart that you will never know, nor understand,' and made a public speech in favour of women's rights; even after she admitted that she loved him, and wrote 'You can scarcely tell me anything I do not know about the emptiness of a single life,' she suffered blinding migraine headaches over the decision to marry him.

At their wedding, the minister Thomas Higginson reported that 'the heroic Lucy cried like any village bride'. The minister also said: 'I never perform the marriage ceremony without a renewed sense of the iniquity of a system by which man and wife are one, and that one is the husband.' And he sent to the newspapers, for other couples to copy, the pact which Lucy

THE FEMININE MYSTIQUE

Stone and Henry Blackwell joined hands to make, before their wedding vows:

> While we acknowledge our mutual affection by publicly assuming the relationship of husband and wife ... we deem it a duty to declare that this act on our part implies no sanction of, nor promise of voluntary obedience to such of the present laws of marriage as refuse to recognize the wife as an independent, rational being, while they confer upon the husband an injurious and unnatural superiority.[7]

Lucy Stone, her friend, the pretty Reverend Antoinette Brown, (who later married Henry's brother), Margaret Fuller, Angelina Grimké, Abbey Kelley Foster – all resisted early marriage, and did not, in fact, marry until in their battle against slavery and for women's rights they had begun to find an identity as women unknown to their mothers. Some, like Susan Anthony and Elizabeth Blackwell, never married; Lucy Stone kept her own name in more than symbolic fear that to become a wife was to die as a person. The concept known as *'femme couverte'* (covered woman), written into the law, suspended the 'very being or legal existence of a woman' upon marriage. 'To a married woman, her new self is her superior, her companion, her master.'

If it is true that the feminists were 'disappointed women', as their enemies said even then, it was because almost all women living under such conditions had reason to be disappointed. In one of the most moving speeches of her life, Lucy Stone said in 1855:

> From the first years to which my memory stretches, I have been a disappointed woman. When, with my brothers, I reached forth after sources of knowledge, I was reproved with 'it isn't fit for you; it doesn't belong to women' ... In education, in marriage, in religion, in everything, disappointment is the lot of woman. It shall be the business of my life to deepen this disappointment in every woman's heart until she bows down to it no longer.[8]

In her own lifetime, Lucy Stone saw the laws of almost every state radically changed in regard to women, high schools opened to them, and two thirds of the colleges in the

United States. Her husband and her daughter, Alice Stone Blackwell, devoted their lives, after her death in 1893, to the unfinished battle for woman's vote. By the end of her passionate journey, she could say she was glad to have been born a woman. She wrote her daughter the day before her seventieth birthday:

I trust my Mother sees and knows how glad I am to have been born, and at a time when there was so much that needed help at which I could lend a hand. Dear Old Mother! She had a hard life, and was sorry she had another girl to share and bear the hard life of a woman. ... But I am wholly glad that I came.[9]

In certain men, at certain times in history, the passion for freedom has been as strong or stronger than the familiar passions of sexual love. That this was so, for many of those women who fought to free women, seems to be a fact, no matter how the strength of that other passion is explained. Despite the frowns and jeers of most of their husbands and fathers, despite the hostility if not outright abuse they got for their 'unwomanly' behaviour, the feminists continued their crusade. They themselves were tortured by soul-searching doubts every step of the way.

The call to that first Woman's Rights Convention came about because an educated woman, who had already participated in shaping society as an abolitionist, came face to face with the realities of a housewife's drudgery and isolation in a small town. Like the college graduate with six children in the suburb of today, Elizabeth Cady Stanton, moved by her husband to the small town of Seneca Falls, was restless in a life of baking, cooking, sewing, washing, and caring for each baby. Her husband, an abolitionist leader, was often away on business. She wrote:

I now understood the practical difficulties most women had to contend with in the isolated household and the impossibility of woman's best development if in contact the chief part of her life with servants and children. ... The general discontent I felt with woman's portion ... and the wearied, anxious look of the majority of women, impressed me with the strong feeling that some active measures should be taken. ... I could not see what to do or where to begin – my only thought was a public meeting for protest and discussion.[10]

She put only one notice in the newspapers, and housewives and daughters who had never known any other kind of life came in wagons from a radius of fifty miles to hear her speak.

However dissimilar their social or psychological roots, all who led the battle for women's rights, early and late, also shared more than common intelligence, fed by more than common education for their time. Otherwise, whatever their emotions, they would not have been able to see through the prejudices which had justified woman's degradation, and to put their dissenting voice into words. Mary Wollstonecraft educated herself and was then educated by that company of English philosophers then preaching the rights of man. Margaret Fuller was taught by her father to read the classics of six languages, and was caught up in the transcendentalist group around Emerson. Elizabeth Cady Stanton's father, a judge, got his daughter the best education then available, and supplemented it by letting her listen to his law cases. Ernestine Rose, the rabbi's daughter who rebelled against her religion's doctrine that decreed woman's inferiority to man, got her education in 'free thinking' from the great Utopian philosopher Robert Owen. She also defied orthodox religious custom to marry a man she loved. She always insisted, in the bitterest days of the fight for women's rights, that woman's enemy was not man. 'We do not fight with man himself, but only with bad principles.'

These women were not man-eaters. Julia Ward Howe, brilliant and beautiful daughter of the New York '400' who studied intensively every field that interested her, wrote the 'Battle Hymn of the Republic' anonymously, because her husband believed her life should be devoted to him and their six children. She took no part in the suffrage movement until 1868, when she met Lucy Stone, who

... had long been the object of one of my imaginary dislikes. As I looked into her sweet, womanly face and heard her earnest voice, I felt that the object of my distaste had been a mere phantom, conjured up by silly and senseless misrepresentations. ... I could only say, 'I am with you.'[11]

The irony of that man-eating myth is that the so-called excesses of the feminists arose from their helplessness. When women are considered to have no rights nor to deserve any, what can they do for themselves? At first, it seemed there was nothing they could do but talk. They held women's rights conventions every year after 1848, in small towns and large, national and state conventions, over and over again – in Ohio, Pennsylvania, Indiana, Massachusetts. They could talk till doomsday about the rights they did not have. But how do women get legislators to let them keep their own earnings, or their own children after divorce, when they do not even have a vote? How can they finance or organize a campaign to get the vote when they have no money of their own, nor even the right to own property?

The very sensitivity to opinion which such complete dependence breeds in women made every step out of their genteel prison a painful one. Even when they tried to change conditions that were within their power to change, they met ridicule. The fantastically uncomfortable dress 'ladies' wore then was a symbol of their bondage: stays so tightly laced they could hardly breathe, half a dozen skirts and petticoats, weighing ten to twelve pounds, so long they swept up refuse from the street. The spectre of the feminists taking the pants off men came partly from the 'Bloomer' dress – a tunic, knee-length skirt, ankle-length pantaloons. Elizabeth Stanton wore it, eagerly at first, to do her housework in comfort, as a young woman today might wear shorts or slacks. But when the feminists wore the Bloomer dress in public, as a symbol of their emancipation, the rude jokes, from newspaper editors, street-corner loafers, and small boys, were unbearable to their feminine sensitivities. 'We put the dress on for greater freedom, but what is physical freedom compared to mental bondage,' said Elizabeth Stanton and discarded her 'Bloomer' dress. Most, like Lucy Stone, stopped wearing it for a feminine reason: it was not very becoming, except to the extremely tiny, pretty Mrs Bloomer herself.

Still, that helpless gentility had to be overcome, in the minds of men, in the minds of other women, in their own minds. When they decided to petition for married women's rights to own property, half the time even the women slammed doors in their faces with the smug remark that they had husbands, they needed no laws to protect them. When Susan Anthony and her women captains collected 6,000 signatures in ten weeks, the New York State Assembly received them with roars of laughter. In mockery, the Assembly recommended that since ladies always get the 'choicest tidbits' at the table, the best seat in the carriage, and their choice of which side of the bed to lie on, 'if there is any inequity or oppression the gentlemen are the sufferers'. However, they would waive 'redress' except where both husband and wife had signed the petition. 'In such case, they would recommend the parties to apply for a law authorizing them to change dresses, that the husband may wear the petticoats and the wife the breeches.'

The wonder is that the feminists were able to win anything at all – that they were not embittered shrews but increasingly zestful women who knew they were making history. There is more spirit than bitterness in Elizabeth Stanton, having babies into her forties, writing Susan Anthony that this one truly will be her last, and the fun is just beginning – 'Courage, Susan, we will not reach our prime until we're fifty.' Painfully insecure and self-conscious about her looks – not because of treatment by men (she had suitors) but because of a beautiful older sister and mother who treated a crossed eye as a tragedy – Susan Anthony, of all the nineteenth-century feminist leaders, was the only one resembling the myth. She felt betrayed when the others started to marry and have babies. But despite the chip on her shoulder, she was no bitter spinster with a cat. Travelling alone from town to town, hammering up her meeting notices, using her abilities to the fullest as organizer and lobbyist and lecturer, she made her own way in a larger and larger world.

In their own lifetime, such women changed the feminine image that had justified woman's degradation. At a meeting while men jeered at trusting the vote to women so helpless that they had to be lifted over mud puddles and handed into carriages, a proud feminist named Sojourner Truth raised her black arm:

> Look at my arm! I have ploughed and planted and gathered into barns ... and ain't I a woman? I could work as much and eat as much as a man – when I could get it – and bear the lash as well ... I have borne thirteen children and seen most of 'em sold into slavery, and when I cried out with my mother's grief, none but Jesus helped me – and ain't I a woman?

That image of empty gentility was also undermined by the growing thousands of women who worked in the red-brick factories: the Lowell mill girls who fought the terrible working conditions which, partly as a result of women's supposed inferiority, were even worse for them than for men. But those women, who after a twelve- or thirteen-hour day in the factory still had household duties, could not take the lead in the passionate journey. Most of the leading feminists were women of the middle class, driven by a complex of motives to educate themselves and smash that empty image.

What drove them on? Lonely and racked with self-doubt, Elizabeth Blackwell, in that unheard-of, monstrous determination to be a woman doctor, ignored sniggers – and tentative passes – to do her anatomical dissections. She battled for the right to witness the dissection of the reproductive organs, but decided against walking in the commencement procession because it would be unladylike. Shunned even by her fellow physicians, she wrote:

> I am woman as well as physician ... I understand now why this life has never been lived before. It is hard, with no support but a high purpose, to live against every species of social opposition ... I should like a little fun now and then. Life is altogether too sober.[12]

In the course of a century of struggle, reality gave the lie to the myth that woman would use her rights for vengeful domination of man. As they won the right to equal education, the right to speak out in public and own property, and the right to work at job or profession and control their own earnings, the feminists felt less reason to be bitter against man.

But there was one more battle to be fought. As M. Carey Thomas, the brilliant first president of Bryn Mawr, said in 1908:

Women are one half the world, but until a century ago ... women lived a twilight life, a half life apart, and looked out and saw men as shadows walking. It was a man's world. The laws were men's laws, the government a man's government, the country a man's country. Now women have won the right to higher education and economic independence. The right to become citizens of the state is the next and inevitable consequence of education and work outside the home. We have gone so far; we must go farther. We cannot go back.[13]

The trouble was, the women's rights movement had become almost too respectable; yet without the right to vote, women could not get any political party to take them seriously. When Elizabeth Stanton's daughter, Harriet Blatch, came home in 1907, the widow of an Englishman, she found the movement in which her mother had raised her in a sterile rut of tea and cookies. She had seen the tactics women used in England to dramatize the issue in a similar stalemate: heckling speakers at public meetings, deliberate provocation of the police, hunger strikes in jail – the kind of dramatic non-violent resistance Gandhi used in India, or that the Freedom Riders now use in the United States when legal tactics leave segregation intact. The American feminists never had to resort to the extremes of their longer-sinned-against English counterparts. But they did dramatize the vote issue until they aroused an opposition far more powerful than the sexual one.

As the battle to free women was fired by the battle to free the slaves in the nineteenth century, it was fired in the twentieth by the battles of social reform, of Jane Addams and Hull House, the rise of the union movement, and the great strikes against intolerable working conditions in the factories. For the Triangle Shirtwaist girls, working for as little as $6 a week, as late as 10 o'clock at night, fined for talking, laughing, or singing, equality was a question of more than education or the vote. They held out on picket lines through bitter cold and hungry months; dozens were clubbed by police and dragged off in Black Marias. The new feminists raised money for the strikers' bail and food, as their mothers had helped the Underground Railroad.

The final battle for the vote was fought in the twentieth century by the growing numbers of college-trained women, led by Carrie Chapman Catt, daughter of the Iowa prairie, educated at Iowa State, a teacher and a newspaperwoman, whose husband, a successful engineer, firmly supported her battles. One group that later called itself the Woman's Party made continual headlines with picket lines around the White House. After the outbreak of the First World War, there was much hysteria about women who chained themselves to the White House fence. Maltreated by police and courts, they went on hunger strikes in jail and were finally martyred by forced feeding. Many of these women were Quakers and pacifists; but the majority of the feminists supported the war even as they continued their campaign for women's rights.

In this final battle, American women over a period of fifty years conducted 56 campaigns of referenda to male voters; 480 campaigns to get legislatures to submit suffrage amendments to voters; 277 campaigns to get state party conventions to include woman's suffrage planks; 30 campaigns to get presidential party conventions to adopt woman's suffrage plans, and 19 campaigns with 19 successive Congresses.[14] Someone had to organize all those parades, speeches, petitions, meetings, lobbying of legislators and Congressmen. The new feminists were no longer a handful of devoted women; thousands, millions of American women with husbands, children, and homes gave as much time as they could spare to the cause. The unpleasant image of the feminists today resembles less the feminists themselves than the image fostered by the interests who so bitterly opposed the vote for women in state after state, lobbying, threatening legislators with business or political ruin, buying votes, even stealing them, until, and even after, 36 states had ratified the amendment.

The ones who fought that battle won more than empty paper rights. They cast off the shadow of contempt and self-contempt that had degraded women for centuries. The joy, the sense of excitement and the personal rewards of that battle are described beautifully by Ida Alexa Ross Wylie, an English feminist:

To my astonishment, I found that women, in spite of knock-knees and the fact that for centuries a respectable woman's leg had not even been mentionable, could at a pinch outrun the average London bobby. Their aim with a little practice became good enough to land ripe vegetables in ministerial eyes, their wits sharp enough to keep Scotland Yard running around in circles and looking very silly. Their capacity for impromptu organization, for secrecy and loyalty, their iconoclastic disregard for class and established order were a revelation to all concerned, but especially themselves. ...

The day that, with a straight left to the jaw, I sent a fair-sized C.I.D. officer into the orchestra pit of the theatre where we were holding one of our belligerent meetings, was the day of my own coming of age. ... Since I was no genius, the episode could not make me one, but it set me free to be whatever I was to the top of my bent. ...

For two years of wild and sometimes dangerous adventure, I worked and fought alongside vigorous, happy, well-adjusted women who laughed instead of tittering, who walked freely instead of teetering, who could outfast Gandhi and come out with a grin and a jest. I slept on hard floors between elderly duchesses, stout cooks, and young shopgirls. We were often tired, hurt and frightened. But we were content as we had never been. We shared a joy of life that we had never known. Most of my fellow-fighters were wives and mothers. And strange things happened to their domestic life. Husbands came home at night with a new eagerness. ... As for children, their attitude changed rapidly from one of affectionate toleration for poor, darling mother to one of wide-eyed wonder. Released from the smother of mother love, for she was too busy to be more than casually concerned with them, they discovered that they liked her. She was a great sport. She had guts. ... Those women who stood outside the fight – I regret to say the vast majority – and who were being more than usually Little Women, hated the fighters with the venomous rage of envy ...[15]

Did women really go home again as a reaction to feminism? The fact is that to women born after 1920, feminism was dead history. It ended as a vital movement in America with the winning of that final right: the vote. In the 1930s and 40s, the sort of woman who fought for woman's rights was still concerned with human rights and freedom – for Negroes, for oppressed workers, for victims of Franco's Spain and Hitler's Germany. But no one was much concerned with rights for women: they had all been won. And yet the man-eating myth prevailed. The feminists had destroyed the old image of woman, but they could not erase the hostility, the prejudice, the discrimination that still remained. Nor could they paint the new image of what women might become when they grew up under conditions that no longer made them inferior to men, dependent, passive, incapable of thought or decision.

Most of the girls who grew up during the years when the feminists were eliminating the causes of that denigrating 'genteel nothingness' got their image of woman from mothers still trapped in it. These mothers were probably the real model for the man-eating myth. The shadow of the contempt and self-contempt which could turn a gentle housewife into a domineering shrew also turned some of their daughters into angry copies of man. The first women in business and the professions were thought to be freaks. Insecure in their new freedom, some perhaps feared to be soft or gentle, love, have children, lest they lose their prized independence, lest they be trapped again as their mothers were. They reinforced the myth.

But the daughters who grew up with the rights the feminists had won could not go back to that old image of genteel nothingness, nor did they have their aunts' or mothers' reasons to be angry copies of man, or fear to love them. They had come unknowing to the turning-point in woman's identity. They had truly outgrown the old image; they were finally free to be what they chose to be. But what choice were they offered? In that corner, the fiery, man-eating feminist, the career woman – loveless, alone. In this corner, the gentle wife and mother – loved and protected by her husband, surrounded by her adoring children. Though many daughters continued on the passionate journey their grandmothers had begun, thousands of others fell out – victims of a mistaken choice.

The real joke that history played on American women is not the one that makes people snigger, with cheap Freudian sophistication, at the dead feminists. It is the joke that Freudian thought played on living women, twisting the memory of the feminists into the man-eating phantom of the feminine mystique, shrivelling the very wish to be more than just a wife and mother. Encouraged by the mystique to evade their identity crisis, permitted to escape identity altogether in the name of sexual fulfilment, women once again are living in the old image of glorified femininity. And it is the same old image, despite its shiny new clothes, that trapped women for centuries and made the feminists rebel.

CHAPTER 5

The Sexual Solipsism of Sigmund Freud

IT would be half-wrong to say it started with Sigmund Freud. It did not really start, in America, until the 1940s. And then again, it was less a start than the prevention of an end. The old prejudices – women are animals, less than human, unable to think like men, born merely to breed and serve men – were not so easily dispelled by the crusading feminists, by science and education, and by the democratic spirit after all. They merely reappeared in the forties, in Freudian disguise. The feminine mystique derived its power from Freudian thought; for it was an idea born of Freud, which led women, and those who studied them, to misinterpret their mothers' frustrations, and their fathers' and brothers' and husbands' resentments and inadequacies, and their own emotions and possible choices in life.

The new mystique is much more difficult for the modern woman to question than the old prejudices, partly because the mystique is broadcast by the very agents of education and social science that are supposed to be the chief enemies of prejudice, partly because the very nature of Freudian thought makes it virtually invulnerable to question. How can an educated American woman, who is not herself an analyst, presume to question a Freudian truth? She knows that Freud's discovery of the unconscious workings of the mind was one of the great breakthroughs in man's pursuit of knowledge. She knows that the science built on that discovery has helped many suffering men and women. She has been taught that only after years of analytic training is one capable of understanding the meaning of Freudian truth. She may even know how the human mind unconsciously resists that truth. How can she presume to tread the sacred ground where only analysts are allowed?

No one can question the basic genius of Freud's discoveries, not the contribution he has made to our culture. Nor do I question the effectiveness of psychoanalysis as it is practised to-day by Freudian or anti-Freudian. But I do question, from my own experience as a woman, and my reporter's knowledge of other women, the application of the Freudian theory of femininity to women today. I question its use, not in therapy, but as it has filtered into the lives of American women through the popular magazines and the opinions and interpretations of so-called experts. I think much of the Freudian theory about women is obsolescent, an obstacle to truth for women in America today, and a major cause of the pervasive problem that has no name.

There are many paradoxes here. Freud's concept of the super-ego helped to free man of the tyranny of the 'shoulds', the tyranny of the past, which prevents the child from becoming an adult. Yet Freudian thought helped create a new super-ego that paralyses educated modern American women – a new tyranny of the 'shoulds', which chains women to an old image, prohibits choice and growth, and denies them individual identity.

Freudian psychology, with its emphasis on freedom from a repressive morality to achieve sexual fulfilment, was part of the ideology of women's emancipation. The lasting American image of the 'emancipated woman' is the flapper of the twenties: burdensome hair shingled off, knees bared, flaunting her new freedom to live in a studio in Greenwich Village or Chicago's near North Side, and drive a car, and drink, and smoke, and enjoy sexual adventures – or talk about them. And yet today, for reasons far removed from the life of Freud himself, Freudian thought has become the ideological bulwark of the sexual counter-revolution in America. Without Freud's definition of the sexual nature of woman to give the conventional image of femininity new authority, I do not think several generations of educated, spirited American women would have been so easily diverted from the dawning realization of who they were and what they could be.

The concept 'penis envy', which Freud coined to describe a phenomenon he observed in women – that is, in the middle-class women who were his patients in Vienna in the Victorian era – was seized in this country in the 1940s as the literal explanation of all that was wrong with American women. Many who preached the doctrine of endangered femininity, reversing the movement of American women towards independence and identity, never knew its Freudian origin. Many who seized on it – not the few psychoanalysts, but the many popularizers, sociologists, educators, ad-agency manipulators, magazine writers, child experts, marriage counsellors, ministers, cocktail-party authorities – could not have known what Freud himself mean by penis envy. One needs only to know what Freud *was* describing, in those Victorian women, to see the fallacy in literally applying his theory of femininity to women today. And one needs only to know *why* he described it in that way to understand that much of it is obsolescent, contradicted by knowledge that is part of every social scientist's thinking today, but was not yet known in Freud's time.

Freud, it is generally agreed, was a most perceptive and accurate observer of important problems of the human personality. But in describing and interpreting those problems, he was a prisoner of his own culture. As he was creating a new framework for our culture, he could not escape the framework of his own. Even his genius could not give him, then, the knowledge of cultural processes which men who are not geniuses grow up with today.

The physicist's relativity, which in recent years has changed our whole approach to scientific knowledge, is harder, and therefore easier to understand, than the social scientist's relativity. It is not a slogan, but a fundamental statement about truth to say that no social scientist can completely free himself from the prison of his own culture; he can only interpret what he observes in the scientific framework of his own time. This is true even of the great innovators. They cannot help but translate their revolutionary observations into language and rubrics that have been determined by the progress of science up until their time. Even those discoveries that create new rubrics are relative to the vantage point of their creator.

Much of what Freud believed to be biological, instinctual, and changeless has been shown by modern research to be a result of specific cultural causes.[1] Much of what Freud described as characteristic of universal human nature was merely characteristic of certain middle-class European men and women at the end of the nineteenth century.

For instance, Freud's theory of the sexual origin of neurosis stems from the fact that many of the patients he first observed suffered from hysteria – and in those cases, he found sexual repression to be the cause. Orthodox Freudians still profess to believe in the sexual origin of all neurosis, and since they look for unconscious sexual memories in their patients, and translate what they hear into sexual symbols, they still manage to find what they are looking for.

But the fact is, cases of hysteria as observed by Freud are much more rare today. In Freud's time, evidently, cultural hypocrisy forced the repression of sex. (Some social theorists even suspect that the very absence of other concerns, in that dying Austrian empire, caused the sexual preoccupation of Freud's patients.[2]) Certainly the fact that his culture denied sex focused Freud's interest on it. He then developed his theory by describing all the stages of growth as sexual, fitting all the phenomena he observed into sexual rubrics.

His attempt to translate all psychological phenomena into sexual terms, and to see all problems of adult personality as the effect of childhood sexual fixations also stemmed, in part, from his own background in medicine, and from the approach to causation implicit in the scientific thought of his time. He had the same diffidence about dealing with psychological phenomena in their own terms which often plagues scientists of human behaviour. Something that could be described in physiological terms, linked to an organ of anatomy, seemed more comfortable, solid, real, scientific, as he moved into the unexplored country of the unconscious mind. As his biographer, Ernest Jones, put it, he made a 'desperate effort to cling to the safety of cerebral anatomy'.[3] Actually, he had the ability to see and describe psychological phenomena so vividly that whether his concepts were given names borrowed from physiology, philosophy, or literature – penis envy, ego, Oedipus complex – they seemed to have a concrete physical reality. Psychological facts, as Jones said, were 'as real and concrete to him as metals are to a metallurgist'.[4] This ability became a source of great confusion as his concepts were passed down by lesser thinkers.

The whole superstructure of Freudian theory rests on the strict determinism that characterized the scientific thinking of the Victorian era. Determinism has been replaced today by a more complex view of cause and effect, in terms of physical processes and phenomena as well as psychological. In the new view, behavioural scientists do not need to borrow language from physiology to explain psychological events, or give them pseudo-reality. Sexual phenomena are no more nor less real than, for instance, the phenomenon of Shakespeare's writing *Hamlet*, which cannot exactly be 'explained' by reducing it to sexual terms. Even Freud himself cannot be explained by his own deterministic, physiological blueprint, though his biographer traces his genius, his 'divine passion for knowledge', to an insatiable sexual curiosity, before the age of three, as to what went on between his mother and father in the bedroom.[5]

Today biologists, social scientists, and increasing numbers of psychoanalysts see the need or impulse to human growth as a primary human need, as basic as sex. The 'oral' and 'anal' stages which Freud described in terms of sexual development – the child gets his sexual pleasure first by mouth, from mother's breast, then from his bowel movements – are now seen as stages of human growth, influenced by cultural circumstances and parental attitudes as well as by sex. When the teeth grow, the mouth can bite as well as suck. Muscle and brain also grow; the child becomes capable of control, mastery, understanding; and his need to grow and learn, at five, twenty-five, or fifty, can be satisfied, denied, repressed, atrophied, evoked, or discouraged by his culture as can his sexual needs.

Child specialists today confirm Freud's observation that

problems between mother and child in the earliest stages are often played out in terms of eating; later in toilet training. And yet in America in recent years there has been a noticeable decline in children's 'eating problems'. Has the child's instinctual development changed? Impossible if, by definition, the oral stage is instinctual. Or has the culture removed eating as a focus for early childhood problems – by the American emphasis on permissiveness in child care, or simply by the fact that in our affluent society food has become less a cause for anxiety in mothers? Because of Freud's own influence on our culture, educated parents are usually careful not to put conflict-producing pressures on toilet training. Such conflicts are more likely to occur today as the child learns to talk or read.[6]

In the 1940s, American social scientists and psychoanalysts had already begun to reinterpret Freudian concepts in the light of their growing cultural awareness. But, curiously, this did not prevent their literal application of Freud's theory of femininity to American women.

The fact is that to Freud, even more than to the magazine editor on Madison Avenue today, women were a strange, inferior, less-than-human species. He saw them as childlike dolls, who existed in terms only of man's love, to love man and serve his needs. It was the same kind of unconscious solipsism that made man for many centuries see the sun only as a bright object that revolved around the earth. Freud grew up with this attitude built in by his culture – not only the culture of Victorian Europe, but that Jewish culture in which men said the daily prayer: 'I thank Thee, Lord, that Thou hast not created me a woman,' and women prayed in submission: 'I thank Thee, Lord, that Thou has created me according to Thy will.'

Freud's mother was the pretty, docile bride of a man twice her age; his father ruled the family with an autocratic authority traditional in Jewish families during those centuries of persecution when the fathers were seldom able to establish authority in the outside world. His mother adored the young Sigmund, her first son, and thought him mystically destined for greatness; she seemed to exist only to gratify his every wish. His own memories of the sexual jealousy he felt for his father, whose wishes she also gratified, were the basis of his theory of the Oedipus complex. With his wife, as with his mother and sisters, his needs, his desires, his wishes, were the sun around which the household revolved. When the noise of his sisters' practising the piano interrupted his studies, 'the piano disappeared,' Anna Freud recalled years later, 'and with it all opportunities for his sisters to become musicians.'

Freud did not see this attitude as a problem, or cause for any problem, in women. It was woman's nature to be ruled by man, and her sickness to envy him. Freud's letters to Martha, his future wife, written during the four years of their engagement (1882–6) have the fond, patronizing sound of Torvald in *A Doll's House*, scolding Nora for her pretences at being human. Freud was beginning to probe the secrets of the human brain in the laboratory at Vienna; Martha was to wait, his 'sweet child', in her mother's custody for four years, until he could come and fetch her. From these letters one can see that to him her identity was defined as child-housewife, even when she was no longer a child and not yet a housewife.

Tables and chairs, beds, mirrors, a clock to remind the happy couple of the passage of time, an armchair for an hour's pleasant daydreaming, carpets to help the housewife keep the floors clean, linen tied with pretty ribbons in the cupboard and dresses of the latest fashion and hats with artificial flowers, pictures on the wall, glasses for everyday and others for wine and festive occasions, plates and dishes ... and the sewing table and the cosy lamp, and everything must be kept in good order or else the housewife who has divided her heart into little bits, one for each piece of furniture, will begin to fret. And this object must bear witness to the serious work that holds the household together, and that object, to a feeling for beauty, to dear friends one likes to remember, to cities one has visited, to hours one wants to recall. ... Are we to hang our hearts on such little things? Yes, and without hesitation. ...

I know, after all, how sweet you are, how you can turn a house into a paradise, how you will share in my interests, how gay yet painstaking you will be. I will let you rule the house as much as you wish, and you will reward me with your sweet love and by rising above all those weaknesses for which women are so often despised. As far as my activities allow, we shall read together what we want to learn, and I will initiate you into things which could not interest a girl as long as she is unfamiliar with her future companion and his occupation ...[7]

On 5 July 1885, he scolds her for continuing to visit Elise, a friend who evidently is less than demure in her regard for men:

What is the good of your feeling that you are now so mature that this relationship can't do you any harm? ... You are far too soft, and this is something I have got to correct, for what one of us does will also be charged to the other's account. You are my precious little woman and even if you make a mistake, you are none the less so. ... But you know all this, my sweet child ...[8]

The Victorian mixture of chivalry and condescension which is found in Freud's scientific theories about women is explicit in a letter he wrote on 5 November 1883 deriding John Stuart Mill's views on 'female emancipation and the woman's question altogether'.

In his whole presentation, it never emerges that women are different beings – we will not say lesser, rather the opposite – from men. He finds the suppression of women an analogy to that of Negroes. Any girl, even without a suffrage or legal competence, whose hand a man kisses and for whose love he is prepared to dare all, could have set him right. It is really a stillborn thought to send women into the struggle for existence exactly as man. If, for instance, I imagined my gentle sweet girl as a competitor, it would only end in my telling her, as I did seventeen months ago, that I am fond of her and that I implore her to withdraw from the strife into the calm, uncompetitive activity of my home. It is possible that changes in upbringing may suppress all a woman's tender attributes, needful of protection and yet so victorious, and that she can then earn a livelihood like men. It is also possible that in such an event one would not be justified in mourning the passing away of the most delightful thing the world can offer us – our ideal of womanhood. I believe that all reforming action in law and education would break down in front of the fact that, long before the age at which a man can earn a position in society, Nature has determined woman's destiny through beauty, charm, and sweetness. Law and custom have much to give women that has been withheld from them, but the position of women will surely be what it is: in youth an adored darling and in mature years a loved wife.[9]

Since all of Freud's theories rested, admittedly, on his own penetrating, unending psychoanalysis of himself, and since sexuality was the focus of all his theories, certain paradoxes about his own sexuality seem pertinent. His writings, as many scholars have noted, give much more attention to infantile sexuality than to its mature expression. His chief biographer, Jones, pointed out that he was, even for those times, exceptionally chaste, puritanical, and moralistic. In his own life, he was relatively uninterested in sex. There were only the adoring mother of his youth, at sixteen a romance that existed purely in fantasy with a girl named Gisele, and his engagement to Martha at twenty-six. The nine months when they both lived in Vienna were not too happy because she was, evidently, uneasy and afraid of him; but separated by a comfortable distance for four years, there was a *grande passion* of 900 love letters. After their marriage, the passion seems to have quickly disappeared, though his biographers note that he was too rigid a moralist to seek sexual satisfaction outside of marriage. The only woman on whom, as an adult, he ever focused the violent passions of love and hate of which he was capable was Martha, during the early years of their engagement. After that, such emotions were focused on men. As Jones, his respectful biographer, said: 'Freud's deviation from the average in this respect, as well as his pronounced mental bisexuality, may well have influenced his theoretical views to some extent.'[10]

Less reverent biographers, and even Jones himself, point out that when one considers Freud's theories in terms of his own life, one is reminded of the puritanical old maid who sees sex everywhere.[11] It is interesting to note that his main complaint about his docile *Hausfrau* was that she was not 'docile' enough – and yet, in interesting ambivalence, that she was not 'at her ease' with him, that she was not able to be a 'comrade-in-arms'.

But, as Freud was painfully to discover, she was not at heart docile and she had a firmness of character that did not readily lend itself to being moulded. Her personality was fully developed and well integrated: it would well deserve the psychoanalyst's highest compliment of being 'normal'.[12]

One gets a glimpse of Freud's 'intention, never to be fulfilled, to mould her to his perfect image', when he wrote her that she must 'become quite young, a sweetheart, only a week old, who will quickly lose every trace of tartness'. But he then reproaches himself:

The loved one is not to become a toy doll, but a good comrade who still has a sensible word left when the strict master has come to the end of his wisdom. And I have been trying to smash her frankness so that she should reserve opinion until she is sure of mine.[13]

As Jones pointed out, Freud was pained when she did not meet his chief test – 'complete identification with himself, his opinions, his feelings, and his intentions. She was not really his unless he could perceive his "stamp" on her.' Freud 'even admitted that it was boring if one could find nothing in the other person to put right'. And he stresses again that Freud's love 'could be set free and displayed only under very favourable conditions. ... Martha was probably afraid of her masterful lover and she would commonly take refuge in silence.'[14]

So, he eventually wrote her, 'I renounce what I demanded. I do not need a comrade-in-arms, such as I hoped to make you into. I am strong enough to fight alone. ... You remain for me a precious sweet, loved one.'[15] Thus evidently ended 'the only time in his life when such emotions [love and hate] centred on a woman'.[16]

The marriage was conventional, but without that passion. As Jones described it:

There can have been few more successful marriages, Martha certainly made an excellent wife and mother. She was an admirable manager – the rare kind of woman who could keep servants indefinitely – but she was never the kind of *Hausfrau* who put things before people. Her husband's comfort and convenience always ranked first. ... It was not to be expected that she should follow the roaming flights of his imagination any more than most of the world could.[17]

She was as devoted to his physical needs as the most doting Jewish mother, organizing each meal on a rigid schedule to fit the convenience of *der Papa*. But she never dreamed of sharing his life as an equal. Nor did Freud consider her a fit guardian for their children, especially of their education, in case of his death. He himself recalls a dream in which he forgets to call for her at the theatre. His associations 'imply that forgetting may be permissible in unimportant matters'.[18]

That limitless subservience of woman taken for granted by Freud's culture, the very lack of opportunity for independent action or personal identity, seems often to have generated that uneasiness and inhibition in the wife, and that irritation in the husband, which characterized Freud's marriage. As Jones summed it up, Freud's attitude towards women 'could probably be called rather old-fashioned, and it would be easy to ascribe this to his social environment and the period in which he grew up rather than to any personal factors'.

Whatever his intellectual opinions may have been in the matter, there are many indications in his writing and correspondence of his emotional attitude. It would certainly be going too far to say that he regarded the male sex as the lords of creation, for there was no tinge of arrogance or superiority in his nature, but it might perhaps be fair to describe his view of the female sex as having as their main function to be ministering angels to the needs and comforts of men. His letters and his love choice make it plain that he had only one type of sexual object in his mind, a gentle feminine one. ...

There is little doubt that Freud found the psychology of women more enigmatic than that of men. He said once to Marie Bonaparte: 'The great question that has never been answered and which I have not yet been able to answer, despite my thirty years of research into the feminine soul, is, what does a woman want?'[19]

Jones also remarked:

Freud was also interested in another type of woman, of a more intellectual and perhaps masculine cast. Such women several times played a part in his life, accessory to his men friends though of a finer calibre, but they had no erotic attraction for him.[20]

These women included his sister-in-law, Minna Bernays, much more intelligent and independent than Martha, and

later women analysts or adherents of the psychoanalytic movement: Marie Bonaparte, Joan Riviere, Lou Andreas-Salomé.
There is no suspicion, however, from either idolators or
hostile biographers that he ever sought sexual satisfaction
outside his marriage. Thus it would seem that sex was completely divorced from his human passions, which he expressed
throughout the productive later years of his long life in his
thought and, to a lesser extent, in friendships with men and
those women he considered his equals, and thus 'masculine'.
He once said: 'I always find it uncanny when I can't understand someone in terms of myself.'[21]

The motive force of woman's personality, in Freud's theory,
was her envy of the penis, which causes her to feel as much
depreciated in her own eyes 'as in the eyes of the boy, and
later perhaps of the man', and leads in normal femininity, to
the wish for the penis of her husband, a wish that is never
really fulfilled until she possesses a penis through giving birth
to a son. In short, she is merely an *homme manqué*, a man with
something missing. As the eminent psychoanalyst Clara
Thompson put it: 'Freud never became free from the Victorian attitude towards women. He accepted as an inevitable
part of the fate of being a woman the limitation of outlook and
life of the Victorian era. . . . The castration complex and penis
envy concepts, two of the most basic ideas in his whole
thinking, are postulated on the assumption that women are
biologically inferior to men.'[22]

What did Freud mean by the concept of penis envy? For
even those who realize that Freud could not escape his culture
do not question that he reported truly what he observed
within it.

In the boy the castration-complex is formed after he has learned
from the sight of the female genitals that the sexual organ which he
prizes so highly is not a necessary part of every woman's body . . .
and thenceforward he comes under the influence of castration-
anxiety, which supplies the strongest motive force for his further
development. The castration-complex in the girl, as well, is started
by the sight of the genital organs of the other sex. She immediately

notices the difference and, it must be admitted, its significance. She feels herself at a great disadvantage, and often declares that she would like to have something like that too and falls a victim to penis envy, which leaves ineradicable traces on her development and character-formation, and even in the most favourable instances, is not overcome without a great expenditure of mental energy. That the girl recognizes the fact that she lacks a penis does not mean that she accepts its absence lightly. On the contrary, she clings for a long time to the desire to get something like it, and believes in that possibility for an extraordinary number of years; and even at a time when her knowledge of reality has long since led her to abandon the fulfilment of this desire as being quite unattainable, analysis proves that it still persists in the unconscious, and retains a considerable charge of energy. The desire after all to obtain the penis for which she so much longs may even contribute to the motives that impel a grown-up woman to come to analysis, and what she quite reasonably expects to get from analysis, such as the capacity to pursue an intellectual career, can often be recognized as a sublimated modification of this repressed wish.[23]

'The discovery of her castration is a turning-point in the life of the girl,' Freud went on to say. 'She is wounded in her self-love by the unfavourable comparison with the boy, who is so much better equipped.' Her mother, and all women, are depreciated in her own eyes, as they are depreciated for the same reason in the eyes of man. This either leads to complete sexual inhibition and neurosis, or to a 'masculinity complex' in which she refuses to give up 'phallic' activity (that is, 'activity such as is usually characteristic of the male') or to 'normal femininity', in which the girl's own impulses to activity are repressed, and she turns to her father in her wish for the penis. 'The feminine situation is, however, only established when the wish for the penis is replaced by the wish for a child – the child taking the place of the penis.' When she played with dolls, this 'was not really an expression of her femininity', since this was activity, not passivity. The 'strongest feminine wish', the desire for a penis, finds real fulfilment only 'if the child is a little boy, who brings the longed-for penis with him. ... The mother can transfer to her son all the ambition she has had to suppress in herself, and she can hope to get from him the satisfaction of all that has remained to her of her masculinity complex.'[24]

But her inherent deficiency, and the resultant penis envy, is so hard to overcome that the woman's super-ego – her conscience, ideals – are never as completely formed as a man's: 'Women have but little sense of justice, and this is no doubt connected with the preponderance of envy in their mental-life.' For the same reason, women's interests in society are weaker than those of men, and 'their capacity for the sublimation of their instincts is less'. Finally, Freud cannot refrain from mentioning 'an impression which one receives over and over again in analytical work' – that not even psychoanalysis can do much for women, because of the inherent deficiency of femininity.

A man of about thirty seems a youthful, and, in a sense, an incompletely developed individual, of whom we expect that he will be able to make good use of the possibilities of development, which analysis lays open to him. But a woman of about the same age, frequently staggers us by her psychological rigidity and unchange-ability.... There are no paths open to her for further development; it is as though the whole process had been gone through and remained unaccessible to influence for the future; as though, in fact, the difficult development which leads to femininity had exhausted all the possibilities of the individual ... even when we are successful in removing the sufferings by solving her neurotic conflict.[25]

What was he really reporting? If one interprets 'penis envy' as other Freudian concepts have been reinterpreted, in the light of our new knowledge that what Freud believed to be biological was often a cultural reaction, one sees simply that Victorian culture gave women many reasons to envy men: the same conditions, in fact, that the feminists fought against. If a woman who was denied the freedom, the status, and the pleasures that men enjoyed wished secretly that she could have these things, in the shorthand of the dream, she might wish herself a man and see herself with that one thing which made men unequivocally different – the penis. She would, of course, have to learn to keep her envy, her anger, hidden: to play the child, the doll, the toy, for her destiny depended on charming man. But underneath, it might still fester, sickening her for love. If she secretly despised herself, and envied man for all she was not, she might go through the motions of love, or even feel a slavish adoration, but would she be capable of free and joyous love? You cannot explain away woman's envy of man, or her contempt for herself, as mere refusal to accept her sexual deformity, unless you think that a woman, by nature, is a being inferior to man. Then, of course, her wish to be equal is neurotic.

It is recognized now that Freud never gave proper attention, even in man, to growth of the ego or self: 'the impulse to master, control or come to self-fulfilling terms with the environment'.[26] Analysts who have freed themselves from Freud's bias and joined other behavioural scientists in studying the human need to grow, are beginning to believe that this is the basic human need, and that interference with it, in any dimension, is the source of psychic trouble. The sexual is only one dimension of the human potential. Freud saw women only in terms of their sexual relationship with men. But in all those women in whom he saw sexual problems, there must have been very severe problems of blocked growth, growth short of full human identity – an immature, incomplete self. Society as it was then, by explicit denial of education and independence, prevented women from realizing their full potential, or from attaining those interests and ideals that might have stimulated their growth. Freud reported these deficiencies, but could only explain them as the toll of 'penis envy'. He saw that women who secretly hungered to be man's equal would not enjoy being his object; and in this, he seemed to be describing a fact. But when he dismissed woman's yearning for equality as 'penis envy', was he not merely stating his own view that women could never really be man's equal, any more than she could wear his penis?

Freud was not concerned with changing society, but in helping man, and woman, adjust to it. Thus he tells of a case of a middle-aged spinster whom he succeeded in freeing from a symptom-complex that prevented her from taking any part in life for fifteen years. Freed of these symptoms she 'plunged into a whirl of activity in order to develop her talents, which were by no means small, and derive a little appreciation, enjoyment, and success from life before it was too late'. But all her attempts ended when she saw that there was no place for her. Since she could no longer relapse into her neurotic symptoms, she began to have accidents; she sprained her ankle, her foot, her hand. When this also was analysed, 'instead of accidents, she contracted on the same occasions slight illnesses, such as catarrh, sore throat, influenzal conditions or rheumatic swellings, until at last, when she made up her mind to resign herself to inactivity, the whole business came to an end'.[27]

Today, when women's equal intelligence has been proved by science, when their equal capacity in every sphere except sheer muscular strength has been demonstrated, a theory explicitly based on woman's natural inferiority would seem as ridiculous as it is hypocritical. But that remains the basis of Freud's theory of women, despite the mask of timeless sexual truth which disguises its elaborations today.

Because Freud's followers could only see woman in the image defined by Freud – inferior, childish, helpless, with no possibility of happiness unless she adjusted to being man's passive object – they wanted to help women get rid of their suppressed envy, their neurotic desire to be equal. They wanted to help women find sexual fulfilment as women, by affirming their natural inferiority.

But society, which defined that inferiority, had changed drastically by the time Freud's followers transposed bodily to twentieth century America the causes as well as the cures of the condition Freud called penis envy. In the light of our new knowledge of cultural processes and of human growth, one would assume that women who grew up with the rights and freedom and education that Victorian women were denied would be different from the women Freud tried to cure. One would assume that they would have much less reason to envy man. But Freud was interpreted to American woman in such curiously literal terms that the concept of penis envy acquired a mystical life of its own, as if it existed quite independent of the women in whom it had been observed. The real injustices life held for women a century ago, compared to men, were dismissed as mere rationalizations of penis envy. And the real opportunities life offered to women now, compared to women then, were forbidden in the name of penis envy.

The literal application of Freudian theory can be seen in these passages from *Modern Woman: The Lost Sex*, by the psychoanalyst Marynia Farnham and the sociologist Ferdinand Lundberg, which was paraphrased *ad nauseam* in the magazines and in marriage courses, until most of its statements became a part of the conventional, accepted truth of our time. Equating feminism with penis envy, they stated categorically:

Feminism, despite the external validity of its political programme and most (not all) of its social programme, was at its core a deep illness. ... The dominant direction of feminine training and development today ... discourages just those traits necessary to the attainment of sexual pleasure: receptivity and passiveness, a willingness to accept dependence without fear or resentment, with a deep inwardness and readiness for the final goal of sexual life – impregnation.

It is not in the capacity of the female organism to attain feelings of well-being by the route of male achievement. ... It was the error of the feminists that they attempted to put women on the essentially male road of exploit, off the female road of nurture. ...

The psychosocial rule that begins to take form, then, is this: the more educated the woman is, the greater chance there is of sexual disorder, more or less severe. The greater the disordered sexuality in a given group of women, the fewer children do they have. ... Fate has granted them the boon importuned by Lady Macbeth; they have been unsexed, not only in the matter of giving birth, but in their feelings of pleasure.[28]

Thus Freud's popularizers embedded his core of unrecognized traditional prejudice against women ever deeper in pseudo-scientific cement. Freud was well aware of his own tendency to build an enormous body of deductions from a single fact – a fertile and creative method, but a two-edged sword, if the significance of that single fact was misinterpreted. Freud wrote Jung in 1909:

Your surmise that after my departure my errors might be

adored as holy relics amused me enormously, but I don't believe it. On the contrary, I think that my followers will hasten to demolish as swiftly as possible everything that is not safe and sound in what I leave behind.[29]

But on the subject of women, Freud's followers not only compounded his errors, but, in their tortuous attempt to fit their observations of real women into his theoretical framework, closed questions that he himself had left open. Thus, for instance, Helene Deutsch, whose definitive two-volume *The Psychology of Woman – A Psychoanalytical Interpretation* appeared in 1944, is not able to trace all women's troubles to penis envy as such. So she does what even Freud found unwise, and equates 'femininity' with 'passivity', and 'masculinity' with 'activity', not only in the sexual sphere, but in all spheres of life.

While fully recognizing that woman's position is subjected to external influence, I venture to say that the fundamental identities 'feminine–passive' and 'masculine–active' assert themselves in all known cultures and races, in various forms and various quantitative proportions.

Very often a woman resists this characteristic given her by nature and in spite of certain advantages she derives from it, displays many modes of behaviour that suggest that she is not entirely content with her own constitution ... the expression of this dissatisfaction, combined with attempts to remedy it, result in woman's 'masculinity complex'.[30]

The 'masculinity complex', as Dr Deutsch refines it, stems directly from the 'female castration complex'. Thus, anatomy is still destiny, woman is still an *homme manqué*. Of course, Dr Deutsch mentions in passing that 'With regard to the girl, however, the environment exerts an inhibiting influence as regards both her aggressions and her activity.' So, penis envy, deficient female anatomy, and society 'all seem to work together to produce femininity'.[31]

'Normal' femininity is achieved, however, only in so far as the woman finally renounces all active goals of her own, all her own 'originality', to identify and fulfil herself through the activities and goals of husband, or son. This process can be sublimated in nonsexual ways – as, for instance, the woman who does the basic research for her male superior's discoveries. The daughter who devotes her life to her father is also making a satisfactory feminine 'sublimation'. Only activity of her own or originality, on a basis of equality, deserves the opprobrium of 'masculinity complex'. This brilliant feminine follower of Freud states categorically that the women who by 1944 in America had achieved eminence by activity of their own in various fields had done so at the expense of their feminine fulfilment. She will mention no names, but they all suffer from the 'masculinity complex'.

How could a girl or woman who was not a psychoanalyst discount such ominous pronouncements, which, in the forties, suddenly began to pour out from all the oracles of sophisticated thought?

It would be ridiculous to suggest that the way Freudian theories were used to brainwash two generations of educated American women was part of a psychoanalytic conspiracy. It was done by well-meaning popularizers and inadvertent distorters; by orthodox converts and bandwagon faddists; by those who suffered and those who cured and those who turned suffering to profit; and, above all, by a congruence of forces and needs peculiar to the American people at that particular time. In fact, the literal acceptance in the American culture of Freud's theory of feminine fulfilment was in tragi-comic contrast to the personal struggle of many American psychoanalysts to reconcile what they saw in their women patients with Freudian theory.

A New York analyst, one of the last trained at Freud's own Psychoanalytic Institute in Vienna, told me:

For twenty years now in analysing American women, I have found myself again and again in the position of having to superimpose Freud's theory of femininity on the psychic life of my patients in a way that I was not willing to do. I have come to the conclusion that penis envy simply does not exist. I have seen women who are completely expressive, sexually, vaginally, and yet who are not mature, integrated, fulfilled. I had a woman patient on the couch for nearly two years before I could face her real problem

– that it was not enough for her to be just a housewife and mother. One day she had a dream that she was teaching a class. I could not dismiss the powerful yearning of this housewife's dream as penis envy. It was the expression of her own need for mature self-fulfilment. I told her: 'I can't analyse this dream away. You must do something about it.'

This same man teaches the young analysts in his postgraduate clinic at a leading Eastern university: 'If the patient doesn't fit the book, throw away the book, and listen to the patient.'

But many analysts threw the book *at* their patients and Freudian theories became accepted fact even among women who never lay down on an analyst's couch, but only knew what they read or heard. To this day, it has not penetrated to the popular culture that the pervasive growing frustration of American women may not be a matter of feminine sexuality. Freud was accepted so quickly and completely at the end of the forties that for over a decade no one even questioned the race of the educated American woman back to the home. When questions finally had to be asked because something was obviously going wrong, they were asked so completely within the Freudian framework that only one answer was possible: education, freedom, rights are wrong for women.

The uncritical acceptance of Freudian doctrine in America was caused, at least in part, by the very relief it provided from uncomfortable questions about objective realities. After the depression, after the war, Freudian psychology became much more than a science of human behaviour, a therapy for the suffering. It became an all-embracing American ideology, a new religion. It provided a convenient escape from the atom bomb, McCarthy, all the disconcerting problems that might spoil the taste of steaks, and cars and colour television and backyard swimming pools. And if the new psychological religion – which made a virtue of sex, removed all sin from private vice, and cast suspicion on high aspirations of the mind and spirit – had a more devastating personal effect on women than men, nobody planned it that way.

But the practice of psychoanalysis as a therapy was not primarily responsible for the feminine mystique. It was the creation of writers and editors in the mass media, ad-agency motivation researchers, and behind them the popularizers and translators of Freudian thought in the colleges and universities. Freudian and pseudo-Freudian theories settled everywhere, like fine volcanic ash. Sociology, anthropology, education, even the study of history and literature became permeated and transfigured by Freudian thought. The most zealous missionaries of the feminine mystique were the functionalists, who seized hasty gulps of pre-digested Freud to start their new departments of 'Marriage and Family-Life Education'. The functional courses in marriage taught American college girls how to 'play the role' of woman – the old role became a new science. Related movements outside the colleges – parent education, child-study groups, prenatal maternity study groups and mental-health education – spread the new psychological super-ego throughout the land, replacing bridge and canasta as an entertainment for educated young wives. And this Freudian super-ego worked for growing numbers of young and impressionable American women as Freud said the super-ego works – to perpetuate the past.

Mankind never lives completely in the present; the ideologies of the super-ego perpetuate the past, the traditions of the race and the people, which yield but slowly to the influence of the present and to new developments, and, so long as they work through the super-ego, play an important part in man's life, quite independently of economic conditions.[32]

The feminine mystique, elevated by Freudian theory into a scientific religion, sounded a single, overprotective, life-restricting, future-denying note for women. Girls who grew up playing baseball, baby-sitting, mastering geometry – almost independent enough, almost resourceful enough, to meet the problems of the fission–fusion era – were told by the most advanced thinkers of our time to go back and live their lives as if they were Noras, restricted to the doll's house by Victorian prejudice. And their own respect and awe for the authority of science – anthropology, sociology, psychology share that authority now – kept them from questioning the feminine mystique.

CHAPTER 6

The Functional Freeze, The Feminine Protest, and Margaret Mead

DURING the last twenty years, under the catalytic impact of Freudian thought, psychoanalysts, anthropologists, sociologists, social psychologists, and other workers in the behavioural sciences have met in professional seminars and foundation-financed conferences in many university centres. Cross-fertilization seemed to make them all bloom, but some strange hybrids were produced. As psychoanalysts began to reinterpret Freudian concepts like 'oral' and 'anal' personality in the light of an awareness, borrowed from anthropology, that cultural processes must have been at work in Freud's Vienna, anthropologists set out for the South Sea islands to chart tribal personality according to literal 'oral' and 'anal' tables. Armed with 'psychological hints for ethnological field workers', the anthropologists often found what they were looking for. Instead of translating, sifting, the cultural bias *out* of Freudian theories, Margaret Mead, and the others who pioneered in the fields of culture and personality, compounded the error by fitting their own anthropological observations into Freudian rubric. But none of this might have had the same freezing effect on women if it had not been for a simultaneous aberration of American social scientists, called functionalism.

Centring primarily on cultural anthropology and sociology and reaching its extremes in the applied field of family-life education, functionalism began as an attempt to make social science more 'scientific' by borrowing from biology the idea of studying institutions as if they were muscles or bones, in terms of their 'structure' and 'function' in the social body. By studying an institution only in terms of its function within its own society, the social scientists intended to avert unscientific value judgements. In practice, functionalism was less a scientific movement than a scientific word-game. 'The function is' was often translated 'the function should be'; the social scientists did not recognize their own prejudices in functional disguise any more than the analysts recognized theirs in Freudian disguise. By giving an absolute meaning and a sanctimonious value to the generic term 'woman's role', functionalism put American women into a kind of deep freeze – like Sleeping Beauties, waiting for a Prince Charming to waken them, while all around the magic circle the world moved on.

The social scientists, male and female, who, in the name of functionalism, drew this torturously tight circle around American women, also seemed to share a certain attitude which I will call 'the feminine protest'. If there is such a thing as a masculine protest – the psychoanalytic concept taken over by the functionalists to describe women who envied men and wanted to be men and therefore denied that they were women and became more manly than any man – its counterpart can be seen today in a feminine protest, made by men and women alike, who deny what women really are and make more of 'being a woman' than it could ever be. The feminine protest, at its most straightforward, is simply a means of protecting women from the dangers inherent in assuming true equality with men. But why should any social scientist, with godlike manipulative superiority, take it upon himself – or herself – to protect women from the pains of growing up?

Protectiveness has often muffled the sound of doors closing against women; it has often cloaked a very real prejudice, even when it is offered in the name of science. If an old-fashioned grandfather frowned at Nora, who is studying calculus because she wants to be a physicist, and muttered, 'woman's place is in the home', Nora would laugh impatiently, 'Grandpa, this is 1963'. But she does not laugh at the urbane pipe-smoking professor of sociology, or the book by Margaret Mead, or the definitive two-volume reference on female sexuality, when they tell her the same thing. The complex, mysterious language of functionalism, Freudian psychology, and cultural anthropology hides from her the fact that they say this with not much more basis than grandpa.

So our Nora would smile at Queen Victoria's letter, written in 1870:

The Queen is most anxious to enlist everyone who can speak or write to join in checking this mad, wicked folly of 'Woman's Rights' with all its attendant horrors, on which her poor feeble sex is bent, forgetting every sense of womanly feeling and propriety. . . . It is a subject which makes the Queen so furious that she cannot contain herself. God created men and women different – then let them remain each in their own position.

But she does not smile when she reads in *Marriage for Moderns*:

The sexes are complementary. It is the works of my watch that move the hands and enable me to tell time. Are the works, therefore, more important than the case? . . . Neither is superior, neither inferior. Each must be judged in terms of its own functions. Together they form a functioning unit. So it is with men and women – together they form a functioning unit. Either alone is in a sense incomplete. They are complementary. . . . When men and women engage in the same occupations or perform common functions, the complementary relationship may break down.[1]

This book was published in 1942. Girls have studied it as a college text for the past twenty years. Under the guise of sociology, or 'Marriage and Family Life', or 'Life Adjustment', they are offered advice of this sort:

The fact remains, however, that we live in a world of reality, a world of the present and the immediate future, on which there rests the heavy hand of the past, a world in which tradition still holds sway and the mores exert a stronger influence than does the theorist . . . a world in which most men and women do marry and in which most married women are homemakers. To talk about what might be done if tradition and the mores were radically changed or what may come about by the year 2000 may be interesting mental gymnastics, but it does not help the young people of today to adjust to the inevitables of life or raise their marriages to a higher plane of satisfaction.[2]

Of course, this 'adjustment to the inevitables of life' denies the speed with which the conditions of life are now changing –

and the fact that many girls who so adjust at twenty will still be alive in the year 2000. This functionalist specifically warns against any and all approaches to the 'differences between men and women' except 'adjustment' to those differences as they now stand. And if, like our Nora, a woman is contemplating a career, he shakes a warning finger.

For the first time in history, American young women in great numbers are being faced with these questions: Shall I voluntarily prepare myself for a lifelong celibate career? Or shall I prepare for a temporary vocation, which I shall give up when I marry and assume the responsibilities of homemaking and motherhood? Or should I attempt to combine homemaking and a career? ... The great majority of married women are homemakers....

If a woman can find adequate self-expression through a career rather than through marriage, well and good. Many young women, however, overlook the fact that there are numerous careers that do not furnish any medium or offer any opportunity for self-expression. Besides they do not realize that only the minority of women, as the minority of men, have anything particularly worth while to express.[3]

And so Nora is left with the cheerful impression that if she chooses a career, she is also choosing celibacy. If she has any illusions about combining marriage and career, the functionalist admonishes her:

How many individuals ... can successfully pursue two careers simultaneously? Not many. The exceptional person can do it, but the ordinary person cannot. The problem of combining marriage and homemaking with another career is especially difficult, since it is likely that the two pursuits will demand qualities of different types. The former, to be successful, requires self-negation; the latter, self-enhancement. The former demands cooperation; the latter competition. ... There is greater opportunity for happiness if husband and wife supplement each other than there is when there is duplication of function ...[4]

This marriage textbook is not the most subtle of its school. It is almost too easy to see that its functional argument is based on no real chain of scientific fact. (It is hardly scientific to say 'this is what is, therefore this is what should be'.) But this is the essence of functionalism as it came to pervade all of

American sociology in this period, whether or not the sociologist called himself a 'functionalist'. In colleges which would never stoop to the 'role-playing lessons' of the so-called functional family course, young women were assigned Talcott Parsons's authoritative 'analysis of sex-roles in the social structure of the United States', which contemplates no alternative for a woman other than the role of 'housewife', patterned with varying emphasis on 'domesticity', 'glamour', and 'good companionship'.

It is perhaps not too much to say that only in very exceptional cases can an adult man be genuinely self-respecting and enjoy a respected status in the eyes of others if he does not 'earn a living' in an approved occupational role. ... In the case of the feminine role the situation is radically different. ... The woman's fundamental status is that of her husband's wife, the mother of his children. ...[5]

Parsons, a highly respected sociologist and the leading functional theoretician, describes with insight and accuracy the sources of strain in this 'segregation of sex roles'. He points out that the 'domestic' aspect of the housewife role 'has declined in importance to the point where it scarcely approaches a full-time occupation for a vigorous person': that the 'glamour pattern' is 'inevitably associated with a rather early age level' and thus 'serious strains result from the problem of adaptation to increasing age', that the 'good companion' pattern – which includes 'humanistic' cultivation of the arts and community welfare – 'suffers from a lack of fully institutionalized status. ... It is only those with the strongest initiative and intelligence who achieve fully satisfying adaptations in this direction.' He states that 'it is quite clear that in the adult feminine role there is quite sufficient strain and insecurity so that widespread manifestations are to be expected in the form of neurotic behaviour'. But Parsons warns:

It is, of course, possible for the adult woman to follow the masculine pattern and seek a career in fields of occupational achievement in direct competition with men of her own class. It is, however, notable that in spite of the very great progress of the emancipation of women from the traditional domestic pattern only a very small fraction have gone very far in this direction. It is also clear that its generalization would only be possible with profound alterations in the structure of the family.

Parsons finds sexual segregation 'functional' in terms of keeping the social structure as it is, which seems to be the functionalist's primary concern.

Absolute equality of opportunity is clearly incompatible with any positive solidarity of the family. ... Where married women are employed outside the home, it is, for the great majority, in occupations which are not in direct competition for status with those of men of their own class. Women's interests, and the standard of judgement applied to them, run, in our society, far more in the direction of personal adornment. ... It is suggested that this difference is functionally related to maintaining family solidarity in our class structure.[6]

Even the eminent woman sociologist Mirra Komarovsky, whose functional analysis of how girls learn to 'play the role of woman' in our society is brilliant indeed, cannot quite escape the rigid mould functionalism imposes: adjustment to the status quo.

A social order can function only because the vast majority have somehow adjusted themselves to their place in society and perform the functions expected of them. ... The differences in the upbringing of the sexes ... are obviously related to their respective roles in adult life. The future homemaker trains for her role within the home, but the boy prepares for his by being given more independence outside the home, by his taking a 'paper route' or a summer job. A provider will profit by independence, dominance, aggressiveness, competitiveness.[7]

The risk of the 'traditional upbringing' of girls, as this sociologist sees it, is its possible 'failure to develop in the girl the independence, inner resources, and that degree of self-assertion which life will demand of her' – in her role as wife. The functional warning follows:

Even if a parent correctly [sic] considers certain conventional attributes of the feminine role to be worthless, he creates risks for the girl in forcing her to stray too far from the accepted mores of her time. ... The steps which parents must take to prepare their daughters to meet economic exigencies and familial responsibilities of modern life – these very steps may awaken aspirations and develop habits which conflict with certain features of their feminine roles, as these are defined today. The very education which is to make the college housewife a cultural leaven of her family and her community may develop in her interests which are frustrated by other phases of housewifery. ... We run the risk of awakening interests and abilities which, again, run counter to the present definition of femininity.[8]

She goes on to cite the recent case of a girl who wanted to be a sociologist. She was engaged to a G.I. who didn't want his wife to work. The girl herself hoped she wouldn't find a good job in sociology.

An unsatisfactory job would, she felt, make it easier for her to comply eventually with her future husband's wishes. The needs of the country for trained workers, the uncertainty of her own future, her current interests notwithstanding, she took a routine job. Only the future will tell whether her decision was prudent. If her fiancé returns from the front, if the marriage takes place, if he is able to provide for the family without her assistance, if her frustrated wishes do not boomerang, then she will not regret her decision. ...

At the present historical moment, the best adjusted girl is probably one who is intelligent enough to do well in school but not so brilliant as to get all As ... capable but not in areas relatively new to women; able to stand on her own two feet and to earn a living, but not so good a living as to compete with men; capable of doing some job well (in case she doesn't marry, or otherwise has to work) but not so identified with a profession as to need it for her happiness.[9]

So, in the name of adjustment to the cultural definition of femininity – in which this brilliant sociologist obviously does not herself believe (that word 'correctly' betrays her) – she ends up virtually endorsing the continued *infantalizing* of American woman, except in so far as it has the unintended consequence of making 'the transition from the role of daughter to that of the spouse more difficult for her than for the son'.

Essentially, it is assumed that to the extent that the woman remains more 'infantile', less able to make her own decisions, more dependent upon one or both parents for initiating and channelling behaviour and attitudes, more closely attached to them so as to find it difficult to part from them or to face their disapproval ... or shows any other indices of lack of emotional emancipation – to that extent she may find it more difficult than the man to conform to the cultural form of primary loyalty to the family she establishes later. It is possible, of course, that the only effect of the greater sheltering is to create in women a generalized dependency which will then be transferred to the husband and which will enable her all the more readily to accept the role of wife in a family which still has many patriarchal features.[10]

She finds evidence in a number of studies that college girls, in fact, are more infantile, dependent, and tied to parents than boys, and do not mature, as boys do, by learning to stand alone. But she can find no evidence – in twenty psychiatric texts – that there are, accordingly, more in-law problems with the wife's parents than the husband's. Evidently, only with such evidence could a functionalist comfortably question the deliberate infantilization of American girls!

Functionalism was an easy out for American sociologists. There can be no doubt that they were describing this 'as they were', but in so doing, they were relieved of the responsibility of building theory from facts, of probing for deeper truth. They were also relieved of the need to formulate questions and answers that would be inevitably controversial (at a time in academic circles, as in America as a whole, when controversy was not welcome). Of course, their reasoning would hold up only as long as the future did not change. As C. P. Snow has pointed out, science and scientists are future-minded. Social scientists under the functional banner were so rigidly present-minded that they denied the future; their theories enforced the prejudices of the past, and actually prevented change.

Sociologists themselves have recently come to the conclusion that functionalism was rather 'embarrassing' because it really said nothing at all. As Kingsley Davis pointed out in his presidential address on 'The Myth of Functional

Analysis as a Special Method in Sociology and Anthropology'
at the American Sociological Association in 1959:

> For more than thirty years now 'functional analysis' has been
> debated among sociologists and anthropologists. ... However
> strategic it may have been in the past, it has now become an im-
> pediment rather than a prop to scientific progress. ... The claim
> that functionalism cannot handle social change because it posits an
> integrated static society is true by definition. ...[11]

Unfortunately, the female objects of functional analysis were
profoundly affected by it. At a time of great change for
women, at a time when education, science, and social science
should have helped women bridge the change, functionalism
transformed 'what is' for women, or 'what was', to 'what
should be'.

The most powerful influence on modern women, in terms
both of functionalism and the feminine protest, was Margaret
Mead. Her work on culture and personality – book after book,
study after study – has had a profound effect on the women in
my generation, the one before it, and the generation now
growing up. She was, and still is, the symbol of the woman
thinker in America.

But her influence, for women, has been a paradox. A mystique takes what it needs from any thinker of the time. The
feminine mystique might have taken from Margaret Mead her
vision of the infinite variety of sexual patterns and the
enormously plasticity of human nature, a vision based on the
differences of sex and temperament she found in three primitive societies: the Arapesh, where both men and women were
'feminine' and 'maternal' in personality and passively sexual,
because both were trained to be cooperative, unaggressive,
responsive to the needs and demands of others; the Mundugumor, where both husband and wife were violent, aggressive, positively sexed, 'masculine'; and the Tchambuli,
where the woman was the dominant, impersonal managing
partner, and the man the less responsible and emotionally
dependent person.

If those temperamental attitudes which we have traditionally regarded as feminine – such as passivity, responsiveness, and a

willingness to cherish children – can so easily be set up as the masculine pattern in one tribe, and in another be outlawed for the majority of women as well as for the majority of men, we no longer have any basis for regarding such aspects of behaviour as sex-linked. ... The material suggests that we may say that many, if not all, of the personality traits which we have called masculine or feminine are as lightly linked to sex, as are the clothing, the manners, and the form of head-dress that a society at a given period assigns to either sex.[12]

From such anthropological observations, she might have passed on to the popular culture a truly revolutionary vision of women finally free to realize their full capabilities in a society which replaced arbitrary sexual definitions with a recognition of genuine individual gifts as they occur in either sex. She had such a vision, more than once:

Where writing is accepted as a profession that may be pursued by either sex with perfect suitability, individuals who have the ability to write need not be debarred from it by their sex, nor need they, if they do write, doubt their essential masculinity or femininity ... and it is here that we can find a ground-plan for building a society that would substitute real differences for arbitrary ones. We must recognize that beneath the superficial classifications of sex and race the same potentialities exist, recurring generation after generation, only to perish because society has no place for them.

Just as society now permits the practice of an art to members of either sex, so it might also permit the development of many contrasting temperamental gifts in each sex. It would abandon its various attempts to make boys fight and to make girls remain passive, or to make all children fight. ... No child would be relentlessly shaped to one pattern of behaviour, but instead there should be many patterns, in a world that had learned to allow to each individual the pattern which was most congenial to his gifts.[13]

But this is not the vision the mystique took from Margaret Mead; nor is it the vision that she continues to offer. Increasingly, in her own pages, her interpretation blurs, is subtly transformed, into a glorification of women in the female role – as defined by their sexual biological function. At times she seems to lose her own anthropological awareness of the malleability of human personality, and to look at anthropological data from the Freudian point of view – sexual biology determines all, anatomy is destiny. At times she seems to be arguing in functional terms, that while woman's potential is as great and various as the unlimited human potential, it is better to preserve the sexual biological limitations established by a culture. At times she says both things in the same page, and even sounds a note of caution, warning of the dangers a woman faces in trying to realize a human potential which her society has defined as masculine.

The difference between the two sexes is one of the important conditions upon which we have built the many varieties of human culture that give human beings dignity and stature. ... Sometimes one quality has been assigned to one sex, sometimes to the other. Now it is boys who are thought of as infinitely vulnerable and in need of special cherishing care, now it is girls. ... Some people think of women as too weak to work out of doors, others regard women as the appropriate bearers of heavy burdens 'because their heads are stronger than men's'. ... Some religions, including our European traditional religions, have assigned women an inferior role in the religious hierarchy, others have built their whole symbolic relationship with the supernatural world upon male imitations of the natural functions of women. ... Whether we deal with small matters or with large, with the frivolities of ornament and cosmetics or the sanctities of man's place in the universe, we find this great variety of ways, often flatly contradictory one to the other, in which the roles of the two sexes have been patterned.

But we always find the patterning. We know of no culture that has said, articulately, that there is no difference between men and women except in the way they contribute to the creation of the next generation; that otherwise in all respects they are simply human beings with varying gifts, no one of which can be exclusively assigned to either sex.

Are we dealing with a must that we dare not flout because it is rooted so deep in our biological mammalian nature that to flout it means individual and social disease? Or with a must that, although not so deeply rooted, still is so very socially convenient and so well tried that it would be uneconomical to flout it – a must which says, for example, that it is easier to get children born and bred if we stylize the behaviour of the sexes very differently, teaching them to walk and dress and act in contrasting ways and to specialize in different kinds of work?[14]

We must also ask: What are the potentialities of sex differences? ... If little boys have to meet and assimilate the early shock of knowing that they can never create a baby with the sureness and incontrovertibility that is a woman's birthright, how does this make them more creatively ambitious, as well as more dependent upon achievement? If little girls have a rhythm of growth which means that their own sex appears to them as initially less sure than their brothers, and so gives them a little false flick towards compensatory achievement that almost always dies down before the certainty of maternity, this probably does mean a limitation on their sense of ambition. But what positive potentialities are there also?[15]

In these passages from *Male and Female*, Margaret Mead betrays her Freudian orientation, even though she cautiously prefaces each statement of apparent scientific fact with the small word 'if'. But it is a very significant 'if'. For when sexual differences become the basis of your approach to culture and personality, and when you assume that sexuality is the driving force of human personality (an assumption that you took from Freud), and when, moreover, as an anthropologist, you know that there are no true-for-every-culture sexual differences except those involved in the act of procreation, you will inevitably give that one biological difference, the difference in reproductive role, increasing importance in the determination of woman's personality.

In discussing men and women, I shall be concerned with the primary differences between them, the difference in their reproductive roles. Out of the bodies fashioned for complementary roles in perpetuating the race, what differences in functioning, in capacities, in sensitivities, in vulnerabilities arise? How is what men can do related to the fact that their reproductive role is over in a single act, what women can do related to the fact that their reproductive role takes nine months of gestation, and until recently many months of breast feeding? What is the contribution of each sex, seen as itself, not as a mere imperfect version of the other?

Living in the modern world, clothed and muffled, forced to convey our sense of our bodies in terms of remote symbols like walking-sticks and umbrellas and handbags, it is easy to lose sight of the immediacy of the human body plan. But when one lives among primitive peoples, where women wear only a pair of little grass aprons, and may discard even these to insult each other or to bathe in a group, and men wear only a very lightly fastened G-string of beaten bark ... and small babies wear nothing at all, the basic communications ... that are conducted between bodies become very real. In our own society, we have now invented a therapeutic method that can laboriously deduce from the recollections of the neurotic, or the untrammelled fantasies of the psychotic, how the human body, its entrances and exits, originally shaped the growing individual's view of the world.[16]

As a matter of fact, the lens of 'anatomy is destiny' seemed to be peculiarly right for viewing the cultures and personalities of Samoa, Manus, Arapesh, Mundugumor, Tchambuli, Iatmul, and Bali; right as perhaps it never was right, in that formulation, for Vienna at the end of the nineteenth century or America in the twentieth.

In the primitive civilizations of the South Sea islands, anatomy was still destiny when Margaret Mead first visited them. Freud's theory that the primitive instincts of the body determined adult personality could find convincing demonstration. The complex goals of more advanced civilizations, in which instinct and environment are increasingly controlled and transformed by the human mind, did not then form the irreversible matrix of every human life. It must have been much easier to see biological differences between men and women as the basic force in life in those unclothed primitive peoples.

Anthropologists today are less inclined to see in primitive civilization a laboratory for the observation of our own civilization, a scale model with all the irrelevancies blotted out; civilization is just not that irrelevant.

Because the human body is the same in primitive South Sea tribes and modern cities, an anthropologist who starts with a psychological theory that reduces human personality and civilization to bodily analogies can end up advising modern women to live through their bodies in the same way as the women of the South Seas. The trouble is that Margaret Mead could not recreate a South Sea world for us to live in: a world where having a baby is the pinnacle of human achievement. (If reproduction were the chief and only fact of human life, would all men today suffer from 'uterus envy'?)

In Bali, little girls between two and three walk much of the time with purposely thrust-out little bellies, and the older women tap them playfully as they pass. 'Pregnant', they tease. So the little girl learns that although the signs of her membership in her own sex are slight, her breasts mere tiny buttons no bigger than her brother's, her genitals a simple inconspicuous fold, some day she will be pregnant, some day she will have a baby, and having a baby is, on the whole, one of the most exciting and conspicuous achievements that can be presented to the eyes of small children in these simple worlds, in some of which the largest buildings are only fifteen feet high, the largest boat some twenty feet long. Furthermore, the little girl learns that she will have a baby not because she is strong or energetic or initiating, not because she works and struggles and tries, and in the end succeeds, but simply because she is a girl and not a boy, and girls turn into women, and in the end – if they protect their femininity – have babies.[17]

To an American woman in the twentieth century competing in a field which demands initiative and energy and work and in which men resent her success, to a woman with less will and ability to compete than Margaret Mead, how tempting is her vision of that South Sea world where a woman succeeds and is envied by man just by being a woman. The yearning is for a return to the Garden of Eden: a garden where women need only forget the 'divine discontent' born of education to return to a world in which male achievement becomes merely a poor substitute for child-bearing.

The recurrent problem of civilization is to define the male role satisfactorily enough – whether it be to build gardens or raise cattle, kill game or kill enemies, build bridges or handle bank shares – so that the male may, in the course of his life, reach a solid sense of irreversible achievement of which his childhood knowledge of the satisfactions of child-bearing has given him a glimpse. In the case of women, it is only necessary that they be permitted by the given social arrangements to fulfil their biological role, to attain this sense of irreversible achievement. If women are to be restless and questing, even in the face of childbearing, they must be made so through education.[18]

What the feminine mystique took from Margaret Mead was not her vision of woman's great untested human potential, but this glorification of the female sexual function that has indeed been tested, in every culture, but seldom, in civilized cultures, valued as highly as the unlimited potential of human creativity, so far mainly displayed by man.

Margaret Mead's eloquent pages made a great many American women envy the serene femininity of a bare-breasted Samoan, and try to make themselves into languorous savages, breasts unfettered by civilization's brassières, and brains undisturbed by pallid man-made knowledge of the goals of human progress.

Woman's biological career-line has a natural climax structure that can be overlaid, muted, muffled and publicly denied, but which remains as an essential element in both sexes' view of themselves. .... The young Balinese girl to whom one says, 'Your name is I Tewa?' and who draws herself up and answers, 'I am Men Bawa' (Mother of Bawa) is speaking absolutely. She is the mother of Bawa; Bawa may die tomorrow, but she remains the mother of Bawa; only if he had died unnamed would her neighbours have called her 'Men Belasin', 'Mother Bereft'. Stage after stage in women's life-histories thus stand, irrevocable, indisputable, accomplished. This gives a natural basis for the little girls' emphasis on being rather than on doing. The little boy learns that he must act like a boy, do things, prove that he is a boy, and prove it over and over again, while the little girl learns that she is a girl, and all she has to do is to refrain from acting like a boy.[19]

Female biology, woman's 'biological career-line', may be changeless – the same in Stone Age women twenty thousand years ago, and Samoan women on remote islands, and American women in the twentieth century – but the nature of the human relationship to biology *has* changed. Our increasing knowledge, the increasing potency of human intelligence, has given us an awareness of purposes and goals beyond the simple biological needs of hunger, thirst, and sex. Even these simple needs, in men or women today, are not the same as they were in the Stone Age or in the South Sea cultures, because they are now part of a more complex pattern of human life.

As an anthropologist, of course, Margaret Mead knew this. And for all her words glorifying the female role, there are other words picturing the wonders of a world in which women would be able to realize their full capabilities. But this picture is almost invariably overlaid with the therapeutic caution, the manipulative superiority, typical of too many American social scientists.

Giving each sex its due, a full recognition of its special vulnerabilities and needs for protection, means looking beyond the superficial resemblances during the period of later childhood when both boys and girls, each having laid many of the problems of sex adjustment aside, seem so eager to learn, and so able to learn the same things. ... But every adjustment that minimizes a difference, a vulnerability, in one sex, a differential strength in the other, diminishes their possibility of complementing each other, and corresponds – symbolically – to sealing off the constructive receptivity of the female and the vigorous outgoing constructive activity of the male, muting them both in the end to a duller version of human life, in which each is denied the fullness of humanity that each might have had.[20]

No human gift is strong enough to flower fully in a person who is threatened with loss of sex membership. ... No matter with what good will we may embark on a programme of actually rearing both men and women to make their full and special contributions in all the complex processes of civilization – medicine and law, education and religion, the arts and sciences – the task will be very difficult. ...

It is of very doubtful value to enlist the gifts of women if bringing women into fields that have been defined as male frightens the men, unsexes the women, muffles and distorts the contribution the women could make, either because their presence excludes men from the occupation or because it changes the quality of the men who enter it. ... It is folly to ignore the signs which warn us that the present terms in which women are lured by their own curiosities and drives developed under the same educational system as boys ... are bad for both men and women.[21]

The role of Margaret Mead as the professional spokesman of femininity would have been less important if American women had taken the example of her own life, instead of listening to what she said in her books. Margaret Mead has lived a life of open challenge, and lived it proudly, if sometimes self-consciously, as a woman. She has moved on the frontiers of thought and added to the superstructure of our knowledge. She has demonstrated feminine capabilities that go far beyond childbirth; she made her way in what was still very much a 'man's world' without denying that she was a woman; in fact, she proclaimed in her work a unique woman's knowledge with which no male anthropologist could compete. After so many centuries of unquestioned masculine authority, how natural for someone to proclaim a feminine authority! But the great human visions of stopping Wars, curing sickness, teaching races to live together, building new and beautiful structures for people to live in, are more than 'other ways of having children'.

It is not easy to combat age-old prejudices. As a social scientist, and as a woman, she struck certain blows against the prejudicial image of woman that may long outlast her own life. In her insistence that women are human beings – unique human beings, not men with something missing – she went a step beyond Freud. And yet, because her observations were based on Freud's bodily analogies, she cut down her own vision of women by glorifying the mysterious miracle of femininity, which a woman realizes simply by being female. In the end she did the very thing that she warned against, re-creating in her work the vicious circle that she broke in her own life:

We may go up the scale from simple physical differences through complementary distinctions that overstress the role of sex difference and extend it inappropriately to other aspects of life, to stereotypes of such complex activities as those involved in the formal use of the intellect, in the arts, in government, and in religion.

In all these complex achievements of civilization, those activities which are mankind's glory, and upon which depends our hope of survival in this world that we have built, there has been this tendency to make artificial definitions that limit an activity to one sex, and by denying the actual potentialities of human beings limit not only both men and women, but also equally the development of the activity itself. . . .

Here is a vicious circle to which it is not possible to assign either a beginning or an end, in which men's overestimation of women's roles, or women's overestimation of men's roles leads one sex or the other to arrogate, to neglect, or even to relinquish part of our so dearly won humanity. Those who would break the circle are themselves a product of it, express some of its defects in their every gesture, may be only strong enough to challenge it, not able actually to break it. Yet once identified, once analysed, it should be possible to create a climate of opinion in which others, a little less the product of the dark past because they have been reared with a light in their hand that can shine backwards as well as forwards, may in turn take the next step.[22]

Margaret Mead was one of the first women to emerge into prominence in American life after rights for women were won. Her mother was a social scientist, her grandmother a teacher; she had private images of women who were fully human, she had education equal to any man's. She made a resounding feminine protest, in her life and in her work. And it was a step forward when she influenced emancipated modern women to choose, with free intelligence, to have babies, bear them with a proud awareness that denied pain, nurse them at the breast, and devote mind and body to their care. It was a step forward in the passionate journey – and one made possible by it – for educated women to say 'yes' to motherhood as a conscious human purpose and not a burden imposed by the flesh. For, of course, the natural-childbirth-breastfeeding movement Margaret Mead helped inspire was not at all a return to primitive earth-mother maternity. It appealed to the independent, educated, spirited American woman – and to her counterparts in western Europe and Russia – because it enabled her to experience childbirth not as a mindless female animal, an object manipulated by the obstetrician, but as a whole person, able to control her own body with her aware mind. Perhaps less important than birth control and the other rights which made woman more equal to man, the work of Margaret Mead helped humanize sex.

It was, perhaps, not her fault that she was taken so literally that procreation became a cult, a career, to the exclusion of every other kind of creative endeavour. She was often quoted out of context by the lesser functionalists and the women's magazines. Those who found in her work confirmation of their own unadmitted prejudices and fears ignored not only the complexity of her total work, but the example of her complex life. With all the difficulties she must have encountered, pioneering as a woman in the realm of abstract thought that was the domain of man she has never retreated from the hard road to self-realization so few women have travelled since.

Margaret Mead and the lesser functionalists knew the pains, the risks, of breaking through age-old social strictures.[23] This awareness was their justification for qualifying their statements of women's potentiality with the advice that women not compete with men, but seek respect for their uniqueness as women.

Ironically, Margaret Mead, in the 1960s, began to voice alarm at the 'return of the cavewoman' – the retreat of American women to narrow domesticity, while the world trembled on the brink of technological holocaust. In an excerpt from a book titled *American Women: The Changing Image*, which appeared in the *Saturday Evening Post* (3 March 1962), she asked:

Why have we returned, despite our advances in technology, to the Stone Age picture? ... Woman has gone back, each to her separate cave, waiting anxiously for her mate and children to return, guarding her mate jealously against other women, almost totally unaware of any life outside her door. ... In this retreat into fecundity, it is not the individual woman who is to blame. It is the climate of opinion that has developed in this country. ...

Apparently she does not acknowledge, or perhaps recognize her own role as a major architect of that 'climate of opinion'.

Even though it would seem that Margaret Mead is now trying to get women out of the home, she still ascribes a sexual specialness to everything a woman does. Trying to seduce them into the modern world of science as 'the teacher-mothers of infant scientists', she is still translating the new possibilities open to women and the new problems facing them as members of the human race into sexual terms. But now 'those roles which have historically belonged to women' are stretched to include political responsibility for nuclear disarmament – 'to cherish not just their own but the children of the enemy'. Since, beginning with the same premise and examining the same body of anthropological evidence, she now arrives at a slightly different sexual role for women, one might seriously question the basis upon which she decides the roles a woman should play – and finds it so easy to change the rules of the game from one decade to the next.

Other social scientists have arrived at the astonishing conclusion that 'being a woman was no more and no less than being human'.[24] But a cultural lag is built into the feminine mystique. By the time a few social scientists were discovering the flaws in 'woman's role', American educators had seized upon it as a magic sesame. Instead of educating women for the greater maturity required to participate in modern society – with all the problems, conflicts, and hard work involved, for educators as well as women – they began educating them to 'play the role of woman'.

CHAPTER 7

The Sex-Directed Educators

IT must have been going on for ten or fifteen years before the educators even suspected it – the old-fashioned educators, that is. The new sex-directed educators were surprised that anyone should be surprised, shocked that anyone should be shocked.

The shock, the mystery, to the naïve who had great hopes for the higher education of women was that more American women than ever before were going to college – but few of them were going on from college to become physicists, philosophers, poets, doctors, lawyers, stateswomen, social pioneers, even college professors. Fewer women in recent college graduating classes have gone on to distinguish themselves in a career or profession than those in the classes graduated before the Second World War, the Great Divide. Fewer and fewer college women were preparing for any career or profession requiring more than the most casual commitment.

Out of loyalty to that more and more futile illusion – the importance of higher education for women – the purist professors kept quiet at first. But the disuse of, the resistance to, higher education by American women finally began to show in the statistics:[1] in the departure of the male presidents, scholars, and educators from women's colleges; in the disillusionment, the mystified frustration or cool cynicism of the ones who stayed; and in the scepticism, finally, in colleges and universities, about the value of a professorial investment in any girl or woman, no matter how apparently able and ambitious. Some women's colleges went out of business; some professors, at co-education universities, said one out of three college places should no longer be wasted on women; the president of Sarah Lawrence, a women's college with high intellectual

132

values, spoke of opening the place to men; the president of
Vassar predicted the end of all the great American women's
colleges which pioneered higher education for women.

I read the first cautious hints of what was happening in the
preliminary report of the psychological–sociological–anthropological Mellon Foundation study of Vassar girls in 1956.

Strong commitment to an activity or career other than that of
housewife is rare. Many students, perhaps a third, are interested in
graduate schooling and in careers, for example, teaching. Few,
however, plan to continue with a career if it should conflict with
family needs. ... As compared to previous periods, however, e.g.,
the 'feminist era', few students are interested in the pursuit of
demanding careers, such as law or medicine, regardless of personal
or social pressures. Similarly, one finds few instances of people like
Edna St Vincent Millay, individuals completely committed to their
art by the time of adolescence and resistant to any attempts to
tamper with it. ...[2]

A later report elaborated:

Vassar students ... are further convinced that the wrongs of
society will gradually right themselves with little or no direct
intervention on the part of women college students. ... Vassar
girls, by and large, do not expect to achieve fame, make an enduring
contribution to society, pioneer any frontiers, or otherwise create
ripples in the placid order of things. ... Not only is spinsterhood
viewed as a personal tragedy but offspring are considered essential
to the full life and the Vassar student believes that she would
willingly adopt children, if it were necessary, to create a family. In
short, her future identity is largely encompassed by the projected
role of wife-mother. ... In describing the qualities to be found in an
ideal husband, the majority of Vassar girls are quite explicit in their
preference for the man who will assume the most important role,
that is, handle his own career and make the majority of decisions
affecting matters outside the home. ... That the female should
attempt, in their thinking, to usurp the prerogatives of the male is a
distasteful notion which would seriously disrupt their own projected role of helpmate and faithful complement to the man of the
house.[3]

I saw the change, a very real one, when I went back to my
own college in 1959, to live for a week with the students in a

campus house at Smith, and then went on to interview girls from colleges and universities all over the United States.

A beloved psychology professor, on the eve of his retirement, complained:

They're bright enough. They have to be, to get here at all now. But they just won't let themselves get interested. They seem to feel it will get in their way when they marry the young executive and raise all those children in the suburbs. I couldn't schedule the final seminar for my senior honour students. Too many kitchen showers interfered. None of them considered the seminar sufficiently important to postpone their kitchen showers.

I picked up a copy of the college newspaper I had once edited. The current student editor described a government class in which fifteen of the twenty girls were knitting 'with the stony-faced concentration of Madame Defarge. The instructor, more in challenge than in seriousness, announced that Western civilization is coming to an end. The students turned to their notebooks and wrote 'Western civ – coming to an end', all without dropping a stitch.'

'What courses are people excited about now?' I asked a blonde senior in cap and gown. Nuclear physics, maybe? Modern art? The civilizations of Africa? Looking at me as if I were some prehistoric dinosaur, she said:

Girls don't get excited about things like that any more. We don't want careers. Our parents expect us to go to college. Everybody goes. You're a social outcast at home if you don't. But a girl who got serious about anything she studied – like wanting to go on and do research – would be peculiar, unfeminine. I guess everybody wants to graduate with a diamond ring on her finger. That's the important thing.

I discovered an unwritten rule barring 'shop talk' about courses, intellectual talk, in some college houses. A cool junior told me:

We never waste time like that. We don't have bull sessions about abstract things. Mostly, we talk about our dates. Anyhow, I spend three days a week off campus. There's a boy I'm interested in. I want to be with him.

A dark-eyed senior in a raincoat admitted, as a kind of secret addiction, that she liked to wander around the stacks in the library and 'pick up books that interest me'.

You learn freshman year to turn up your nose at the library. Lately though – well, it hits you, that you won't be at college next year. Suddenly you wish you'd read more, talked more, taken hard courses you skipped. So you'd know what you're interested in. But I guess those things don't matter when you're married. You're interested in your home and teaching your children how to swim and skate, and at night you talk to your husband. I think we'll be happier than college women used to be.

These girls behaved as if college were an interval to be got through impatiently, efficiently, bored but businesslike, so 'real' life could begin. And real life was when you married and lived in a suburban house with your husband and children. Was it quite natural, this boredom, this businesslike haste? Was it real, this preoccupation with marriage? The girls who glibly disclaimed any serious interest in their education with talk of 'when I'm married' often were not seriously interested in any particular man, I discovered. The ones who were rushing to get their college work done, to spend three days a week off campus, sometimes had no real date they wanted to keep.

In my time, popular girls who spent many weekends at Yale were often just as serious about their work as the 'brains'. Even if you were temporarily, or quite seriously, in love, during the week at college you lived the life of the mind – and found it absorbing, demanding, sometimes exciting, always real. Could these girls who now must work so much harder, have so much more ability to get into such a college against the growing competition, really be so bored with the life of the mind?

Gradually, I sensed the tension, the almost sullen protest, the deliberate effort – or effort deliberately avoided – behind their cool façades. Their boredom was not quite what it seemed. It was a defence, a refusal to become involved. As a woman who unconsciously thinks sex a sin is not there, is somewhere else, as she goes through the motions of sex, so these girls are somewhere else. They go through the motions, but they defend themselves against the impersonal passions of mind and spirit that college might instil in them – the dangerous nonsexual passions of the intellect.

A pretty sophomore explained to me:

The idea is to be casual, very sophisticated. Don't be too enthusiastic about your work or anything. People who take things too seriously are more or less pitied or laughed at. Like wanting to sing, being so intent about it you make other people uncomfortable. An oddball.

Another girl elaborated:

They might feel sorry for you. I think you can be serious about your work and not be looked down upon as a total intellectual, if you stop now and then and think isn't this too hysterical. Because you do it with tongue in cheek, it's O.K.

A girl with a fraternity pin on her pink sweater said:

Maybe we should take it more seriously. But nobody wants to graduate and get into something where they can't use it. If your husband is going to be an organization man, you can't be too educated. The wife is awfully important for the husband's career. You can't be too interested in art, or something like that.

A girl who had dropped out of honours in history told me:

I loved it. I got so excited about my work I would sometimes go into the library at eight in the morning and not come out till ten at night. I even thought I might want to go on to graduate school or law school and really use my mind. Suddenly, I was afraid of what would happen. I wanted to lead a rich full life. I want to marry, have children, have a nice house. Suddenly I felt, what am I beating my brains out for. So this year I'm trying to lead a well-rounded life. I take courses, but I don't read eight books and still feel like reading the ninth. I stop and go to the movies. The other way was harder, and more exciting. I don't know why I stopped. Maybe I just lost courage.

The phenomenon does not seem confined to any particular college; one finds it among the girls in any college, or department of a college, which still exposes students to the life of the mind. A junior from a Southern university said:

Ever since I was a little girl, science has had a fascination for me. I was going to major in bacteriology and go into cancer research. Now I've switched to home economics. I realized I don't want to go into something that deep. If I went on, I'd have been one of those dedicated people. I got so caught up in the first two years, I never got out of the laboratory. I loved it, but I was missing so many things. If the girls were off swimming in the afternoon, I'd be working on my smears and slides. There aren't any girls in bacteriology here, sixty boys and me in the lab. I couldn't get on with the girls any more who don't understand science. I'm not so intensely interested in home economics as I was in bacteriology, but I realize it was better for me to change, and get out with people. I realized I shouldn't be that serious. I'll go home and work in a department store until I get married.

The mystery to me is not that these girls defend themselves against an involvement with the life of the mind, but that educators should be mystified by their defence, or blame it on the 'student culture', as certain educators do. The one lesson a girl could hardly avoid learning, if she went to college between 1945 and 1960, was *not* to get interested, seriously interested, in anything besides getting married and having children, if she wanted to be normal, happy, adjusted, feminine, have a successful husband, successful children, and a normal, feminine, adjusted, successful sex life. She might have learned some of this lesson at home, and some of it from the other girls in college, but she also learned it, incontrovertibly, from those entrusted with developing her critical, creative intelligence: her college professors.

A subtle and almost unnoticed change had taken place in the academic culture for American women in the last fifteen years: the new sex-direction of their educators. Under the influence of the feminine mystique, some college presidents and professors charged with the education of women had become more concerned with their students' future capacity for sexual orgasm than with their future use of trained intelligence. In fact, some leading educators of women began to concern themselves, conscientiously, with protecting students from the temptation to use their critical, creative intelligence –

by the ingenious method of educating it *not* to be critical or creative.

The new sex-direction of women's education was not, however, confined to any specific course or academic department. It was implicit in all the social sciences; but more than that, it became a part of education itself, not only because the English professor, or the guidance counsellor, or the college president read Freud and Mead, but because education was the prime target of the new mystique – the education of American girls with, or like, boys. If the Freudians and the functionalists were right, educators were guilty of defeminizing American women, of dooming them to frustration as housewives and mothers, or to celibate careers, to life without orgasm. It was a damning indictment; many college presidents and educational theorists confessed their guilt without a murmur and fell into the sex-directed line. There were a few cries of outrage, of course, from the old-fashioned educators who still believed the mind was more important than the marriage bed, but they were often near retirement and soon to be replaced by younger, more thoroughly sex-indoctrinated teachers, or they were so wrapped up in their special subjects that they had little say in over-all school policies.

The general educational climate was ripe for the new sex-directed line, with its emphasis on adjustment. The old aim of education, the development of intelligence through vigorous mastery of the major intellectual disciplines, was already in disfavour among the child-centred educators. Teachers College at Columbia was the natural breeding ground for educational functionalism. As psychology and anthropology and sociology permeated the total scholarly atmosphere, education for femininity also spread from Mills, Stephens, and the finishing schools (where its basis was more traditional than theoretical) to the proudest bastions of the women's Ivy League, the colleges which pioneered higher education for women in America, and were noted for their uncompromising intellectual standards.

The few college presidents and professors who were women either fell into line or had their authority – as teachers and as women – questioned. If they were spinsters, if they had not had babies, they were forbidden by the mystique to speak as women. (*Modern Woman: The Lost Sex* would forbid them even to teach.) The brilliant scholar, who did not marry but inspired many generations of college women to the pursuit of truth, was sullied as an educator of women. She was not named president of the women's college whose intellectual tradition she carried to its highest point; the girls' education was put in the hands of a handsome, husbandly man, more suitable to indoctrinating girls for their proper feminine role. The scholar often left the woman's college to head a department in a great university, where the potential Ph.Ds. were safely men, for whom the lure of scholarship, the pursuit of truth, was not deemed a deterrent to sexual fulfilment.

In building the sex-directed curriculum, not everyone went as far as Lynn White, former president of Mills College, but if you started with the premise that women should no longer be educated like men, but for their role as women, you almost had to end with his curriculum – which amounted to re-placing college chemistry with a course in advanced cooking.

The sex-directed educator begins by accepting education's responsibility for the frustration, general and sexual, of American women.

On my desk lies a letter from a young mother, a few years out of college:

'I have come to realize that I was educated to be a successful man and must now learn by myself to be a successful woman.' The basic irrelevance of much of what passes as women's education in America could not be more compactly phrased. ... The failure of our edu-cational system to take into account these simple and basic differ-ences between the life patterns of average men and women is at least in part responsible for the deep discontent and restlessness which affects millions of women. ...

It would seem that if women are to restore their self-respect they must reverse the tactics of the older feminism which indignantly denied inherent differences in the intellectual and emotional tendencies of men and women. Only by recognizing and insisting upon the importance of such differences can women save themselves, in their own eyes, of conviction as inferiors.[4]

The sex-directed educator equates as masculine our 'vastly overrated cultural creativity', 'our uncritical acceptance of "progress" as good in itself', 'egotistic individualism', 'innovation', 'abstract construction', 'quantitative thinking' – of which, of course, the dread symbol is either communism or the atom bomb. Against these, equated as feminine, are 'the sense of persons, of the immediate, of intangible qualitative relationships, an aversion for statistics and quantities', 'the intuitive', 'the emotional', and all the forces that 'cherish' and 'conserve' what is 'good, true, beautiful, useful, and holy'.

A feminized higher education might include sociology, anthropology, psychology. It would hardly include either pure science (since abstract theory and quantitative thinking are unfeminine) or fine art, which is masculine, 'flamboyant and abstract'. The applied or minor arts, however, are feminine: ceramics, textiles, work shaped more by the hand than the brain.

The sex-directed educator cites approvingly Cardinal Tisserand's saying, 'Women should be educated so that they can argue with their husbands.' Let us stop altogether professional training for women, he insists: all women must be educated to be housewives. Even home economics and domestic science, as they are now taught at college, are masculine because 'they have been pitched at the level of professional training'.[5]

Here is a truly feminine education:

One may prophesy with confidence that as women begin to make their distinctive wishes felt in curricular terms, not merely will every women's college and coeducational institution offer a firm nuclear course in the Family, but from it will radiate curricular series dealing with food and nutrition, textiles and clothing, health and nursing, houseplanning and interior decoration, garden design and applied botany, and child-development. ... Would it be impossible to present a beginning course in foods as exciting and as difficult to work up after college, as a course in post-Kantian philosophy would be? ... Let's abandon talk of proteins, carbohydrates and the like, save inadvertently, as for example, when we point out that a British hyper-boiled brussels sprout is not merely inferior in flavour and texture, but in vitamin content. Why not study the theory and preparation of a Basque paella, of a well-marinated shish kebab, lamb kidneys sauteed in sherry, an authoritative curry, the use of herbs, even such simple sophistications as serving cold artichokes with fresh milk.[6]

This kind of education, in the name of life-adjustment, became a fact on many campuses, high-school as well as college. When American educators finally began to investigate the waste of our national resources of creative intelligence, they found that the lost Einsteins, Schweitzers, Roosevelts, Edisons, Fords, Fermis, Frosts were feminine. Of the brightest forty per cent of U.S. high-school graduates, only half went on to college; of the half who stopped, *two out of three were girls.*[7] When Dr James B. Conant went across the nation to find out what was wrong with the American high school, he discovered too many students were taking easy how-to courses which didn't really stretch their minds. Again, most of those who should have been studying physics, advanced algebra, analytic geometry, four years of language – and were not – were girls. They had the intelligence, the special gift which was not sex-directed, but they also had the sex-directed attitude that such studies were 'unfeminine'.

Sometimes a girl wanted to take a hard subject, but was advised by a guidance counsellor or teacher that it was a waste of time – as, for instance, the girl in a good Eastern high school who wanted to be an architect. Her counsellor strongly advised her against applying for admission anywhere in architecture, on the grounds that women are rare in that profession, and she would never get in anyhow. She stubbornly applied to two universities who give degrees in architecture; both, to her amazement, accepted her. Then her counsellor told her that even though she had been accepted, there was really no future for women in architecture; she would spend her life in a drafting room. She was advised to go to a junior college where the work would be much easier than in architecture and where she would learn all she needed to know when she married.[8]

The influence of sex-directed education was perhaps even more insidious on the high-school level than it was in the colleges, for many girls who were subjected to it never got to college. I picked up a lesson plan for one of these life-adjustment courses now taught in junior high in the suburban county where I live. Entitled 'The Slick Chick', it gives functional 'dos and don'ts for dating' to girls of eleven, twelve, thirteen – a kind of early or forced recognition of their sexual function. Though many have nothing yet with which to fill a brassière, they are told archly not to wear a sweater without one, and to be sure to wear slips so boys can't see through their skirts. It is hardly surprising that by the sophomore year many bright girls in this high school are more than conscious of their sexual function, bored with all the subjects in school, and have no ambition other than to marry and have babies. One cannot help wondering (especially when some of these girls get pregnant as high-school sophomores and marry at fifteen or sixteen) if they have not been educated for their sexual function too soon, while their other abilities go unrecognized.

This stunting of able girls from nonsexual growth is nationwide. Of the top ten per cent of graduates of Indiana high schools in 1955, only fifteen per cent of the boys did not continue their education: thirty-six per cent of the girls did not go on.[9] In the very years in which higher education has become a necessity for almost everyone who wants a real function in our exploding society, *the proportion of women among college students has declined, year by year*. In the fifties, women also dropped out of college at a faster rate than the men: only thirty-seven per cent of the women graduated, in contrast to fifty-five per cent of the men.[10] By the sixties, an equal proportion of boys was dropping out of college.[11] But, in this era of keen competition for college seats, the one girl who enters college for every two boys is 'more highly selected', and less likely to be dropped from college for academic failure. Women drop out, as David Riesman says, either to marry or because they fear too much education is a 'marriage bar'. The average age of first marriage, in the last fifteen years, has dropped to the youngest in the history of this country, the youngest in any of the countries of the Western world, almost as young as it used to be in the so-called underdeveloped countries.[12]

Education should, and can, make a person 'broad in outlook, and open to new experience, independent and disciplined in his thinking, deeply committed to some productive activity, possessed of convictions based on understanding of the world and on his own integration of personality.'[13] The main barrier to such growth in girls is their own rigid preconception of woman's role, which sex-directed educators reinforce, either explicitly or by not facing their own ability, and responsibility, to break through it.

Such a sex-directed impasse is revealed in the massive depths of that thousand-page study, *The American College*, when 'motivational factors in college entrance' are analysed from research among 1,045 boys and 1,925 girls. The study recognizes that it is the need to be independent, and find identity in society not primarily through the sex role but through work, which makes boys grow in college. The girl's evasion of growth in college is explained by the fact that for a girl, identity is exclusively sexual; for the girl, college itself is seen even by these scholars not as the key to larger identity but as a disguised 'outlet for sexual impulses'.

The dream of college apparently serves as a substitute for more direct preoccupation with marriage: girls who do not plan to go to college are more explicit in their desire to marry, and have a more developed sense of their own sex role. They are more aware of and more frankly concerned with sexuality. ... The view of fantasy as an outlet for sexual impulses follows the general psychoanalytic conception that impulses denied direct expression will seek some disguised mode of gratification.[14]

Thus, it did not surprise them that seventy per cent of freshmen women at a Midwestern university answered the question, 'What do you hope to get out of college?' with, among other things, 'The man for me.' They also interpreted answers indicating a wish to 'leave home', 'travel', and answers relating to potential occupations which were given by half the girls as symbolizing 'curiosity about the sexual mysteries'.

College and travel are alternatives to a more open interest in sexuality. Girls who complete their schooling with high school are closer to assuming an adult sex role in early marriages, and they have more developed conceptions of their sexual impulses and sex roles. Girls who will enter college, on the other hand, will delay direct realization and settlement of sexual identity, at least for a while. During the interim, sexual energy is converted and gratified through a fantasy system that focuses on college, the glamour of college life, and a sublimation to general sensuous experience.[15]

Why do the educators view girls, and only girls, in such completely sexual terms? Adolescent boys also have sexual urges whose fulfilment may be delayed by college. But for boys the educators are not concerned with sexual 'fantasy'; they are concerned with 'reality', and boys are expected to achieve personal autonomy and identity by 'committing themselves in the sphere of our culture that is most morally worthwhile – the world of work – in which they will be acknowledged as persons with recognized achievements and potentials'. Even if the boys' own vocational images and goals are not realistic in the beginning – and this study showed that they were not – the sex-directed educators recognize, for boys, that motives, goals, interests, childish preconceptions, can change. They also recognize that, for most, the crucial last chance for change is in college. But apparently girls are not expected to change, nor are they given the opportunity. Even at co-educational colleges, very few girls get the same education as boys. Instead of stimulating what psychologists have suggested might be a 'latent' desire for autonomy in the girls, the sex-directed educators stimulated their sexual fantasy of fulfilling all desire for achievement, status, and identity vicariously through a man. Instead of challenging the girls' childish, rigid, parochial preconception of woman's role, they cater to it by offering them a potpourri of liberal-arts courses, suitable only for a wifely veneer, or narrow programmes such as 'institutional dietetics', well beneath their abilities and suitable only for a 'stop-gap' job between college and marriage.

As educators themselves admit, women's college training does not often equip them to enter the business or professional world at a meaningful level, either at graduation or afterwards.

Presumably, if the campus is 'the world's best marriage mart', as one educator remarked, both sexes are affected. On college campuses today, professor and student agree, the girls are the aggressors in the marriage hunt. The boys, married or not, are there to stretch their minds, to find their own identity, to fill out their life plan; the girls are there only to fulfil their sexual function.

Research reveals that ninety per cent or more of the rising number of campus wives who were motivated for marriage by 'fantasy and the need to conform' are literally working their husbands' way through college.[16]

During the period when the sex-directed educators were devoting themselves to women's sexual adjustment and femininity, economists charted a new and revolutionary change in American employment: beneath the ebb and flow of boom and recession, they found an absolute, spiralling decline in employment possibilities for the uneducated and the unskilled. But when the government economists on the 'womanpower' study visited college campuses, they found the girls unaffected by the statistical probability that they will spend twenty-five years or more of their adult lives in jobs outside the home. Even when it is virtually certain that most women will no longer spend their lives as full-time housewives, the sex-directed educators have told them not to plan for a career for fear of hampering their sexual adjustment.

A few years ago, sex-directed education finally infiltrated a famous women's college, which had been proud in the past of its large share of graduates who went on to play leading roles in education and law and medicine, the arts and sciences, government and social welfare. This college had an ex-feminist woman president, who was perhaps beginning to suffer a slight guilt at the thought of all those women educated like men. A questionnaire, sent to alumnae of all ages, indicated that the great majority were satisfied with their non-sex-directed education; but a minority complained that their education had made them overly conscious of women's rights and equality with men, too interested in careers, possessed of a nagging feeling that they should do something in the community, that they should at least keep on reading, study-ing, developing their own abilities and, interests. Why hadn't they been educated to be happy housewives and mothers?

The guilty woman college president – guilty personally of being a college president, besides having a large number of children and a successful husband; guilty also of having been an ardent feminist in her time and of having advanced a good way in her career before she married; barraged by the thera-peutic social scientists who accused her of trying to mould these young girls in her own impossible, unrealistic, out-moded, energetic, self-demanding, visionary, unfeminine image – introduced a functional course in marriage and the family, compulsory for all sophomores.

The circumstances which led to the college's decision, two years later, to *drop* that functional course are shrouded in secrecy. Nobody officially connected with the college will talk. But a neighbouring educator, a functionalist crusader himself, said with a certain contempt for naïve wrong-thinking that they were evidently shocked over there that the girls who took the functional course got married so quickly. (The class of 1959 at that college included a record number of 75 wives, nearly a quarter of the girls who still remained in the class.) He told me calmly:

Why should it upset them, over there, that the girls got married a little early? There's nothing wrong with early marriage, with the proper preparation. I guess they can't get over the old notion that women should be educated to develop their minds. They deny it, but one can't help suspecting that they still believe in careers for women. Unfortunately, the idea that women go to college to get a husband is anathema to some educators.

At the college in question, 'Marriage and the Family' is taught once again as a course in sociology, geared to critical analysis of these changing social institutions, and not to functional action, or group therapy. But in the neighbouring institution, my professor-informant is second in command of a booming department of 'family-life education', which is currently readying a hundred graduate students to teach functional marriage courses in colleges, state teachers' colleges, junior colleges, community colleges, and high schools across America. As my informant elaborated:

> These kids are concerned about dating and sex, how to get along with boys, is it all right to have premarital relations. Maybe a girl is trying to decide about her major; she's thinking about a career, and she's also thinking about marriage. You set up a role-playing situation to help her work it out – so she sees the effect on the children. She sees she need not feel guilty about being just a housewife.

There often is an air of defensiveness, when a sex-directed educator is asked to define, for the uninitiated, the 'functional approach'. One told a reporter:

> It's all very well to talk big talk – intellectual generalizations, abstract concepts, the United Nations – but somewhere we have to start facing these problems of interpersonal relations on a more modest scale. We have to stop being so teacher-centred, and become student-centred. It's not what you think they need, but what they think they need. That's the functional approach. You walk into a class, and your aim is no longer to cover a certain content, but to set up an atmosphere that makes your students feel comfortable and talk freely about interpersonal relations, in basic terms, not high-falutin generalizations.
>
> Kids tend in adolescence to be very idealistic. They think they can acquire a different set of values, marry a boy from a different background, and that it won't matter later on. We make them aware it will matter, so they won't walk so lightly into mixed marriages, and other traps.[17]

The reporter asked why 'Mate Selection', 'Adjustment to Marriage', and 'Education for Family Living' are taught in colleges at all, if the teacher is committed not to teach, if no material is to be learned or covered, and if the only aim is to help the student understand personal problems and emotions. After surveying a number of marriage courses for *Mademoiselle*, she concluded:

> Only in America would you overhear one undergraduate say to another with total ingenuousness, 'You should have been in class today. We talked about male role-playing and a couple of people really opened up and got personal.'

The point of role-playing, a technique adapted from group therapy, is to get students to understand problems 'on a feeling level'. Emotions more heady than those of the usual college classroom are undoubtedly stirred up when the professor invites them to 'role-play' the feelings of 'a boy and a girl on their wedding night'.

There is a pseudotherapeutic air, as the professor listens patiently to endless self-conscious student speeches about personal feelings ('verbalizing') in the hopes of sparking a 'group insight'. But though the functional course is not group therapy, it is certainly an indoctrination of opinions and values through manipulation of the students' emotions; and in this manipulative disguise, it is no longer subject to the critical thinking demanded in other academic disciplines.

The students take as gospel the bits and pieces assigned in text books that explain Freud or quote Margaret Mead; they do not have the frame of reference that comes from the actual study of psychology or anthropology. In fact, by explicitly banning the usual critical attitudes of college study, these courses give what is often no more than popular opinion the fiat of scientific law.

The discussion on premarital intercourse usually leads to the scientific conclusion that it is wrong. One professor builds up his case against sexual intercourse before marriage with statistics chosen to demonstrate that premarital sexual experience tends to make marital adjustment more difficult. The student will not know of the other statistics which refute this point; if the professor knows of them, he can in the functional marriage course feel free to disregard them as unfunctional. ('Ours is a sick society. The students need some accurate definitive kind of knowledge.') It is functional 'knowledge' that 'only the exceptional woman can make a go of a commitment to a career'. Of course, since most women in the past have not had careers, the few who did were all 'exceptional' – as a mixed marriage is 'exceptional', and premarital intercourse for a girl is exceptional. All are phenomena of less than 51 per cent. The whole point of functional education often

148

seems to be: what 51 per cent of the population does today, 100 per cent should do tomorrow.

So the sex-directed educator promotes a girl's adjustment by dissuading her from any but the 'normal' commitment to marriage and the family. One such educator goes farther than imaginary role-playing; she brings real ex-working mothers to class to talk about their guilt at leaving their children in the morning. Somehow, the students seldom hear about a woman who has successfully broken convention – the young woman doctor whose sister handled her practice when her babies were born, the mother who adjusted her babies' sleeping hours to her work schedule without problems, the happy Protestant girl who married a Catholic, the sexually serene wife whose premarital experience did not seem to hurt her marriage. 'Exceptional' cases are of no practical concern to the functionalist, though he often acknowledges scrupulously that there *are* exceptions. (The 'exceptional child', in educational jargon, bears a connotation of handicap: the blind, the crippled, the retarded, the genius, the defier of convention – anyone who is different from the crowd, in any way unique – bears a common shame; he is 'exceptional'.) Somehow, the student gets the point that she does not want to be the 'exceptional woman'.

This is not to say that the study of a social science, as such, produces conformity in woman or man. This is hardly the effect when it is studied critically and motivated by the usual aims of intellectual discipline, or when it is mastered for professional use. But for girls forbidden both professional and intellectual commitment by the new mystique, the study of sociology, anthropology, psychology is often merely 'functional'. And in the functional course itself, the girls take those bits and pieces from Freud and Mead, the sexual statistics, the role-playing insights, not only literally and out of context, but personally – to be acted upon in their own lives. That, after all, is the whole point of life-adjustment education. It can happen among adolescents in almost any course that involves basic emotional material. It will certainly happen when the material

THE FEMININE MYSTIQUE

is deliberately used not to build critical knowledge but to stir up personal emotions. Therapy, in the orthodox psycho-analytic tradition, requires the suppression of critical thinking (intellectual resistance) for the proper emotions to come out and be worked through. In therapy, this may work. But does education work, mixed up with therapy? One course could hardly be crucial, in any man or woman's life, but when it is decided that the very aim of woman's education should not be intellectual growth, but sexual adjustment, certain questions could be very crucial.

One might ask: if an education geared to the growth of the human mind weakens femininity, will an education geared to femininity weaken the growth of the mind? What is femininity, if it can be destroyed by an education which makes the mind grow, or induced by not letting the mind grow?

One might even ask a question in Freudian terms: what happens when sex becomes not only id for women, but ego and super-ego as well; when education, instead of developing the self, is concentrated on developing the sexual functions? What happens when education gives new authority to the feminine 'shoulds' – which already have the authority of tradition, convention, prejudice, popular opinion – instead of giving women the power of critical thought, the independence and autonomy to question blind authority, new or old? At Pembroke, the women's college at Brown University in Providence, R.I., a guest psychoanalyst was recently invited to lead a buzz session on 'what it means to be a woman'. The students seemed disconcerted when the guest analyst, Dr Margaret Lawrence, said, in simple, un-Freudian English, that it was rather silly to tell women today that their main place is in the home, when most of the work women used to do is now done outside the home, and everyone else in the family spends most of his time outside the house. Hadn't they better be educated to join the rest of the family, out there in the world?

This, somehow, was not what the girls expected to hear from a lady psychoanalyst. Unlike the usual functional, sex-directed lesson, it upset a conventional feminine 'should'. It also implied that they should begin to make certain decisions of their own, about their education and their future.

The functional lesson is much more soothing to the unsure sophomore who has not yet quite made the break from childhood. It does not defy the comfortable, safe conventions; it gives her sophisticated words for accepting her parents' view, the popular view, without having to figure out views of her own. It also reassures her that she doesn't have to work in college; that she can be lazy, follow impulse. She doesn't have to postpone present pleasure for future goals; she doesn't have to read eight books for a history paper, take the tough physics course. It might give her a masculinity complex. After all, didn't the book say:

Woman's intellectuality is to a large extent paid for by the loss of valuable feminine qualities. ... All observations point to the fact that the intellectual woman is masculinized; in her warm, intuitive knowledge has yielded to cold unproductive thinking.[18]

A girl doesn't have to be very lazy, very unsure, to take the hint. Thinking, after all, is hard work. In fact, she would have to do some very cold hard thinking about her own warm, intuitive knowledge to challenge this authoritative statement.

It is no wonder that several generations of American college girls of fine mind and fiery spirit took the message of the sex-directed educators, and fled college and career to marry and have babies before they became so 'intellectual' that, heaven forbid, they wouldn't be able to enjoy sex 'in a feminine way'.

Even without the help of sex-directed educators, the girl growing up with brains and spirit in America learns soon enough to watch her step, 'to be like all the others', not to be herself. She learns not to work too hard, think too often, ask too many questions. In high schools, in co-educational colleges, girls are reluctant to speak out in class for fear of being typed as 'brains'. This phenomenon has been borne out by many studies;[19] any bright girl or woman can document it from personal experience. Bryn Mawr girls have a special term for the way they talk when boys are around, compared to the real talk they can permit themselves when they are not afraid to let their intelligence show.

These are exceptions, of course. The Mellon study found that some Vassar seniors, as compared with freshmen, showed an enormous growth in four years – the kind of growth towards identity and self-realization which scientists now know takes place in people in their twenties and even thirties, forties, and fifties, long after the period of physical growth is over. But many girls showed no signs of growth. These were the ones who resisted, successfully, involvement with ideas, the academic work of the college, the intellectual disciplines, the larger values. It was not that their actual sexual interests interfered; in fact, the psychologists got the impression that with many of these girls, 'interest in men and marriage is a kind of defence against intellectual development'. For such girls, even sex is not real, merely a kind of conformity. The sex-directed educator would find no fault in this kind of adjustment. But in view of other evidence, one might ask: could such an adjustment mask a failure to grow that becomes finally a human deformity?

Several years ago a team of California psychologists who had been following the development of 140 bright youngsters noticed a sudden sharp drop in I.Q. curves in some of the teenage records. When they investigated this, they found that while most of the youngsters' curves remained at the same high level, year after year, those whose curves dropped were all girls. The drop had nothing to do with the physiological changes of adolescence; it was not found in all girls. But in the records of those girls whose intelligence dropped were found repeated statements to the effect that 'it isn't too smart for a girl to be smart'. In a very real sense, these girls were arrested in their mental growth, at age fourteen or fifteen, by conformity to the feminine image.[20]

The fact is, girls today and those responsible for their education do face a choice. They must decide between adjustment, conformity, avoidance of conflict, therapy – or individuality, human identity, education in the truest sense, with all its pains of growth. But they do not have to face the mistaken choice painted by the sex-directed educators, with their dire warnings against loss of femininity and sexual frustration. For the perceptive psychologist who studied the Vassar girls uncovered some startling new evidence about the students who chose to become truly involved with their education. It seems that those seniors who showed the greatest signs of growth were more 'masculine' in the sense of being less passive and conventional; but they were more 'feminine' in inner emotional life, and the ability to gratify it. They also scored higher, far higher than as freshmen, on certain scales commonly supposed to measure neuroses. The psychologist commented: 'We have come to regard elevations on such scales as evidence that education is taking place.'[21] He found girls with conflicts showed more growth than the adjusted ones, who had no wish to become independent. The least adjusted were also the more developed – 'already prepared for even further changes and more independence'. In summing up the Vassar study, its director could not avoid the psychological paradox: education for women does make them less feminine, less adjusted – but it makes them grow.

Being less 'feminine' is closely related to being more educated and more mature. ... It is interesting to note, however, that Feminine Sensitivity, which may well have sources in physiology and in early identifications, does not decrease during the four years; 'feminine' interests and feminine role behaviour, i.e., conventionality and passivity, can be understood as later and more superficial acquisitions, and, hence, more susceptible to decrease as the individual becomes more mature and more educated. ...
One might say that if we were interested in stability alone, we would do well to plan a programme to keep freshmen as they are, rather than to try to increase their education, their maturity and their flexibility with regard to sex-role behaviour. Seniors are more unstable because there is more to be stabilized, less certain of their identities because more possibilities are open to them.[22]

At graduation, such women were, however, only at a 'halfway point' in their growth to autonomy. Their fate depended on 'whether they now enter a situation in which they can continue to grow or whether they find some quick but regressive means for relieving the stress'. The flight into marriage is the easiest, quickest way to relieve that stress. To the educator, bent on women's growth to autonomy, such a marriage is 'regressive'. To the sex-directed educator, it is femininity fulfilled.

A therapist at another college told me of girls who had never committed themselves, either to their work or any other activity of the college, and who felt that they would 'go to pieces' when their parents refused to let them leave college to marry the boys in whom they found 'security'. When these girls, with help, finally applied themselves to work – or even began to feel a sense of self by taking part in an activity such as student government or the school newspaper – they lost their desperate need for 'security'. They finished college, worked, went out with more mature young men, and are now marrying on quite a different emotional basis.

Unlike the sex-directed educator, this professional therapist felt that the girl who suffers almost to the point of breakdown in the senior year, and who faces a personal decision about her own future – faces even an irreconcilable conflict between the values and interests and abilities her education has given her, and the conventional role of housewife – is still 'healthier' than the adjusted, calm, stable girl in whom education did not 'take' at all and who steps smoothly from her role as parents' child to husband's wife, conventionally feminine, without ever waking up to painful individual identity.

The Vassar study showed that just as girls begin to feel the conflicts, the growing pains of identity, they stop growing. They more or less consciously stop their own growth to play the feminine role. Or, to put it in another way, they evade further experiences conducive to growth. Until now this stunting or evasion of growth has been considered normal feminine adjustment. But when the Vassar study followed women past the senior year – where they were on the verge of this painful crucial step in personal growth – out into life, where most of them were playing the conventional feminine role, these facts emerged:

1. Twenty or twenty-five years out of college, these women measured lower than seniors on the 'Development Scale' which covered the whole gamut of mental, emotional, and

personal growth. They did not lose all the growth achieved in college (alumnae scored higher than freshmen) but – in spite of the psychological readiness for further growth at twenty-one – they did not keep growing.

2. These women were, for the most part, adjusted as suburban housewives, conscientious mothers, active in their communities. But, except for the professional career women, they had not continued to pursue deep interests of their own. There seemed some reason to believe that the cessation of growth was related to the lack of deep personal interests, the lack of an individual commitment.

3. The women who, twenty years later, were most troubling to the psychologist were the most conventionally feminine – the ones who were not interested, even in college, in anything except finding a husband.[23]

There was one group of students who in senior year neither suffered conflict to the point of near-breakdown nor stopped their own growth to flee into marriage. These were students who were preparing for a profession; they had gained, in college, interests deep enough to commit themselves to a career. The study revealed that virtually all such students with professional ambitions plan to marry, but marriage is for them an activity in which they will voluntarily choose to participate rather than something that is necessary for any sense of personal identity. Such students have a greater degree of independence and self-confidence than most. They may be engaged or deeply in love, but they do not feel they must sacrifice their own individualities or their career ambitions if they wish to marry. With these girls, the psychologists did not get the impression, as they did with so many, that interest in men and in marriage was a kind of defence against intellectual development. Their interest in some particular man was real. At the same time, it did not interfere with their education.

But the degree to which the feminine mystique has brainwashed American educators was shown when the director of the Vassar study described to a panel of his colleagues such a girl, who 'not only makes top grades, but in whose case there is high probability that a scholarly or professional career will be followed'.

Julie B's mother is a teacher and scholar and the driving force in the family. ... Mother gets after father for being too easy-going. Father doesn't mind if his wife and daughter have highbrow tastes and ideas, only such are not for him. Julie becomes out-door girl, nonconformist, dominates her older brother, but is conscience-stricken if she doesn't do required reading or if grade average slips. Sticks to her intention to do graduate work and become teacher. Older brother now college teacher and Julie, herself a graduate student now, is married to a graduate student in natural science.

When she was a freshman we presented her interview data, without interpretation, to a group of psychiatrists, psychologists, social scientists. Our idea of a really promising girl. Common question: 'What's wrong with her?' Common opinion: she would need psychotherapy. Actually she got engaged to her budding scientist in her sophomore year, became increasingly conscious of herself as an intellectual and outsider, but still couldn't neglect her work. 'If only I could flunk something,' she said.

It takes a very daring educator today to attack the sex-directed line, for he must challenge, in essence, the conventional image of femininity. The image says that women are passive, dependent, conformist, incapable of critical thought or original contribution to society; and, in the best traditions of the self-fulfilling prophecy, sex-directed education continues to make them so, as, in an earlier era, lack of education made, them so. No one asks whether a passively feminine, uncomplicated, dependent woman – in a primitive village or in a suburb – actually enjoys greater happiness, greater sexual fulfilment than a woman who commits herself in college to serious interests beyond the home. No one, until very recently when Russians orbited moons and put men in space, asked whether adjustment should be education's aim. In fact, the sex-directed educators, so bent on women's feminine adjustment, could gaily cite the most ominous facts about American housewives – their emptiness, idleness, boredom, alcoholism, drug addiction, disintegration to fat, disease, and despair after forty, when their sexual function has been filled – without deviating a bit from their crusade to educate all women to this sole end.

So the sex-directed educator disposes of the thirty years women are likely to live after forty with three blithe proposals:

1. A course in 'Law and Order for the Housewife' to enable her to deal, as a widow, with insurances, taxes, wills, investments.

2. Men might retire earlier to help keep their wives company.

3. A brief fling in 'volunteer community services, politics, the arts or the like' – though, since the woman will be untrained the main value will be personal therapy.

To choose only one example, a woman who wants some really novel experience may start a campaign to rid her city or country of that nauseous eczema of our modern world, the billboard.

The billboards will remain and multiply like bacteria infesting the landscape, but at least she will have had a vigorous adult education course in local politics. Then she can relax and devote herself to the alumnae activities of the institution from which she graduated. Many a woman approaching middle years has found new vigour and enthusiasm in identifying herself with the on-going life of her college and in expanding her maternal instincts, now that her own children are grown, to encompass the new generations of students which inhabit its campus.[24]

She could also take a part-time job, he said, but she shouldn't take work away from men who must feed their families, and, in fact, she won't have the skills or experience for a very 'exciting' job.

There is great demand for experienced and reliable women who can relieve younger women of family responsibilities on regular days or afternoons, so that they may either develop community interests or hold part-time jobs of their own. . . . There is no reason why women of culture and breeding, who in any case for years have probably done most of their own housework, should recoil from such arrangements.[25]

If the feminine mystique has not destroyed her sense of humour, a woman might laugh at such a candid description of the life her expensive sex-directed education fits her for: an occasional alumnae reunion and someone else's housework. The sad fact is, in the era of Freud and functionalism and the feminine mystique, few educators escaped such a sex-distortion of their own values. Max Lerner,[26] even Riesman in *The*

Lonely Crowd, suggested that women need not seek their own autonomy through productive contribution to society – they might better help their husbands hold on to theirs, through play. And so sex-directed education segregated recent generations of able American women as surely as separate-but-equal education segregated able American Negroes from the opportunity to realize their full abilities in the mainstream of American life.

It does not explain anything to say that in this era of conformity colleges did not really educate anybody. The Jacob report,[27] which levelled this indictment against American colleges generally, and even the more sophisticated indictment by Sanford and his group, does not recognize that the colleges' failure to educate women for an identity beyond their sexual role was undoubtedly a crucial factor in perpetuating, if not creating, that conformity which educators now so fashionably rail against. For it is impossible to educate women to devote themselves so early and completely to their sexual role – women who, as Freud said, can be very active indeed in achieving a passive end – without pulling men into the same comfortable trap. In effect, sex-directed education led to a lack of identity in women most easily solved by early marriage. And a premature commitment to any role – marriage or vocation – closes off the experiences, the testing, the failures and successes in various spheres of activity that are necessary for a person to achieve full maturity, individual identity.

The danger of stunting of boys' growth by early domesticity was recognized by the sex-directed educators. As Margaret Mead put it recently:

Early domesticity has always been characteristic of most savages, of most peasants and of the urban poor. ... If there are babies, it means, you know, the father's term paper gets all mixed up with the babies' bottle. ... Early student marriage is domesticating boys so early they don't have a chance for full intellectual development. They don't have a chance to give their entire time, not necessarily to study in the sense of staying in the library – but in the sense that the married students don't have time to experience, to think, to sit up all night in bull sessions, to develop as individuals. This is not

THE SEX-DIRECTED EDUCATORS

only important for the intellectuals, but also the boys who are going to be the future statesmen of the country and lawyers and doctors and all sorts of professional men.[28]

But what of the girls who will never even write the term papers because of the baby's bottle? Advanced educators in the early 1960s have their own cheerful fantasies about postponing women's education until after they have had their babies; they thereby acknowledge that they have resigned themselves almost unanimously to the early marriages, which continue unabated.

Still, it is too easy to make education the scapegoat. Whatever the mistakes of the sex-directed educators, other educators have fought a futile, frustrating rear-guard battle trying to make able women 'envision new goals and grow by reaching for them'. In the last analysis, millions of able women in this free land chose, themselves, not to use the door education could have opened for them. The choice – and the responsibility – for the race back home was finally their own.

CHAPTER 8

The Mistaken Choice

A MYSTIQUE does not compel its own acceptance. For the feminine mystique to have 'brainwashed' American women of nonsexual human purposes for more than fifteen years, it must have filled real needs in those who seized on it for others and those who accepted it for themselves. Those needs may not have been the same in all the women or in all the purveyors of the mystique. But there were many needs, at this particular time in America, that made us pushovers for the mystique: needs so compelling that we suspended critical thought, as one does in the face of an intuitive truth. The trouble is, when need is strong enough, intuition can also lie.

There was, just before the feminine mystique took hold in America, a war, which followed a depression and ended with the explosion of an atom bomb. After the loneliness of war and the unspeakableness of the bomb, against the frightening uncertainty, the cold immensity of the changing world, women as well as men sought the comforting reality of home and children. In the foxholes, the G.I.s had pinned up pictures of Betty Grable, but the songs they asked to hear were lullabies. And when they got out of the army they were too old to go home to their mothers. The needs of sex and love are undeniably real in men and women, boys and girls, but why at this time did they seem to so many the *only* needs?

A pent-up hunger for marriage, home, and children was felt simultaneously by several different generations; a hunger which, in the prosperity of postwar America, everyone could suddenly satisfy. The young G.I., made older than his years by the war, could meet his lonely need for love and mother by re-creating his childhood home. Instead of dating many girls until college and profession were achieved, he could marry on the

G.I. bill, and give his own babies the tender mother love he was no longer baby enough to seek for himself. Then there were the slightly older men: men of twenty-five whose marriages had been postponed by the war and who now felt they must make up for lost time; men in their thirties, kept first by depression and then by war from marrying, or, if married, from enjoying the comforts of home.

For the girls, these lonely years added an extra urgency to their search for love. Those who married in the thirties saw their husbands off to war; those who grew up in the forties were afraid, with reason, that they might never have the love, the homes, and children which few women would willingly miss. When the men came back, there was a headlong rush into marriage.

The baby boom of the immediate postwar years took place in every country. But it was not permeated, in most other countries, with the mystique of feminine fulfilment. It did not in other countries lead to the even greater baby boom of the fifties, with the rise in teenage marriages and pregnancies, and the increase in family size. The number of American women with three or more children doubled in twenty years. And educated women, after the war, led all the others in the race to have more babies.[1] (The generation before mine, the women born between 1910 and 1919, showed the change most sharply. During their twenties, their low pregnancy rate led to warnings that education was going to wipe out the human race; in their thirties, they suddenly showed a sharp *increase* in pregnancies, despite the lowered biological capacity that makes the pregnancy rate decline with age.)

Today the American population explosion comes in large part from teenage marriages. The number of children born to teenagers rose 165 per cent between 1940 and 1957, according to Metropolitan Life Insurance figures. The girls who would normally go to college but leave or forgo it to marry (eighteen and nineteen are the most frequent ages of marriage of American girls today; half of all American women are married by twenty) are products of the mystique. They give up education without a qualm, truly believing that they will find 'fulfilment' as wives and mothers. I suppose a girl today, who knows from statistics or merely from observation that if she waits to marry until she finishes college, or trains for a profession, most of the men will be married to someone else, has as much reason to fear she may miss feminine fulfilment as the war gave the girls in the forties. But this does not explain why they drop out of college to support their husbands, while the boys continue with their education.

War made women particularly vulnerable to the mystique, but the war, with all its frustrations, was not the only reason they went home again. Nor can it be explained by 'the servant problem', which is an excuse the educated woman often gives to herself. During the war, when the cooks and maids went to work in the war plants, the servant problem was even more severe than in recent years. But at that time, women of spirit often worked out unconventional domestic arrangements to keep their professional commitments. (I knew two young wartime mothers who pooled forces while their husbands were overseas. One, an actress, took both babies in the morning, while the other did graduate work; the second took over in the afternoon, when the other had a rehearsal or matinée. I also knew a woman who switched her baby's night-and-day so he would sleep at a neighbour's house during the hours she was at medical school.) And in the cities, then, the need for nurseries and day-care centres for the children of working mothers was seen, and met.

But in the years of postwar femininity, even women who could afford, and find, a full-time nurse or housekeeper chose to take care of house and children themselves. And in the cities, during the fifties, the nursery and day-care centres for the children of working mothers all but disappeared; the very suggestion of their need brought hysterical outcries from educated housewives as well as the purveyors of the mystique.[2]

When the war ended, of course, G.I.s came back to take the jobs and fill the seats in colleges and universities that for a while had been occupied largely by girls. For a short time, competition was keen and the resurgence of the old anti-feminine prejudices in business and the professions made it difficult for a girl to keep or advance in a job. This undoubtedly sent many women scurrying for the cover of marriage and home. Subtle discrimination against women, to say nothing of the sex wage differential, is still an unwritten law today, and its effects are almost as devastating and as hard to fight as the flagrant opposition faced by the feminists. A woman researcher on *Time* magazine, for instance, cannot, no matter what her ability, aspire to be a writer; the unwritten law makes the men writers and editors, the women researchers. She doesn't get mad; she likes her job, she likes her boss. She is not a crusader for women's rights; it isn't a case for the Newspaper Guild. But it is discouraging nevertheless. If she is never going to get anywhere, why keep on?

Women were often driven embittered from their chosen fields when, ready and able to handle a better job, they were passed over for a man. In some jobs a woman had to be content to do the work while the man got the credit. Or if she got the better job, she had to face the bitterness and hostility of the man. Because the race to get ahead, in the big organization, in every profession in America, is so terribly competitive for men, competition from women is somehow the last straw – and much easier to fight by simply evoking that unwritten law. During the war, women's abilities, and the inevitable competition, were welcome; after the war they were confronted with that polite but impenetrable curtain of hostility.

Still, during the depression, able, spirited girls sacrificed, fought prejudice, and braved competition in order to pursue their careers, even though there were fewer places to compete for. Nor did many see any conflict between career and love. In the prosperous postwar years, there were plenty of jobs, plenty of places in all the professions; there was no real need to give up everything for love and marriage. The less-educated girls, after all, did not leave the factories and go back to being maids. The proportion of women in industry has steadily increased since the war – but not of women in careers or professions requiring training, effort, personal commitment.[3] 'I live through my husband and children,' a frank member of my own generation told me. 'It's easier that way.

In this world now, it's easier to be a woman, if you take advantage of it.'

In this sense, what happened to women is part of what happened to all of us in the years after the war. We found excuses for not facing the problems we once had the courage to face. The American spirit fell into a strange sleep; men as well as women, scared liberals, disillusioned radicals, conservatives bewildered and frustrated by change – the whole nation stopped growing up.

Women went home again just as men shrugged off the bomb, forgot the concentration camps, condoned corruption, and fell into helpless conformity; just as the thinkers avoided the complex larger problems of the postwar world. It was easier, safer, to think about love and sex than about communism, McCarthy, and the uncontrolled bomb. It was easier to look for Freudian sexual roots in man's behaviour, his ideas, and his wars than to look critically at his society and act constructively to right its wrongs.

We can see all this now, in retrospect. For the social worker, the psychologist and the numerous 'family' counsellors, analytically oriented therapy for private patients on personal problems of sex, personality, and interpersonal relations was safer and more lucrative than probing too deeply for the common causes of man's suffering. If you no longer wanted to think about the whole of mankind, at least you could 'help' individuals without getting into trouble. Irwin Shaw, who once goaded the American conscience on the great issues of war and peace and racial prejudice, now wrote about sex and adultery; Norman Mailer and the young beatnik writers confined their revolutionary spirit to sex and kicks and drugs and advertising themselves in four-letter words. It was easier and more fashionable for writers to think about psychology than politics, about private motives than public purposes. Painters retreated into an abstract expressionism that flaunted discipline and glorified the evasion of meaning. Dramatists reduced human purpose to bitter, pretentious nonsense: 'the theatre of the absurd'. Freudian thought gave this whole process of escape its dimension of endless, tantalizing, intellectual mystery: process within process, meaning hidden within meaning, until meaning itself disappeared and the hopeless, dull outside world hardly existed at all.

The Freudian mania in the American culture, apart from the practice of psychotherapy itself, also filled a real need in the forties and fifties: the need for an ideology, a national purpose, an application of the mind to the problems of people. Analysts themselves have recently suggested that the lack of an ideology or national purpose may be partially responsible for the personal emptiness which sends many men and women into psychotherapy; they are actually looking for an identity which therapy alone can never give. The religious revival in America coincided with the rush to psychoanalysis, and perhaps came about for the same reason. It is significant that many ministers now spend much of their time in giving psychotherapy – pastoral counselling – to members of their congregations. Do they thereby also evade the larger questions, the real search?

When I was interviewing on college campuses in the late fifties, chaplains and sociologists alike testified to the younger generation's 'privatism'. A major reason for the early marriage movement, they felt, was that the young saw no other true value in contemporary society.

The five babies, the movement to suburbia, do-it-yourself, and even beatnikery filled homely needs; they also took the place of those larger needs and purposes with which the most spirited in this nation were once concerned. The family and its loves and problems – this, at least, was good and true.

Under the Freudian microscope, however, a very different concept of family began to emerge. Oedipus conflict and sibling rivalry became household words. Frustration was as great a peril to childhood as scarlet fever. And singled out for special attention was the 'mother'. It was suddenly discovered that the mother could be blamed for almost everything. In every case history of troubled child; alcoholic, suicidal, schizophrenic, psychopathic, neurotic adult; impotent, homosexual male; frigid, promiscuous female; ulcerous, asthmatic, and otherwise disturbed American, could be found a mother. A frustrated, repressed, disturbed, martyred, never satisfied, unhappy woman. A demanding, nagging, shrewish wife. A rejecting, overprotecting, dominating mother. The Second World War revealed that millions of American men were psychologically incapable of facing the shock of war, of facing life away from their 'moms'. Clearly something was 'wrong' with American women.

By unfortunate coincidence, this attack against mothers came about at the same time that American women were beginning to use the rights of their emancipation, to go in increasing numbers to college and professional schools, to rise in industry and the professions in inevitable competition with men. It was apparent to the naked eye, obvious to the returning G.I., that these American women were indeed more independent, strong-minded, assertive of will and opinion, less passive and feminine than, for instance, the German and Japanese girls who, the G.I.s boasted, 'even washed our backs for us'. It was less apparent, however, that these girls were different from their mothers. Perhaps that is why, by some strange distortion of logic, all the neuroses of children past and present were blamed on the independence and individuality of this new generation of American girls – independence and individuality which the housewife-mothers of the previous generation had never had.

The evidence seemed inescapable: the figures on the psychiatric discharges in the war and the mothers in their case histories; the early Kinsey figures on the incapacity of American women to enjoy sexual orgasm, especially educated women; the fact that so many women *were* frustrated, and took it out on their husbands and children. More and more men in America did feel inadequate, impotent. Many of those first generations of career women did miss love and children, resented and were resented by the men they competed with. More and more American men, women, children were going to mental hospitals, clinics, psychiatrists. All this was laid at the doorstep of the frustrated American mother, 'masculinized' by her education, prevented by her insistence on equality and independence from finding sexual fulfilment as a woman.

It all fitted so neatly with the Freudian rationale that no one stopped to investigate what these pre-war mothers were really like. They were indeed frustrated. But the mothers of the maladjusted soldiers, the insecure and impotent postwar males, were not independent educated career women, but self-sacrificing, dependent, martyred-housewife 'moms'.

In 1940, less than a fourth of American women worked outside the home; those who did were for the most part unmarried. A minuscule 2.5 per cent of mothers were 'career women'. The mothers of the G.I.s who were 18–30 in 1940 were born in the nineteenth century, or the early 1900s, and were grown up before American women won the right to vote, or enjoyed the independence, the sexual freedom, the educational or the career opportunities of the twenties. By and large, these 'moms' were neither feminists, nor products of feminism, but American women leading the traditional feminine life of housewife and mother. Was it really education, career dreams, independence, which made the 'moms' frustrated, and take it out on their children? Even a book that helped build the new mystique – Edward Strecker's *Their Mothers' Sons* – confirms the fact that the 'moms' were neither career women, nor feminists, nor used their education, if they had it; they lived for their children, they had no interests beyond home, children, family, or their own beauty. In fact, they fit the very image of the feminine mystique.

Here is the 'mom' whom Dr Strecker, as consultant to the Surgeon General of the Army and Navy, found guilty in the case histories of the vast majority of the 1,825,000 men rejected for military service because of psychiatric disorders, the 600,000 discharged from the Army for neuro-psychiatric reasons, and the 500,000 more who tried to evade the draft – almost 3,000,000 men, out of 15,000,000 in the service, who retreated into psychoneurosis, often only a few days after induction, because they lacked maturity, 'the ability to face life, live with others, think for themselves and stand on their own two feet'.

A mom is a woman whose maternal behaviour is motivated by the seeking of emotional recompense for the buffets which life has dealt her own ego. In her relationship with her children, every deed and almost every breath are designed unconsciously but exclusively to absorb her children emotionally and to bind them to her securely. In order to achieve this purpose, she must stamp a pattern of immature behaviour on her children. ... The mothers of men and women capable of facing life maturely are not apt to be the traditional mom type. More likely mom is sweet, doting, self-sacrificing. ... takes no end of trouble and spares herself no pains in selecting clothes for her grown-up children. She supervises the curl of their hair, the selection of their friends and companions, their sports, and their social attitudes and opinions. By and large she does all their thinking for them. ... [This domination] is sometimes hard and arbitrary, more often soft, persuasive and somewhat devious. ... Most frequent is the method of indirection in which in some way the child is made to feel that mom's hurt and trying ever so hard to conceal that hurt. The soft method is infinitely more successful in blocking manifestations of youthful thought and action. ...

The 'self-sacrificing' mom when hard-pressed may admit hesitatingly that perhaps she does look 'played out' and is actually a bit tired, but she chirps brightly 'What of it?' ... The implication is that she does not care how she looks or feels, for in her heart there is the unselfish joy of service. From dawn until late at night she finds her happiness in doing for her children. The house belongs to them. It must be 'just so'; the meals on the minute, hot and tempting. Food is available at all hours. ... No buttons missing from garments in this orderly house. Everything is in its proper place. Mom knows where it is. Uncomplainingly, gladly, she puts things where they belong after the children have strewn them about, here, there, and everywhere. ... Anything the children need or want, mom will cheerfully get for them. It is the perfect home. ... Failing to find a comparable peaceful haven in the outside world, it is quite likely that one or more of the brood will remain in or return to the happy home, forever enwombed.[4]

These were the 'moms' of the sons who could not be men at the front or at home, in bed or out, because they really wanted to be babies. All these moms had one thing in common:

... the emotional satisfaction, almost repletion, she derives from keeping her children paddling about in a kind of psychological amniotic fluid rather than letting them swim away with the bold and decisive strokes of maturity from the emotional maternal womb. . . . Being immature herself, she breeds immaturity in her children and, by and large, they are doomed to lives of personal and social insufficiency and unhappiness. . . .[5]

I quote Dr Strecker at length because he was, oddly enough, one of the psychiatric authorities most frequently cited in the spate of postwar articles and speeches condemning American women for their lost femininity – and bidding them rush back home again and devote their lives to their children. Actually, the moral of Strecker's cases was just the opposite; those immature sons had mothers who devoted *too* much of their lives to their children, mothers who had to keep their children babies or they themselves would have no lives at all, mothers who never themselves reached or were encouraged to reach maturity: 'ripeness, full development . . . independence of thought and action' – the quality of being fully human. Which is not quite the same as femininity.

Facts are swallowed by a mystique in much the same way, I guess, as the strange phenomenon by which hamburger eaten by a dog becomes dog, and hamburger eaten by a human becomes human. The facts of the G.I.s' neurosis became, in the 1940s, 'proof' that American women had been seduced from feminine fulfilment by an education geared to career, independence, equality with men, 'self-realization at any cost' – even though most of these frustrated women were simply housewives. By some fascinating paradox, the massive evidence of psychological damage done to boys and girls by frustrated mothers who devoted all their days to filling children's needs was twisted by the feminine mystique to a summons to the new generation of girls to go back home and devote *their* days to filling children's needs.

Nothing made that hamburger more palatable than the early Kinsey figures which showed that sexual frustration in women was related to their education. As *Modern Woman: The Lost Sex* interpreted these early Kinsey returns:

Among women with a grade school education or less, complete failure to achieve orgasm diminished towards the vanishing point. Dr Kinsey and his colleagues reported that practically 100 per cent full orgastic reaction had been found among uneducated Negro women. .... The psychosexual rule that begins to take form, then, is this: the more educated the woman is, the greater chance there is of sexual disorder, more or less severe. ....[6]

Nearly a decade went by before publication of the full Kinsey report on women, which completely contradicted those earlier findings. How many women realize, even now, that Kinsey's 5,940 case histories of American women showed that the number of females reaching orgasm in marriage, and the number of females reaching orgasm nearly 100 per cent of the time, *was* related to education, but the more educated the woman, the greater chance of sexual fulfilment? The woman with only a grade-school education was more likely never to experience orgasm, while the woman who finished college, and who went on to graduate or professional school, was far more likely to achieve full orgasm nearly 100 per cent of the time. In Kinsey's words:

We found that the number of females reaching orgasm within any five-year period was rather distinctly higher among those with upper educational backgrounds. ... In every period of marriage, from the first until at least the fifteenth year, a larger number of the females in the sample who had more limited educational backgrounds had completely failed to respond to orgasm in their marital coitus, and a small number of the better educated females had so completely failed. ...

These data are not in accord with a preliminary, unpublished calculation which we made some years ago. On the basis of a smaller sample, and on the basis of a less adequate method of calculation, we seemed to find a larger number of the females of the lower educational levels responding to orgasm in the marital coitus. These data now need correction. ...[7]

But the mystique nourished by the early incorrect figures was not so easily corrected.

And then there were the frightening figures and case histories of children abandoned and rejected because their mothers worked. How many women realize, even now, that the babies in those publicized cases, who withered away from lack of maternal affection, were not the children of educated, middle-class mothers who left them in others' care certain hours of the day to practise a profession or write a poem, or fight a political battle – but truly abandoned children: foundlings often deserted at birth by unwed mothers and drunken fathers, children who never had a home or tender loving care. Headlines were made by any study which implied that working mothers were responsible for juvenile delinquency, school difficulties or emotional disturbance in their children. Recently a psychologist, Dr Lois Meek Stolz, of Stanford University, analysed all the evidence from such studies. She discovered that at the present time one can say *anything* – good or bad – about children of employed mothers and support the statement by *some* research findings. But there is no definitive evidence that children are less happy, healthy, adjusted, *because* their mothers work.[8]

The studies that show working women to be happier, better, more mature mothers do not get much publicity. Since juvenile delinquency is increasing, and more women work or 'are educated for some kind of intellectual work', there is surely a direct cause-and-effect relationship, one says. Except that evidence indicates there is not. Several years ago, much publicity was given to a study comparing matched groups of delinquent and non-delinquent boys. It was found, among other things, that there was no more delinquency, or school truancy, when the mothers worked regularly than when they were housewives. But, spectacular headlines warned, significantly more delinquents had mothers who worked irregularly. This finding brought guilt and gloom to the educated mothers who had given up full-fledged careers, but managed to keep on in their fields by working part-time, by free-lancing, or by taking temporary jobs with periods at home in between. 'Here for years I've been purposely taking temporary jobs and part-time jobs, trying to arrange my working life in the boys' best interests,' one such mother was quoted by the *New York Times*, 'and now it looks as though I've been doing the worst possible thing!'[9]

Actually, this mother, a woman with professional training who lived in a comfortable middle-class neighbourhood, was equating herself with mothers in that study who, it turned out, not only lived in poor socio-economic circumstances, but had in many cases been juvenile delinquents themselves. And they often had husbands who were emotionally disturbed.

The researchers who did that study suggested that the sons of these women had emotional conflicts because the mother was motivated to her sporadic work 'not so much to supplement family income as to escape household and maternal responsibilities'. But another specialist, analysing the same findings, thought the basic cause both of the mother's sporadic employment and the son's delinquency was the emotional instability of both parents. Whatever the reason, the situation was in no way comparable to that of most educated women who read themselves into it. In fact, as Dr Stolz shows, many studies misinterpreted as 'proof' that women cannot combine careers and motherhood actually indicate that, where other conditions are equal, the children of mothers who work because they want to are less likely to be disturbed, have problems in school, or to 'lack a sense of personal worth' than housewives' children.

The early studies of children of working mothers were done in an era when few married women worked, at day nurseries which served working mothers who were without husbands due to death, divorce or desertion. These studies were done by social workers and economists in order to press for such reforms as mothers' pensions. The disturbances and higher death rate in such children were not found in studies done in this recent decade, when of the millions of married women working, only 1 out of 8 was not living with her husband.

In one such recent study, based on 2,000 mothers, the only significant differences were that more housewife-mothers stated 'the children make me nervous' than working mothers; and the housewives seemed to have 'more children'. A famous study in Chicago which had seemed to show more mothers of delinquents were working outside the home, turned out to show only that more delinquents come from broken homes. Another study of 400 seriously disturbed children (of a school population of 16,000) showed that where no broken home was involved, three times as many of the disturbed children's mothers were housewives as working mothers.

Other studies showed that children of working mothers were less likely to be either extremely aggressive or extremely inhibited, less likely to do poorly in school, or to 'lack a sense of personal worth' than children of housewives, and that mothers who worked were more likely to be 'delighted' at becoming pregnant, and less likely to suffer conflict over the 'role of mother' than housewives.

There also seemed to be a closer and more positive relationship to children among working mothers who liked their work, than among housewife-mothers or mothers who did not like their work. And a study during the thirties of college-educated mothers, who are more able to choose work they like, showed no adverse effect of their employment on their marital and emotional adjustment, or on number or seriousness of children's problems. In general, women who work shared only two attributes; they were more likely to have higher education and to live in cities.[10]

In our own era, however, as droves of educated women have become suburban housewives, who among them did not worry that their child's bedwetting, thumbsucking, overeating, refusal to eat, withdrawal, lack of friends, inability to be alone, aggressiveness, timidity, slow reading, too much reading, lack of discipline, rigidity, inhibition, exhibitionism, sexual precociousness, or sexual lack of interest was a sign of incipient neurosis. Parenthood, and especially motherhood, under the Freudian spotlight, had to become a full-time job and career if not a religious cult. One false step could mean disaster. Without careers, without any commitment other than their homes, mothers could devote every moment to their children; their full attention could be given to finding signs of incipient neurosis – and perhaps to producing it.

In every case history, of course, you can always find significant facts about the mother, especially if you are looking for facts, or memories, of those supposedly crucial first five years. In America, after all, the mother is always there; she is *supposed* to be there. Is the fact that they are always there, and there only as mothers, somehow linked to the neuroses of their children? Many cultures pass on their conflicts to children through the mothers, but in the modern cultures of the civilized world not many educate their strongest, ablest women to make a career of their own children.

Not long ago Dr Spock confessed, a bit uneasily, that Russian children, whose mothers usually have some purpose in their lives besides motherhood – they work in medicine, science, education, industry, government, art – seemed somehow more stable, adjusted, mature, than American children, whose full-time mothers do nothing but worry about them. Could it be that Russian women are somehow better mothers because they have a serious purpose in their own lives? At least, said the good Dr Spock, these mothers are more sure of themselves as mothers. They are not, like American mothers, dependent on the latest word from the experts, the newest child-care fad.[11] It is clearly a terrible burden on Dr Spock to have 13,500,000 mothers so unsure of themselves that they bring up their children literally according to his book – and call piteously to him for help when the book does not work.

No headlines marked the growing concern of psychiatrists with the problem of 'dependence' in American children and grown-up children. The psychiatrist David Levy, in a very famous study of 'maternal overprotection', studied in exhaustive detail twenty mothers who had damaged their children to a pathological extent by 'maternal infantilization, indulgence and overprotection'.[12] A typical case was a twelve-year-old boy who had

... infantile temper tantrums in his eleventh year when his mother refused to butter his bread for him. He still demanded her help in dressing. ... He summed up his requirements in life very neatly by saying that his mother would butter his bread for him until he married, after which his wife would do so. ...

All these mothers – according to physiological indexes such as menstrual flow, breast milk and early indications of a 'maternal type of behaviour' – were unusually strong in their feminine or maternal instinctual base, if it can be described that way. All but two of the twenty, as Dr Levy himself described it, were responsible, stable, and aggressive. In none was there any tinge of unconscious rejection of the child or motherhood.

What made these twenty strongly maternal women (evidently strength, even aggression, is not masculine when a psychiatrist considers it part of the maternal instinct) produce such pathologically infantile sons? For one thing, the 'child was utilized as a means of satisfying an abnormal craving for love'. These mothers freshened up, put lipstick on when the son was due home from school, as a wife for a husband or a girl for her date, because they had no other life besides the child. Most, Levy said, had thwarted career ambitions. The 'maternal overprotection' was actually caused by these mothers' strength, by their basic feminine energy – responsible, stable, active, and aggressive – producing pathology in the child when the mother was blocked from 'other channels of expression'.

Most of these mothers also had dominating mothers and submissive fathers of their own, and their husbands had also been obedient sons of dominating mothers; in Freudian terms, the castrativeness all around was rather extreme. The sons and mothers were given intensive psychoanalytical therapy for years, which, it was hoped, would break the pathological cycle. But when, some years after the original study, research workers checked on these women and the children they had pathologically overprotected, the results were not quite what was expected. In most cases psychotherapy had not been effective. Yet some of the children, miraculously, did not become pathological adults; not because of therapy, but because by circumstance the mother had acquired an interest or activity in her own life and had simply stopped living the child's life for him. In a few other cases, the child survived because, through his own ability, he had staked out an area of independence of which his mother was not a part.

Other clues to the real problem of the mother–child relationship in America have been seen by social scientists without ever penetrating the mystique. A sociologist named Arnold Green almost by accident discovered another dimension to the relationship between nurturing mother love, or its lack, and neurosis.

It seems that in the Massachusetts industrial town where Green grew up an entire generation was raised under psychological conditions which should have been traumatic. The parents, Polish immigrants, tried to enforce rigid old-world rules which their American children did not respect.

In exasperation and fear of losing all control over their Americanized youngsters, parents apply the fist and whip rather indiscriminately. The sound of blows, screams, howls, vexations, wails of torment and hatred are so commonplace along the rows of dilapidated millhouses that the passersby pay them scant attention.[13]

Surely, here were the seeds of future neuroses, as all good post-Freudian parents in America understand them. But to Green's amazement, when he went back and checked as a sociologist on the neuroses which according to the book must surely be flourishing, he found no known case of Army rejection because of psychoneurosis in the local Polish community, and in the overt behaviour of an entire generation in the village 'no expression of anxiety, guilty feelings, rigidity of response, repressed hostility – the various symptoms described as characteristic of the basic neurotic character'. Green wondered. Why didn't those children become neurotic, why weren't they destroyed by that brutal, irrational parental authority?

They had none of that constant and watchful nurturing love that is urged on middle-class mothers by the child psychologizers; their mothers, like their fathers, worked all day in the factory; they had been left in the care of older sisters or brothers, had run free in fields and woods, had avoided their parents wherever possible. In these families, stress was placed upon work, rather than personal sentiment: 'Respect, not love is the tie that binds.' Demonstrations of affection were not altogether lacking, Green said, 'but they had little in common with the definitions of parent–child love found in the middle-class women's magazines.'

It occurred to the sociologist that perhaps the very absence of this omnipresent nurturing mother love might explain why these children did not suffer the neurotic symptoms so commonly found in the sons of middle-class parents. The Polish parents' authority, however brutal and irrational, was 'external to the core of the self', as Green put it. The Polish parents did not have the technique or opportunity to 'absorb the personality of the child'. Perhaps, Green suggested, 'lack of love' and 'irrational authority' do not in themselves cause neurosis, but only within a certain context of 'personality absorption' – the physical and emotional blanketing of the child which brings about that slavish dependence upon the parents found among children of the native white American urban college-educated middle class.

Green wanted to 'find out what there is to being a modern middle-class parent that fertilizes the soil of the child's neurosis, however the individual seed is planted'.

As usual, the arrow pointed unerringly to the mother. But Green was not concerned with helping the modern American mother adjust to her role; on the contrary, he found that she lacked any real 'role' as a woman in modern society.

She enters marriage and perhaps bears a child with no definite role and series of functions, as formerly.... She feels inferior to man because comparatively she has been and is more restricted. The extent of the actual emancipation of women has been commonly exaggerated....

Through a 'good' marriage the middle-class girl attains far more status than is possible through a career of her own. But the period of phantom dalliance with a career, or an embarkation upon one, leave her ill-fitted for the drudgery of housecleaning, diapers, and the preparation of meals.... The mother has little to do, in or out of the home; she is her single child's sole companion. Modern 'scientific child care' enforces a constant supervision and diffused worrying over the child's health, eating spinach, and ego development; this is complicated by the fact that much energy is spent forcing early walking, toilet-training, talking, because in an intensively competitive milieu middle-class parents from the day of birth are constantly comparing their own child's development with that of the neighbours' children.

Perhaps, Green speculates, middle-class mothers

... have made 'love' of supreme importance in their relation to the child, theirs for him and his for them, partly because of the love-complex of our time, which is particularly ramified within the middle class, and partly as a compensation for them any sacrifices they have made for the child. The child's need for love is experienced precisely because he has been conditioned to need it ... conditioned to a slavish emotional dependence. ... Not the need for parental love, but the constant threat of its withdrawal after the child has been conditioned to the need, lies at the root of the most character-istic modern neuroses; Mamma won't like you if you don't eat your spinach, or stop dribbling your milk, or get down from that davenport. To the extent that a child's personality has been absorbed, he will be thrown into a panic by this sort of treatment. ... In such a child, a disapproving glance may produce more terror – than a twenty-minute lashing in little Stanislaus Wojcik.

Green was only concerned with mothers in terms of their effect on their sons. But it occurred to him that 'personality absorption' alone cannot, after all, explain neurosis. Because otherwise, he says, middle-class women of the previous gene-ration would all have suffered such neuroses – and nobody recorded such suffering in those women. Certainly the person-ality of the middle-class girl of the late nineteenth century was 'absorbed' by her parents, by the demands of 'love' and un-questioning obedience. However, 'the rate of neurosis under those conditions was probably not too high', the sociologist concludes, because even though the woman's own personality was 'absorbed', it was consistently absorbed 'within a role which changed relatively slightly from childhood into adoles-cence, courtship, and finally into marriage'; she never could be her own person.

It is provocative, this speculation made by a sociologist in 1946, but it never penetrated far beyond the inner circles of social theory, never permeated the bulwarks of the feminine mystique, despite increasing national awareness that some-thing was wrong with American mothers. Even this sociolo-gist, who managed to get behind the mystique and see children in terms other than their need for more mother love, was con-cerned only with the problem of the sons. But was not the real implication that the role of the middle-class American housewife forces many a mother to smother, absorb, the personality of both her sons and daughters? Many saw the tragic waste of American sons who were made incapable of achievement, individual values, independent action; but they did not see as tragic the waste of the daughters, or of the mothers to whom it happened generations earlier. If a culture does not expect human maturity from its women, it does not see its lack as a waste, or as a possible cause of neurosis or conflict. The insult, the real reflection on our culture's definition of the role of women, is that as a nation we only noticed that something was wrong with women when we saw its effects on their sons.

The unremitting attack on women which has become an American preoccupation in recent years might also stem from the same escapist motives that sent men and women back to the security of the home. Mother love is said to be sacred in America, but with all the reverence and lip service she is paid, mom is a pretty safe target, no matter how correctly or incorrectly her failures are interpreted. Apart from the psychological pressures from mothers or wives, there have been plenty of nonsexual pressures in the America of the last decade – the compromising, never-ceasing competition, the anonymous and often purposeless work in the big organization – that also kept a man from feeling like a man. Safer to take it out on his wife and his mother than to recognize a failure in himself or in the sacred American way of life. The men were not always kidding when they said their wives were lucky to be able to stay home all day. It was also soothing to rationalize the rat race by telling themselves that they were in it 'for the wife and kids'. And so men re-created their own childhood in suburbia, and made mothers of their wives.

But why did women sit still for this barrage of blame? When a culture has erected barrier after barrier against women as separate selves; when a culture has erected legal, political, social, economic, and educational barriers to women's own acceptance of maturity – even after most of those barriers are down it is still easier for a woman to seek the sanctuary of the home. It is easier to live through her husband and children

than to make a road of her own in the world. For she is the
daughter of that same mom who made it so hard for girl as
well as boy to grow up. And freedom is a frightening thing.
Why should a woman bother to be anything more than a wife
and mother if all the forces of her culture tell her she doesn't
have to, will be better off not to, grow up?

And so the American woman made her mistaken choice.
She ran back home again to live by sex alone, trading in her
individuality for security. Her husband was drawn in after her,
and the door was shut against the outside world. They began
to live the pretty lie of the feminine mystique, but could either
of them really believe it? She was, after all, an American
woman, an irreversible product of a culture that stops just
short of giving her a separate identity. He was, after all, an
American man whose respect for individuality and freedom
of choice are his nation's pride. They went to school together;
he knows who she is. Does his meek willingness to wax the
floor and wash the dishes when he comes home tired on the
6.55 hide from both their guilty awareness of the reality
behind the pretty lie? What keeps them believing it, in spite
of the warning signs that have cropped up all over the suburban lot? What keeps the women home? What force in our
culture is strong enough to write 'Occupation: housewife' so
large that all the other possibilities for women have been
almost obscured?

CHAPTER 9

The Sexual Sell

SOME months ago, as I began to fit together the puzzle of
women's retreat to home, I had the feeling I was missing
something. If, despite the nameless desperation of so many
American housewives, despite the opportunities open to all
women now, so few have any purpose in life other than to be
a wife and mother, somebody, something pretty powerful
must be at work.

There are certain facts of life so obvious and mundane that
one never talks about them. Only the child blurts out: 'Why
do people in books never go to the toilet?' Why is it never
said that the really crucial function, the really important role
that women serve as housewives is *to buy more things for the
house?* In all the talk of femininity and woman's role, one
forgets that the real business of America is business. But the
perpetuation of housewifery, the growth of the feminine mystique, makes sense (and dollars) when one realizes that women
are the chief customers of American business. Somehow,
somewhere, someone must have figured out that women will
buy more things if they are kept in the underused, nameless-
yearning, energy-to-get-rid-of state of being housewives.

It was not an economic conspiracy directed against women.
It was a byproduct of our general confusion lately of means
with ends; just something that happened to women when the
business of producing and selling and investing in business
for profit – which is merely the way our economy is organized
to serve man's needs efficiently – began to be confused with the
purpose of our nation, the end of life itself. No more surprising, the subversion of women's lives in America to the
ends of business, than the subversion of the sciences of
human behaviour to the business of deluding women about

their real needs. It would take a clever economist to figure out what would keep our affluent economy going if the housewife market began to fall off, just as an economist would have to figure out what to do if there were no threat of war.

It is easy to see why it happened. I learned *how* it happened when I went to see a man who is paid approximately a million dollars a year for his professional services in manipulating the emotions of American women to serve the needs of business. This particular man got in on the ground floor of the hidden-persuasion business in 1945, and kept going. The head-quarters of his institute for motivational manipulation is a baronial mansion in upper Westchester. The walls of a ball-room two storeys high are filled with steel shelves holding a thousand-odd studies for business and industry, 300,000 indi-vidual 'depth interviews', mostly with American housewives.[1]

He let me see what I wanted, said I could use anything that was not confidential to a specific company. Nothing there for anyone to hide, to feel guilty about – only, in page after page of those depth studies, a shrewd cheerful awareness of the empty, purposeless, uncreative, even sexually joyless lives that most American housewives lead. In his own unabashed terms, this most helpful of hidden persuaders showed me the function served by keeping American women housewives – the reservoir that their lack of identity, lack of purpose, creates, to be manipulated into dollars at the point of pur-chase.

Properly manipulated ('if you are not afraid of that word,' he said), American housewives can be given the sense of identity, purpose, creativity, the self-realization, even the sex-ual joy they lack – by the buying of things. I suddenly realized the significance of the boast that women wield seventy-five per cent of the purchasing power in America. I suddenly saw American women as *victims* of that ghastly gift, that power at the point of purchase. The insights he shared with me so liberally revealed many things. ...

The dilemma of business was spelled out in a survey made in 1945 for the publisher of a leading women's magazine on the attitudes of women towards electrical appliances. The message was considered of interest to all the companies that, with the war about to end, were going to have to make consumer sales take the place of war contracts. It was a study of 'the psychology of housekeeping'; 'a woman's attitude towards housekeeping appliances cannot be separated from her attitude towards homemaking in general,' it warned.

On the basis of a national sample of 4,500 wives (middle-class, high-school or college-educated), American women were divided into three categories: 'The True Housewife Type', 'The Career Woman', and 'The Balanced Home-maker'. While 51 per cent of the women then fitted 'The True Housewife Type' ('From the psychological point of view, housekeeping is this woman's dominating interest. She takes the utmost pride and satisfaction in maintaining a comfortable and well-run home for her family. Consciously or subconsciously, she feels that she is indispensable and that no one else can take over her job. She has little, if any, desire for a position outside the home, and if she has one it is through force of circumstances or necessity'), it was apparent that this group was diminishing, and probably would continue to do so as new fields, interests, education were now open to women.

The largest market for appliances, however, was this 'True Housewife' – though she had a certain 'reluctance' to accept new devices that had to be recognized and overcome. ('She may even fear that they [appliances] will render unnecessary the old-fashioned way of doing things that has always suited her.') After all, housework was the justification for her whole existence. ('I don't think there is any way to make housework easier for myself,' one True Housewife said, 'because I don't believe that a machine can take the place of hard work.')

The second type – The Career Woman or Would-Be Career Woman – was a minority, but an extremely 'unhealthy' one from the sellers' standpoint; advertisers were warned that it would be to their advantage not to let this group get any larger. For such women, though not necessarily job-holders, 'do not believe that a woman's place is primarily in the home'. ('Many in this group have never actually worked, but their attitude is: "I think housekeeping is a horrible waste of time. If my youngsters were old enough and I were free to leave the house, I would use my time to better advantage. If my family's meals and laundry could be taken care of, I would be delighted to go out and get a job." ') The point to bear in mind regarding career women, the study said, is that, while they buy modern appliances, they are not the ideal type of customer. *They are too critical.*

The third type – 'The Balanced Homemaker' – is 'from the market standpoint, the ideal type'. She has some outside interests, or has held a job before turning exclusively to homemaking; she 'readily accepts' the help mechanical appliances can give – but 'does not expect them to do the impossible' because she needs to use her own executive ability 'in managing a well-run household'.

The moral of the study was explicit:

Since the Balanced Homemaker represents the market with the greatest future potential, it would be to the advantage of the appliance manufacturer to make more and more women aware of the desirability of belonging to this group. Educate them through advertising that it is possible to have outside interests and become alert to wider intellectual influences (without becoming a Career Woman). The art of good homemaking should be the goal of every normal woman.

The problem – which, if recognized at that time by one hidden persuader for the home-appliance industry, was surely recognized by others with products for the home – was that 'a whole new generation of women is being educated to do work outside the home. Furthermore, an increased desire for emancipation is evident.' The solution, quite simply, was to encourage them to be 'modern' housewives. The Career or Would-Be Career Woman who frankly dislikes cleaning, dusting, ironing, washing clothes, is less interested in a new wax, a new soap powder. Unlike 'The True Housewife' and the 'Balanced Homemaker' who prefer to have sufficient appliances and do the housework themselves, the Career Woman would 'prefer servants – housework takes too much time and energy'. She buys appliances, however, whether or not she has servants, but she is 'more likely to complain about the service they give', and to be 'harder to sell'.

It was too late – impossible – to turn these modern could-or-would-be career women back into True Housewives, but the study pointed out, in 1945, the potential for Balanced House-wifery – the home career. Let them 'want to have their cake and eat it too ... save time, have more comfort, avoid dirt and disorder, have mechanized supervision, yet not want to give up the feeling of personal achievement and pride in a well-run household, which comes from "doing it yourself". As one young housewife said: "It's nice to be modern – it's like running a factory in which you have all the latest machinery."'

But it was not an easy job, either for business or advertisers. New gadgets that were able to do almost all the housework crowded the market; increased ingenuity was needed to give American women that 'feeling of achievement', and yet keep housework their main purpose in life. Education, independence, growing individuality, everything that made them ready for other purposes had constantly to be countered, channelled back to the home.

The manipulator's services became increasingly valuable. In later surveys, he no longer interviewed professional women; they were not at home during the day. The women in his samples were deliberately True or Balanced Housewives, the new suburban housewives. Household and consumer products are, after all, geared to women; seventy-five per cent of all consumer advertising budgets is spent to appeal to women; that is, to housewives, the women who are available during the day to be interviewed, the women with the time for shopping. Naturally, his depth interviews, projective tests, 'living laboratories', were designed to impress his clients, but more often than not they contained the shrewd insights of a skilled social scientist, insights that could be used with profit.

He wrote in one report, for example:

Every effort must be made to sell X Mix, as a base upon which the woman's creative effort is used.

The appeal should emphasize the fact that X Mix aids the woman in expressing her creativity because it takes the drudgery away. At the same time, stress should be laid upon the cooking manipulations, the fun that goes with them, permitting you to feel that X Mix baking is real baking.

But the dilemma again: how to make her spend money on the mix that takes some of the drudgery out of baking by telling her 'she can utilize her energy where it really counts' – and yet keep her from being 'too busy to bake'? ('I don't use the mix because I don't do any baking at all. It's too much trouble. I live in a sprawled-out apartment and what with keeping it clean and looking after my child and my part-time job, I don't have time for baking.') What to do about their 'feeling of disappointment' when the biscuits come out of the oven, and they're really only bread and there is no feeling of creative achievement? ('Why should I bake my own biscuits when there are so many good things on the market that just need to be heated up? It just doesn't make any sense at all to go through all the trouble of mixing your own and then greasing the tin and baking them.') What to do when the woman doesn't get the feeling her mother got, when the cake *had* to be made from scratch? ('The way my mother made them, you had to sift the flour yourself and add the eggs and the butter and you knew you'd really made something you could be proud of.')

The problem can be handled, the report assured:

By using X Mix the woman can prove herself as a wife and mother, not only by baking, but by spending more time with her family. . . . Of course, it must also be made clear that home-baked foods are in every way preferable to bakery-shop foods . . .

Above all, give X Mix 'a therapeutic value' by downplaying the easy recipes, emphasizing instead 'the stimulating effort of baking'. From an advertising viewpoint, this means stressing that 'with X Mix in the home, you will be a different woman . . . a happier woman'.

Further, the client was told that a phrase in his ad, 'and you make that cake the easiest, laziest way there is', evoked a 'negative response' in American housewives – it hit too close to their 'underlying guilt'. ('Since they never feel that they are

really exerting sufficient effort, it is certainly wrong to tell
them that baking with X Mix is the lazy way.') Supposing, he
suggested, that this devoted wife and mother behind the
kitchen stove, anxiously preparing a cake or pie for her
husband or children 'is simply indulging her own hunger for
sweets'. The very fact that baking is work for the housewife
helps her dispel any doubts that she might have about her real
motivations.

But there are even ways to manipulate the housewives' guilt,
the report said:

It might be possible to suggest through advertising that not to
take advantage of all 12 uses of X Mix is to limit your efforts to give
pleasure to your family. A transfer of guilt might be achieved.
Rather than feeling guilty about using X Mix for dessert food, the
woman would be made to feel guilty if she doesn't take advantage
of this opportunity to give her family 12 different and delicious
treats. 'Don't waste your skill; don't limit yourself.'

By the mid fifties, the surveys reported with pleasure that
the Career Woman ('the woman who clamoured for equality –
almost for identity in every sphere of life, the woman who
reacted to "domestic slavery" with indignation and vehe-
mence') was gone, replaced by the 'less worldly, less sophisticated' woman whose activity in P.T.A. gives her 'broad contacts with the world outside her home', but who 'finds in
housework a medium of expression for her femininity and
individuality'. She's not like the old-fashioned self-sacrificing
housewife; she considers herself the equal of man. But she
still feels 'lazy, neglectful, haunted by guilt feelings' because
she doesn't have enough work to do.

After an initial resistance, she now tends to accept instant coffee,
frozen foods, precooked foods, and labour-saving items as part of
her routine. But she needs a justification and she finds it in the
thought that 'by using frozen foods I'm freeing myself to accomplish other important tasks as a modern mother and wife'.

Creativeness is the modern woman's dialectical answer to the
problem of her changed position in the household. Thesis: I'm a
housewife. Antithesis: I hate drudgery. Synthesis: I'm creative!

This means, essentially that even though the housewife may buy canned food, for instance, and thus save time and effort, she doesn't let it go at that. She has a great need for 'doctoring up' the can and thus prove her personal participation and her concern with giving satisfaction to her family.

The feeling of creativeness also serves another purpose: it is an outlet for the liberated talents, the better taste, the freer imagination, the greater initiative of the modern woman. It permits her to use at home *all the faculties that she would display in an outside career*.

The yearning for creative opportunities and moments is a major aspect of buying motivations.

The only trouble, the surveys warned, is that she 'tries to use her own mind and her own judgement. She is fast getting away from judging by collective or majority standards. She is developing independent standards.' ('Never mind the neighbours. I don't want to "live up" to them or compare myself to them at every turn.') She can't always be reached now with 'keep up with the Joneses' – the advertiser must appeal to her *own* need to live.

Appeal to this thirst. . . . Tell her that you are adding more zest, more enjoyment to her life, that it is within her reach now to taste new experiences and that she is entitled to taste these experiences. Even more positively, you should convey that you are giving her 'lessons in living'.

'House cleaning should be fun,' the manufacturer of a certain cleaning device was advised. Even though his product was, perhaps, less efficient than the vacuum cleaner, it let the housewife use more of her own energy in the work. Further, it let the housewife have the illusion that she has become 'a professional, an expert in determining which cleaning tools to use for specific jobs'.

This professionalization is a psychological defence of the house-wife against being a general 'cleaner-upper' and menial servant for her family in a day and age of general work emancipation.

The role of expert serves a two-fold emotional function: (1) it helps the housewife achieve status, and (2) she moves beyond the orbit of her home, into the world of modern science in her search for new and better ways of doing things.

As a result, there has never been a more favourable psychological climate for household appliances and products. The modern housewife ... is actually aggressive in her efforts to find those household products which, in her expert opinion, really meet her need. This trend accounts for the popularity of different waxes and polishes for different materials in the home, for the growing use of floor polishers, and for the variety of mops and cleaning implements for floors and walls.

The difficulty is to give her the 'sense of achievement', of 'ego enhancement', she has been persuaded to seek in the housewife 'profession', when, in actuality, 'her time-consuming task, housekeeping, is not only endless, it is a task for which society hires the lowliest, least-trained, most trod-upon individuals and groups. ... Anyone with a strong enough back (and a small enough brain) can do these menial chores.' But even this difficulty can be manipulated to sell her more things:

One of the ways that the housewife raises her own prestige as a cleaner of her home is through the use of specialized products for specialized tasks. ...

When she uses one product for washing clothes, a second for dishes, a third for walls, a fourth for floors, a fifth for venetian blinds, etc., rather than an all-purpose cleaner, she feels less like an unskilled labourer, more like an engineer, an expert.

A second way of raising her own stature is to 'do things my way' – to establish an expert's role for herself by creating her own 'tricks of the trade'. For example, she may 'always put a bit of bleach in all my washing – even coloured, to make them *really* clean'!

Help her to 'justify her menial task by building up her role as the protector of her family – the killer of millions of microbes and germs', this report advised. 'Emphasize her king-pin role in the family ... help her be an expert rather than a menial worker ... make housework a matter of knowledge and skill, rather than a matter of brawn and dull, unremitting effort.' An effective way of doing this is to bring out a *new* product. For, it seems, there's a growing wave of housewives 'who look forward to new products which not only decrease their daily work load, but actually engage their emotional and intellectual interest in the world of scientific development outside the home'.

The question of letting the woman use her mind and even participate in science through housework is, however, not without its drawbacks. Science should not relieve housewives of too much drudgery; it must concentrate instead on creating the *illusion* of that sense of achievement that housewives seem to need.

To prove this point, 250 housewives were given a depth test: they were asked to choose among four imaginary methods of cleaning. The first was a completely automatic dust-and-dirt-removal system which operated continuously like a home-heating system. The second, the housewife had to press a button to start. The third was portable; she had to carry it around and point it at an area to remove the dirt. The fourth was a brand new, modern object with which she could sweep the dirt away herself. The housewives spoke up in favour of this last appliance. If it 'appears new, modern' she would rather have the one that lets her work herself, this report said. 'One compelling reason is her desire to be a participant, not just a button-pusher.' As one housewife remarked, 'As for some magical push-button cleaning system, well, what would happen to my exercise, my feeling of accomplishment, and what would I do with my mornings?'

This fascinating study incidentally revealed that a certain electronic cleaning appliance – long considered one of our great labour savers – actually made 'housekeeping more difficult than it need be'. From the response of eighty per cent of those housewives, it seemed that once a woman got this appliance going, she 'felt compelled to do cleaning that wasn't really necessary'. The electronic appliance actually dictated the extent and type of cleaning to be done.

Should the housewife then be encouraged to go back to that simple cheap sweeper that let her clean only as much as she felt necessary? No, said the report, of course not. Simply give that old-fashioned sweeper the 'status' of the electronic appliance as a 'labour-saving necessity' for the modern housewife 'and then indicate that the modern homemaker would, naturally, own both'.

No one, not even the depth researchers, denied that house-work was endless, and its boring repetition just did not give that much satisfaction, did not require that much vaunted expert knowledge. But the endlessness of it all was an advantage from the seller's point of view. The problem was to keep at bay the underlying realization which was lurking dangerously in 'thousands of depth interviews which we have conducted for dozens of different kinds of house-cleaning products' – the realization that, as one housewife said, 'It stinks! I have to do it, so I do it. It's a necessary evil, that's all.' What to do? For one thing, put out more and more products, make the directions more complicated, make it really necessary for the housewife to 'be an expert'. (Washing clothes, the report advised, must become more than a matter of throwing clothes into a machine and pouring in soap. Garments must be carefully sorted, one load given treatment A, a second load treatment B, some washed by hand. The house-wife can then 'take great pride in knowing just which of the arsenal of products to use on each occasion'.)

Capitalize, the report continued, on housewives' 'guilt over the hidden dirt' so she will rip her house to shreds in a 'deep cleaning' operation, which will give her a 'sense of complete-ness' for a few weeks. ('The times of thorough cleaning are the points at which she is most willing to try new products and "deep clean" advertising holds out the promise of com-pletion.')

The seller must also stress the joys of completing each separate task, remembering that 'nearly all housekeepers, even those who thoroughly detest their job, paradoxically find escape from their endless fate by accepting it – by "throwing myself into it," as she says'.

Losing herself in her work – surrounded by all the implements, creams, powders, soaps, she forgets for a time how soon she will have to re-do the task. ... she seizes the moment of completion of a task as a moment of pleasure as pure as if she had just finished a masterpiece of art which would stand as a monument to her credit forever.

This is the kind of creative experience the seller of things can give the housewife. In one housewife's own words:

I don't like housework at all. I'm a lousy houseworker. But once in a while I get pepped up and I'll really go to town. ... When I have some new kind of cleaning material – like when Glass Wax first came out or those silicone furniture polishes – I got a real kick out of it, and I went through the house shining everything. I like to see the things shine. I feel so good when I see the bathroom just glistening.

And so the manipulator advised:

Identify your product with the physical and spiritual rewards she derives from the almost religious feeling of basic security provided by her home. Talk about her 'light, happy, peaceful feelings'; her 'deep sense of achievement'. ... But remember she doesn't really want praise for the sake of praise ... also remember that her mood is not simply 'gay'. She is tired and a bit solemn. Superficially cheerful adjectives or colours will not reflect her feelings. She will react much more favourably to simple, warm and sincere messages.

In the fifties came the revolutionary discovery of the teenage market. Teenagers and young marrieds began to figure prominently in the surveys. It was discovered that young wives, who had only been to high school and had never worked, were more 'insecure', less independent, easier to sell. These young people could be told that, by buying the right things, they could achieve middle-class status, without work or study. The keep-up-with-the-Joneses sell would work again; the individuality and independence which American women had been getting from education and work outside the home was not such a problem with the teenage brides. In fact, the surveys said, if the pattern of 'happiness through things' could be established when these women were young enough, they could be safely encouraged to go out and get a part-time job to help their husbands pay for all the things they buy. The main point now was to convince the teenagers that 'happiness through things' is no longer the prerogative of the rich or the talented; it can be enjoyed by all, if they learn 'the right way', the way the others do it, if they learn the embarrassment of being different.

In the words of one of these reports:

49 per cent of the new brides were teenagers, and more girls marry at the age of 18 than at any other age. This early family formation yields a larger number of young people who are on the threshold of their own responsibilities and decision-making in purchases. ...

But the most important fact is of a psychological nature: marriage today is not only the culmination of a romantic attachment; more consciously and more clear-headedly than in the past, it is also a decision to create a partnership in establishing a comfortable home, equipped with a great number of desirable products.

In talking to scores of young couples and brides-to-be, we found that, as a rule, their conversations and dreams centred to a very large degree around their future homes and their furnishings, around shopping 'to get an idea', around discussing the advantages and disadvantages of various products. ...

The modern bride is deeply convinced of the unique value of married love, of the possibilities of finding real happiness in marriage and of fulfilling her personal destiny in it and through it.

But the engagement period today is a romantic, dreamy and heady period only to a limited extent. It is probably safe to say that the period of engagement tends to be a rehearsal of the material duties and responsibilities of marriage. While waiting for the nuptials, couples work hard, put aside money for definite purchases, or even begin buying on an instalment plan.

What is the deeper meaning of this new combination of an almost religious belief in the importance and beauty of married life on the one hand, and the product-centred outlook, on the other? ...

The modern bride seeks as a conscious goal that which in many cases her grandmother saw as a blind fate and her mother as slavery: to belong to a man, to have a home and children of her own, to choose among all possible careers the career of wife–mother–homemaker.

All these meanings she seeks in her marriage, even her fear that she will be 'left behind', can be channelled into the purchase of products. For example, a manufacturer of sterling silver, a product that is very difficult to sell, was told:

Reassure her that only with sterling can she be fully secure in her new role ... it symbolizes her success as a modern woman. Above all, dramatize the fun and pride that derive from the job of cleaning silver. Stimulate the pride of achievement. 'How much pride you get from the brief task that's so much fun ...'

Concentrate on the very young teenage girls, this report further advised. The young ones will want what 'the others' want, even if their mothers don't. ('As one of our teenagers said: "All the gang has started their own sets of sterling. We're real keen about it – compare patterns and go through the ads together. My own family never had any sterling and they think I'm showing off when I spend my money on it – they think plated's just as good. But the kids think they're way off base."') Get them in schools, churches, sororities, social clubs; get them through home-economics teachers, group leaders, teenage TV programmes, and teenage advertising. 'This is the big market of the future and word-of-mouth advertising, along with group pressure, is not only the most potent influence but, in the absence of tradition, a most necessary one.'

As for the more independent older wife, that unfortunate tendency to use materials that require little care – stainless steel, plastic dishes, paper napkins – can be met by making her feel guilty about the effects on the children. ('As one young wife told us: "I'm out of the house all day long, so I can't prepare and serve meals the way I want to. I don't like it that way – my husband and the children deserve a better break. Sometimes I think it'd be better if we tried to get along on one salary and have a real home life but there are always so many things we need."') Such guilt, the report maintained, can be used to make her see the product, silver, as a means of holding the family together; it gives 'added psychological value'. What's more, the product can even fill the housewife's need for identity: 'Suggest that it becomes truly a part of *you*, reflecting *you*. Do not be afraid to suggest mystically that sterling will adapt itself to any house and any person.'

The fur industry is in trouble, another survey reported, because young high school and college girls equate fur coats with 'uselessness' and 'a kept woman'. Again the advice was to get to the very young before these unfortunate connotations have formed. ('By introducing youngsters to positive fur experiences, the probabilities of easing their way into garment purchasing in their teens is enhanced.') Point out that 'the wearing of a fur garment actually establishes femininity and sexuality for a woman'. ('It's the kind of thing a girl looks forward to. It means something. It's feminine.' 'I'm bringing my daughter up right. She always wants to put on "mommy's coat". She'll want them. She's a real girl.') But keep in mind that 'Mink has contributed a negative feminine symbolism to the whole fur market.' Unfortunately, two out of three women felt mink-wearers were 'predatory ... exploitative ... dependent ... socially non-productive ...'

And so fur's 'ego-orientation' must be reduced and replaced with the new femininity of the housewife, for whom ego-orientation must be translated into togetherness, family-orientation.

Begin to create the feeling that fur is a necessity – a delightful necessity ... thus providing the consumer with moral permission to purchase something she now feels is ego-oriented.... Give fur femininity a broader character, developing some of the following status and prestige symbols ... an emotionally happy woman ... wife and mother who wins the affection and respect of her husband and her children because of the kind of person she is, and the kind of role she performs. ...

Place furs in a family setting; show the pleasure and admiration of a fur garment derived by family members, husband and children; their pride in their mother's appearance, in her ownership of a fur garment. Develop fur garments as 'family' gifts – enable the whole family to enjoy that garment at Christmas, etc., thus reducing its ego-orientation for the owner and eliminating her guilt over her alleged self-indulgence.

Thus, the only way that the young housewife was supposed to express herself, and not feel guilty about it, was in buying products for the home-and-family. Any creative urges she may have should also be home-and-family oriented, as still another survey reported to the home sewing industry.

Such activities as sewing achieve a new meaning and a new status. Sewing is no longer associated with absolute need. . . . Moreover, with the moral elevation of home-oriented activities, sewing, along with cooking, gardening, and home decorating – is recognized as a means of expressing creativity and individuality and also as a means of achieving the 'quality' which a new taste level dictates.

The women who sew, this survey discovered, are the active, energetic, intelligent modern housewives, the new home-oriented modern American women, who have a great unfulfilled need to create, and achieve, and realize their own individuality – which must be filled by some home activity. The big problem for the home-sewing industry was that the 'image' of sewing was too 'dull'; somehow it didn't achieve the feeling of creating something important. In selling their products, the industry must emphasize the 'lasting creativeness' of sewing.

But even sewing can't be too creative, too individual, according to the advice offered to one pattern manufacturer. His patterns required some intelligence to follow, left quite a lot of room for individual expression, and the manufacturer was in trouble for that very reason; his patterns implied that a woman 'would know what she likes and would probably have definite ideas'. He was advised to widen this 'far too limited fashion personality' and get one with 'fashion conformity' – appeal to the 'fashion-insecure woman', 'the conformist element in fashion', who feels 'it is not smart to be dressed too differently'.

Time and time again, the surveys shrewdly analysed the needs, and even the secret frustrations of the American housewife; and each time if these needs were properly manipulated, she could be induced to buy more 'things'. In 1957, a survey told the department stores that their role in this new world was not only to 'sell' the housewife but to satisfy her need for 'education'.

Most women have not only a material need, but a psychological compulsion to visit department stores. They live in comparative isolation. Their vista and experiences are limited. They know that there is a vaster life beyond their horizon and they fear that life will pass them by.

Department stores break down that isolation. The woman entering a department store suddenly has the feeling she knows what is going on in the world. Department stores, more than magazines, TV, or any other medium of mass communication, are most women's main source of information about the various aspects of life. . . .

There are many needs that the department store must fill, this report continued. For one, the housewife's 'need to learn and to advance in life'.

We symbolize our social position by the objects with which we surround ourselves. A woman whose husband was making $6,000 a few years ago and is making $10,000 now needs to learn a whole new set of symbols. Department stores are her best teachers of this subject.

For another, there is the need for achievement, which for the new modern housewife is primarily filled by a 'bargain'.

We have found that in our economy of abundance, preoccupation with prices is not so much a financial as a psychological need for the majority of women. . . . Increasingly a 'bargain' means not that 'I can now buy something which I could not afford at a higher price'; it mainly means 'I'm doing a good job as a housewife; I'm contributing to the welfare of the family just as my husband does when he works and brings home the pay cheque.'

The price itself hardly matters, the report said:

Since buying is only the climax of a complicated relationship, based to a large extent on the woman's yearning to know how to be a more attractive woman, a better housewife, a superior mother, etc., use this motivation in all your promotion and advertising. Take every opportunity to explain how your store will help her fulfil her most cherished roles in life. . . .

If the stores are women's school of life, ads are the textbooks. They have an inexhaustible avidity for these ads which give them the illusion that they are in contact with what is going on in the world of inanimate objects, objects through which they express so much of so many of their drives. . . .

Again, in 1957, a survey very correctly reported that despite the 'many positive aspects' of the 'new home-centred era', unfortunately too many needs were now centred on the home – that home was not able to fill. A cause for alarm? No indeed; even these needs are grist for manipulation.

The family is not always the psychological pot of gold at the end of the rainbow of promise of modern life as it has sometimes been represented. In fact, psychological demands are being made upon the family today which it cannot fulfil. ...

Fortunately for the producers and advertisers of America (and also for the family and the psychological well-being of our citizens) much of this gap may be filled, and is being filled, by the acquisition of consumer goods.

Hundreds of products fulfil a whole set of psychological functions that producers and advertisers should know of and use in the development of more effective sales approaches. Just as producing once served as an outlet for social tension, now consumption serves the same purpose.

'The frustrated need for privacy in the family life', in this era of 'togetherness', was another secret wish uncovered in a depth survey. This need, however, might be used to sell a second car. ...

In addition to the car the whole family enjoys together, the car for the husband and wife separately – 'Alone in the car, one may get the breathing spell one needs so badly and may come to consider the car as one's castle, or the instrument of one's reconquered privacy.' Or 'individual' 'personal' toothpaste, soap, shampoo.

Another survey reported that there was a puzzling 'de-sexualization of married life' despite the great emphasis on marriage and family and sex. The problem: what can supply what the report diagnosed as a 'missing sexual spark'? The solution: the report advised sellers to 'put the libido back into advertising'. Despite the feeling that our manufacturers are trying to sell everything through sex, sex as found on TV commercials and ads in national magazines is too tame, the report said, too narrow. 'Consumerism' is desexing the American libido because it 'has failed to reflect the powerful life forces in every individual which range far beyond the relationship between the sexes'.

Most modern advertising reflects and grossly exaggerates our present national tendency to downgrade, simplify and water down the passionate, turbulent and electrifying aspects of the life urges of mankind. ... No one suggests that advertising can or should become obscene or salacious. The trouble lies with the fact that through its timidity and lack of imagination, it faces the danger of becoming libido-poor and consequently unreal, inhuman and tedious.

How to put the libido back, restore the lost spontaneity, drive, love of life, the individuality, that sex in America seems to lack? In an absent-minded moment, the report concludes that 'love of life, as of the other sex, should remain unsoiled by exterior motives ... let the wife be more than a housewife ... a woman ...'

One day, having immersed myself in the varied insights these reports have been giving American advertisers for the last fifteen years, I was invited to have lunch with the man who runs this motivational research operation. He had been so helpful in showing me the commercial forces behind the feminine mystique, perhaps I could be helpful to him. Naïvely I asked why, since he found it so difficult to give women a true feeling of creativeness and achievement in housework, and tried to assuage their guilt and disillusion and frustrations by getting them to buy more 'things' – why didn't he encourage them to buy things for all they were worth, so they would have time to get out of the home and pursue truly creative goals in the outside world?

'But we have helped her rediscover the home as the expression of her creativeness,' he said. 'We help her think of the modern home as the artist's studio, the scientist's laboratory. Besides,' he shrugged, 'most of the manufacturers we deal with are producing things which have to do with homemaking.'

'In a free enterprise economy,' he went on,

we have to develop the need for new products. And to do that we have to liberate women to desire these new products. We help them rediscover that homemaking is more creative than to compete with men. This can be manipulated. We sell them what they ought to want, speed up the unconscious, move it along. The big problem is to liberate the woman not to be afraid of what is going to happen to her, if she doesn't have to spend so much time cooking, cleaning.

'That's what I mean,' I said. 'Why doesn't the pie-mix ad tell the woman she could use the time saved to be an astronomer?'

'It wouldn't be too difficult,' he replied. 'A few images – the astronomer gets her man, the astronomer as the heroine, make it glamorous for a woman to be an astronomer ... but no,' he shrugged again. 'The client would be too frightened. He wants to sell pie mix. The woman has to want to stay in the kitchen. The manufacturer wants to intrigue her back into the kitchen – and we show him how to do it the right way. If he tells her that all she can be is a wife and mother, she will spit in his face.'

The motivational researchers must be given credit for their insights into the reality of the housewife's life and needs – a reality that often escaped their colleagues in academic sociology and therapeutic psychology, who saw women through the Freudian-functional veil. To their own profit, and that of their clients, the manipulators discovered that millions of supposedly happy American housewives have complex needs which home-and-family, love-and-children, cannot fill. But by a morality that goes beyond the dollar, the manipulators are guilty of using their insights to sell women things which, no matter how ingenious, will never satisfy those increasingly desperate needs. They are guilty of persuading housewives to stay at home, mesmerized in front of a television set, their nonsexual human needs unnamed, unsatisfied, drained by the sexual sell into the buying of things.

The manipulators and their clients in American business can hardly be accused of creating the feminine mystique. But they are the most powerful of its perpetuators; it is their millions which blanket the land with persuasive images, flattering the American housewife, diverting her guilt and disguising her

growing sense of emptiness. They have done this so successfully, employing the techniques and concepts of modern social
science, and transposing them into those deceptively simple,
clever, outrageous ads and commercials, that an observer of
the American scene today accepts as fact that the great
majority of American women have no ambition other than to
be housewives. If they are not solely responsible for sending
women home, they are surely responsible for keeping them
there.

Love is said in many ways. It's giving and accepting. It's protecting and selecting ... knowing what's safest for those you love.
Their bathroom tissue is Scott tissue always. ... Now in four
colours and white.

How skilfully they divert her need for achievement into
sexual fantasies which promise her eternal youth, dulling her
sense of passing time:

Does she ... or doesn't she? She's as full of fun as her kids – and
just as fresh looking! Her naturalness, the way her hair sparkles and
catches the light – as though she's found the secret of making time
stand still. And in a way she has. ...

With increasing skill, the ads glorify her 'role' as an American housewife – knowing that her very lack of identity in that
role will make her fall for whatever they are selling.

Who is she? She gets as excited as her six-year-old about the
opening of school. She reckons her days in trains met, lunches
packed, fingers bandaged, and 1,001 details. She could be you,
needing a special kind of clothes for your busy, rewarding life.

Are you this woman? Giving your kids the fun and advantages
you want for them? Taking them places and helping them do
things? Taking the part that's expected of you in church and
community affairs ... developing your talents so you'll be more
interesting? You can be the woman you yearn to be with a Plymouth
all your own. ... Go where you want, when you want in a beautiful
Plymouth that's yours and nobody else's ...

But a softer toilet paper does not make a woman a better
wife or mother, even if she thinks that's what she needs to be.

Dyeing her hair cannot stop time; buying a Plymouth will not give her a new identity; smoking a Marlboro will not get her an invitation to bed, even if that's what she thinks she wants. But those unfulfilled promises can keep her endlessly hungry for things, keep her from ever knowing what she really needs or wants.

A full-page ad in the *New York Times*, 10 June 1962, was 'Dedicated to the woman who spends a lifetime living up to her potential!' Under the picture of a beautiful woman, adorned by evening dress and jewels and two handsome children, it said: 'The only totally integrated programme of nutrient make-up and skin care – designed to lift a woman's good looks to their absolute peak. The woman who uses "Ultima" feels a deep sense of fulfilment. A new kind of pride. For this luxurious Cosmetic Collection is the *ultimate* ... beyond it there is nothing.'

It all seems so ludicrous when you understand what they are up to. Perhaps the housewife has no one but herself to blame if she lets the manipulators flatter or threaten her into buying things that neither fill her family's needs nor her own. But if the ads and commercials are a clear case of *caveat emptor*, the same sexual sell disguised in the editorial content of a magazine or a television programme is both less ridiculous and more insidious. Here the housewife is often an unaware victim. I have written for some of the magazines in which the sexual sell is inextricably linked with the editorial content. Consciously or unconsciously, the editors know what the advertiser wants.

The heart of X magazine is service – complete service to the whole woman who is the American homemaker; service in all the areas of greatest interest to advertisers, who are also businessmen. It delivers to the advertiser a strong concentration of serious, conscientious, dedicated homemakers. Women more interested in the home and products for the home. Women more willing and able to pay ...

A memo need never be written, a sentence need never be spoken at an editorial conference; the men and women who make the editorial decisions often compromise their own very high standards in the interests of the advertising dollar. Often, as a former editor of *McCall's* recently revealed,[2] the advertiser's influence is less than subtle. The kind of home pictured in the 'service' pages is dictated in no uncertain terms by the boys over in advertising.

The real crime, no matter how profitable for the American economy, is the callous and growing acceptance of the manipulator's advice 'to get them young' – the television commercials that children sing or recite even before they learn to read, the big beautiful ads almost as easy as 'Look, Sally, Look', the magazines deliberately designed to turn teenage girls into housewife buyers of things before they grow up to be women:

> She reads X Magazine from beginning to end ... She learns how to market, to cook and to sew and everything else a young woman should know. She plans her wardrobe round X Magazine's clothes, heeds X Magazine's counsel on beauty and beaux ... consults X Magazine for the latest teen fads ... and oh, how she buys from those X Magazine ads! Buying habits start in X Magazine. It's easier to START a habit than to STOP one! (Learn how X Magazine's unique publication, X Magazine-at-school, carries your advertising into high-school home-economics classrooms.)

Like a primitive culture which sacrificed little girls to its tribal gods, we sacrifice our girls to the feminine mystique, grooming them ever more efficiently through the sexual sell to become consumers of the things to whose profitable sale our nation is dedicated. Two ads recently appeared in a national news magazine, geared not to teenage girls but to executives who produce and sell things. One of them showed the picture of a boy:

> I am *so* going to the moon ... and you can't go, 'cause you're a girl! Children are growing faster today, their interests can cover such a wide range – from roller skates to rockets. X company too has grown, with a broad spectrum of electronic products for worldwide governmental, industrial and space application.

The other showed the face of a girl:

> Should a gifted child grow up to be a housewife? Educational

experts estimate that the gift of high intelligence is bestowed upon only one out of every 50 children in our nation. When that gifted child is a girl, one question is inevitably asked: 'Will this rare gift be wasted if she becomes a housewife?' Let these gifted girls answer that question themselves. Over 90 per cent of them marry, and the majority find the job of being a housewife challenging and rewarding enough to make full use of all their intelligence, time and energy. . . . In her daily roles of nurse, educator, economist and just plain housewife, she is constantly seeking ways to improve her family's life. . . . Millions of women – shopping for half the families in America – do so by saving X Stamps.

If that gifted girl-child grows up to be a housewife, can even the manipulator make supermarket stamps use all of her human intelligence, her human energy, in the century she may live while that boy goes to the moon?

Never underestimate the power of a woman, says another ad. But that power was and is underestimated in America. Or rather, it is only estimated in terms that can be manipulated at the point of purchase. Woman's human intelligence and energy do not really figure in. And yet, they exist, to be used for some higher purpose than housework and thing-buying – or wasted. Perhaps it is only a sick society, unwilling to face its own problems and unable to conceive of goals and purposes equal to the ability and knowledge of its members, that chooses to ignore the strength of women.

CHAPTER 10

Housewifery Expands to Fill the Time Available

WITH a vision of the happy modern housewife as she is described by the magazines and television, by the functional sociologists, the sex-directed educators, and the manipulators dancing before my eyes, I went in search of one of those mystical creatures. I went as a reporter from suburb to suburb, searching for a woman of ability and education who was fulfilled as a housewife.

'I know many such housewives who have found fulfilment as women,' one psychoanalyst said. I asked him to name four, and went to see them.

One, after five years of therapy, was no longer a driven woman, but neither was she a full-time housewife; she had become a computer programmer. The second was a gloriously exuberant woman, with a fine successful husband and three able, exuberant children. Throughout her married life she had been a professional psychoanalyst. The third, between pregnancies, continued seriously her career as a dancer. And the fourth, after psychotherapy, was moving with an increasingly serious commitment into politics.

I reported back to my guide and said that while all four seemed 'fulfilled' women, none were full-time housewives and one, after all, was a member of his own profession. 'That's a coincidence with those four,' he said. But I wondered if it *was* a coincidence.

In another community, I was directed to a woman who, my informant said, was truly fulfilled as a housewife ('she even bakes her own bread'). I discovered that during the years when her four children were under six and she wrote on the census blank 'Occupation: housewife', she had learned a new language (with certification to teach) and had used her previous training in music first as volunteer church organist and then as a paid professional. Shortly after I interviewed her, she took a teaching position.

In many instances, however, the women I interviewed truly fitted the new image of feminine fulfilment – four, five, or six children, baked their own bread, helped build the house with their own hands, sewed all their children's clothes. These women had had no dreams of career, no visions of a world larger than the home; all energy was centred on their lives as housewives and mothers; their only ambition, their only dream already realized. But were they fulfilled women?

In one upper-income development where I interviewed, there were twenty-eight wives. Some were college graduates in their thirties or early forties; the younger wives had usually quit college to marry. Their husbands were, to a rather high degree, engrossed in challenging professional work. Only one of these wives worked professionally; most had made a career of motherhood with a dash of community activity. Nineteen out of the twenty-eight had had natural childbirth (at dinner parties there, a few years ago, wives and husbands often got down on the floor to practise the proper relaxing exercises together). Twenty of the twenty-eight breastfed their babies. At or near forty, many of these women were pregnant. The mystique of feminine fulfilment was so literally followed in this community that if a little girl said: 'When I grow up, I'm going to be a doctor', her mother would correct her: 'No, dear, you're a girl. You're going to be a wife and mother, like mummy.'

But what was mummy really like? Sixteen out of the twenty-eight were in analysis or analytical psychotherapy. Eighteen were taking tranquillizers; several had tried suicide; and some had been hospitalized for varying periods, for depression or vaguely diagnosed psychotic states. ('You'd be surprised at the number of these happy suburban wives who simply go berserk one night, and run shrieking through the street without any clothes on,' said the local doctor, not a psychiatrist, who had been called in, in such emergencies.) Of the women who breastfed their babies, one had continued, desperately, until the child was so undernourished that her doctor intervened by force. Twelve were engaged in extra-marital affairs in fact or in fantasy.

These were fine, intelligent American women, to be envied for their homes, husbands, children, and for their personal gifts of mind and spirit. Why were so many of them driven women? Later, when I saw this same pattern repeated over and over again in similar suburbs, I knew it could hardly be coincidence. These women were alike mainly in one regard: they had uncommon gifts of intelligence and ability nourished by at least the beginnings of higher education – and the life they were leading as suburban housewives denied them the full use of their gifts.

It was in these women that I first began to notice the tell-tale signs of the problem that has no name; their voices were dull and flat, or nervous and jittery; they were listless and bored, or frantically 'busy' around the house or community. They talked about 'fulfilment' in the wife-and-mother terms of the mystique, but they were desperately eager to talk about this other 'problem', with which they seemed very familiar indeed.

One woman had pioneered the search for good teachers in her community's backward school system; she had served her term on the school board. When her children had all started school, she had thought seriously at thirty-nine about her own future: should she go back to college, get an M.A., and become a professional teacher herself? But then, suddenly, she had decided not to go on – she had a late baby instead, her fifth. I heard that flat tone in her voice when she told me she had now retired from community leadership to 'major again in the home'.

I heard the same sad, flat tone in an older woman's voice as she told me:

I'm looking for something to satisfy me. I think it would be the most wonderful thing in the world to work, to be useful. But I don't know how to do anything. My husband doesn't believe in wives working. I'd cut off both my arms if I could have my children little, and at home again. My husband says, find something to occupy yourself that you'll enjoy, why should you work? So now I play golf, nearly every day, just myself. When you walk three, four hours a day, at least you can sleep at night.

I interviewed another woman in the huge kitchen of a house she had helped build herself. She was busily kneading the dough for her famous homemade bread; a dress she was making for a daughter was half-finished on the sewing mach-ine; a handloom stood in one corner. Children's art materials and toys were strewn all over the floor of the house, from front door to stove: in this expensive modern house, like many of the open-plan houses in this era, there was no door at all between kitchen and living-room. Nor did this mother have any dream or wish or thought or frustration of her own to separate her from her children. She was pregnant now with her seventh; her happiness was complete, she said, spending her days with her children. Perhaps here was a happy house-wife.

But just before I left, I said, as an afterthought, that I guessed she was joking when she mentioned that she envied her neigh-bour, who was a professional designer as well as the mother of three children. 'No, I wasn't joking,' she said; and this serene housewife, kneading the dough for the bread she always made herself, started to cry. 'I envy her terribly,' she said. 'She knows what she wants to do. I don't know. I never have. When I'm pregnant and the babies are little, I'm *somebody*, finally, a mother. But then, they get older. I can't just keep on having babies.'

While I never found a woman who actually fitted that 'happy housewife' image, I noticed something else about these able women who were leading their lifes in the protec-tive shade of the feminine mystique. They were so *busy* – busy shopping, chauffeuring, using their dishwashers and dryers and electric mixers, busy gardening, waxing, polishing, help-ing with the children's homework, collecting for mental health, and doing thousands of little chores. In the course of my interviews with these women, I began to see that there was something peculiar about the *time* housework takes today.

On one suburban road there were two colonial houses, each with a big, comfortable living-room, a small library, a formal dining-room, a big cheerful kitchen, four bedrooms, an acre of garden and lawn, and, in each family, one commuting husband and three school-age children. Both houses were well-kept, with a cleaning woman two days a week; but the cooking and the other housework was done by the wife, who in each case was in her late thirties, intelligent, healthy, attractive, and well-educated.

In the first house, Mrs W., a full-time housewife, was busy most of every day with cooking, cleaning, shopping, chauffeuring, taking care of the children. Next door Mrs D., a microbiologist, got most of these chores done before she left for her laboratory at nine, or after she got home at five-thirty. In neither family were the children neglected, though Mrs D.'s were slightly more self-reliant. Both women entertained a fair amount. Mrs W., the housewife, did a lot of routine community work, but she did not 'have time' to take a policy-making office – which she was often offered as an intelligent capable woman. At most, she headed a committee to run a dance, or a P.T.A. fair. Mrs D., the scientist, did no routine community work, but, in addition to her job and home, played in a dedicated string quintet (music was her main interest outside of science), and held a policy-making post in the world-affairs organization which had been an interest since college.

How could the same size house and the same size family, under almost identical conditions of income, outside help, style of life, take so much more of Mrs W.'s time than of Mrs D.'s? And Mrs W. was never idle, really. She never had time in the evening to 'just read', as Mrs D. often did.

In a large, modern apartment building in a big eastern city, there were two six-room apartments, both a little untidy, except when the cleaning woman had just left, or before a party. Both the G.'s and the R.'s had three children under ten, one still a baby. Both husbands were in their early thirties, and both were in demanding professional work. But Mr G., whose wife is a full-time housewife, was expected to do, and did, much more housework when he got home at night or on

Saturday than Mr R., whose wife was a free-lance illustrator and evidently had to get the same amount of housework done in between the hours she spent at her drawing table. Mrs G. somehow couldn't get her housework done before her husband came home at night and was so tired then that he had to do it. Why did Mrs R., who did not count the housework as her main job, get it done in so much less time?

I noticed this pattern again and again, as I interviewed women who defined themselves as 'housewives', and compared them to the few who pursued professions, part or full time. The same pattern held even where both housewife and professional had full-time domestic help, though more often the 'housewives' chose to do their own housework, full time, even when they could well afford two servants. But I also discovered that many frantically busy full-time housewives were amazed to find that they could polish off in one hour the housework that used to take them six – or was still undone at dinnertime – as soon as they started studying, or working, or had some other serious interest outside the home.

Toying with the question, how can one hour of housework expand to fill six hours (same house, same work, same wife), I came back again to the basic paradox of the feminine mystique: that it emerged to glorify woman's role as housewife at the very moment when the barriers to her full participation in society were lowered, at the very moment when science and education and her own ingenuity made it possible for a woman to be both wife and mother and to take an active part in the world outside the home. The glorification of 'woman's role', then, seems to be in proportion to society's reluctance to treat women as complete human beings; for the less real function that role has, the more it is decorated with meaningless details to conceal its emptiness. This phenomenon has been noted, in general terms, in the annals of social science and in history – the chivalry of the Middle Ages, for example, and the artificial pedestal of the Victorian woman – but it may come as somewhat of a shock to the emancipated American woman to discover that it applies in a concrete and extreme degree to the housewife's situation in America today.

Did the new mystique of separate-but-equal femininity arise because the growth of women in America could no longer be repressed by the old mystique of feminine inferiority? Could women be prevented from realizing their full capabilities by making their role in the home *equal* to man's role in society? 'Woman's place is in the home' could no longer be said in tones of contempt. Housework, washing dishes, diaper-changing had to be dressed up by the new mystique to become equal to splitting atoms, penetrating outer space, creating art that illuminates human destiny, pioneering on the frontiers of society. It had to become the very end of life itself to conceal the obvious fact that it is barely the beginning.

When you look at it this way, the double deception of the feminine mystique becomes quite apparent:

1. The more a woman is deprived of function in society at the level of her own ability, the more her housework, mother-work, wife-work, will expand – and the more she will resist finishing her housework or mother-work, and being without any function at all. (Evidently human nature also abhors a vacuum, even in women.)

2. The time required to do the housework for any given woman varies inversely with the challenge of the other work to which she is committed. Without any outside interests, a woman is virtually forced to devote her every moment to the trivia of keeping house.

The simple principle that 'Work Expands to Fill the Time Available' was first formulated by the Englishman C. Northcote Parkinson on the basis of his experience with administrative bureaucracy in the Second World War. Parkinson's Law can easily be re-formulated for the American housewife. This is, without question, the true explanation for the fact that, even with all the new labour-saving appliances, the modern American housewife probably spends more time on housework than her grandmother. It is also part of the explanation for our national preoccupation with sex and love, and for the continued baby boom.

Tabling for the moment the sexual implications, which are vast, let's consider some of the dynamics of the law itself, as an explanation for the disposal of feminine energy in America. To go back several generations: I have suggested that the real cause both of feminism and of women's frustration was the emptiness of the housewife's role. The major work and decisions of society were taking place outside the home, and women felt the need, or fought for the right, to participate in this work. If women had gone on to use their newly-won education and find new identity in this work outside the home, the mechanics of housewifery would have taken the same subsidiary place in their lives as car and garden and workbench in man's life. Motherhood, wifehood, sexual love, family responsibility, would merely have acquired a new emotional importance, as they have for men. (Many observers have noticed the new joy American men have been taking in their children – as their own work week is shortened – without that edge of anger women whose children *are* their work seem to feel.)

But when the mystique of feminine fulfilment sent women back home again, housewifery had to expand into a full-time career. Sexual love and motherhood had to become all of life, had to use up, to dispose of, women's creative energies. The very nature of family responsibility had to expand to take the place of responsibility to society. As this began to happen, each labour-saving appliance brought a labour-demanding elaboration of housework.

The automatic clothes-dryer does not save a woman the four or five hours a week she used to spend at the clothes-line, if, for instance, she runs her washing machine and dryer every day. After all, she still has to load and unload the machine herself, sort the clothes and put them away. As a young mother said, ' Clean sheets twice a week are now possible. Last week, when my dryer broke down, the sheets didn't get changed for eight days. Everyone complained. We all felt dirty. I felt guilty. Isn't that silly?'[1]

According to a Bryn Mawr survey made just after the war, in a typical United States farm family, housework took 60.55 hours a week; 78.35 hours in cities under 100,000; 80.57 in cities of over 100,000.[2] With all their appliances, the suburban and city housewives spend more time on housework than the busy farmer's wife. That farmer's wife, of course, has quite a lot of other work to do.

In the 1950s, sociologists and home economists reported puzzlement, and baffling inconsistencies, as to the amount of time American women were still spending on housework. Study after study revealed that American housewives were spending almost as many, or even more, hours a day on housekeeping as women thirty years earlier, despite the smaller, easier-to-care-for homes, and despite the fact that they had seven times as much capital equipment in housekeeping appliances. There were, however, some exceptions. Women who worked many hours a week outside the home – either in paid jobs or community work – did the housekeeping, on which the full-time housewife still spent sixty hours a week, in half the time. They still seemed to do all the home-making activities of the housewife – meals, shopping, cleaning, the children – but even with a thirty-five-hour work week on the job, their work took only an hour and a half a day longer than the housewife's. That this strange phenomenon caused so little comment was due to the relative scarcity of such women. For the even stranger phenomenon, the real significance of which the mystique hid, was the fact that, despite the growth of the American population and the movement of that population from farm to city with the parallel growth of American industry and professions, in the first fifty years of the twentieth century the proportion of American women working outside the home increased very little indeed, while the proportion of American women in the professions actually declined.[3] From nearly half the nation's professional force in 1930, women had dropped to only 35 per cent in 1960, despite the fact that the number of women college graduates had nearly tripled.

And yet, for the suburban and city housewife, the fact remains that more and more of the jobs that used to be performed in the home have been taken away. It is possible for women to reverse history – or kid themselves that they can reverse it – by baking their own bread, but the law does not permit them to teach their own children at home, and few housewives would match their so-called generalist's skill with the professional expertise of doctor and hospital to nurse a child through tonsillitis or pneumonia at home.

There is a real basis, then, for the complaint that so many housewives have: 'I feel so empty somehow, useless, as if I don't exist.' 'At times I feel as though the world is going past my door while I just sit and watch.' This very sense of emptiness, this uneasy denial of the world outside the home, often drives the housewife to even more effort, more frantic housework to keep the future out of sight.

The woman with two children, for example, bored and restive in her city apartment, is driven by her sense of futility and emptiness to move, 'for the children's sake', to a spacious house in the suburbs. The house takes longer to clean, the shopping and gardening and chauffeuring and do-it-yourself routines are so time-consuming that, for a while, the emptiness seems solved. But when the house is furnished, and the children are in school and the family's place in the community has jelled, there is 'nothing to look forward to', as one woman I interviewed put it. The empty feeling returns, and so she must redecorate the living-room, or wax the kitchen floor more often than necessary – or have another baby. Yet none of it is quite as real, quite as necessary, as it seems.

One of the great changes in America, since the Second World War, has been the explosive movement to the suburbs, those ugly and endless sprawls which are becoming a national problem. Sociologists point out that a distinguishing feature of these suburbs is the fact that the women who live there are better educated than city women, and that the great majority are full-time housewives.[4]

At first glance, one might suspect that the very growth and existence of the suburbs causes educated modern American women to become and remain full-time housewives. Or did the postwar suburban explosion come, at least in part, as a result of the coincidental choice of millions of American women to 'seek fulfilment in the home'? Among the women I interviewed, the decision to move to the suburbs 'for the children's sake' followed the decision to give up job or profession and become a full-time housewife, usually after the birth of the first baby, or the second, depending on the age of the woman when the mystique hit.

In the city, of course, there are more and better jobs for educated women; more universities, sometimes free, with evening courses, geared to men who work during the day, and often more convenient than the conventional daytime programme for a young mother who wants to finish college or work towards a graduate degree. There is also a better supply of full or part-time nurses and cleaning help, nursery schools, day-care centres, after-school play programmes. But these considerations are only important to the woman who has commitments outside the home.

There is also less room for housewifery to expand to fill the time available, in the city. That sense of restless 'marking time' comes early to the educated, able city housewife. It is not surprising, then, that many young wives vote for a move to the suburbs as soon as possible. Like the empty plains of Kansas that tempted the restless immigrant, the suburbs in their very newness and lack of structured service offered, at least at first, a limitless challenge to the energy of educated American women. The women who were strong enough, independent enough, seized the opportunity and were leaders and innovators in these new communities. But, in most cases, these were women educated before the era of feminine fulfilment. The ability of suburban life to fulfil, or truly use, the potential of the able, educated American woman seems to depend on her own previous autonomy or self-realization – that is, on her strength to resist the pressures to conform, resist the time-filling busywork of suburban house and community, and find, or make, the same kind of serious commitment outside the home that she would have made in the city.

When the mystique took over, however, a new breed of women came to the suburbs. They were looking for sanctuary; they were perfectly willing to accept the suburban community as they found it (their only problem was 'how to fit in'); they were perfectly willing to fill their days with the trivia of housewifery. Women of this kind, and most of those that I interviewed were of the post-1950 college generation, refuse to take policy-making positions in community organizations; they will only collect for Red Cross or March of Dimes or Scouts or be den mothers or take the lesser P.T.A. jobs. Their resistance to serious community responsibility is usually explained by 'I can't take the time from my family.' But much of their time is spent in meaningless busywork. The kind of community work they choose does not challenge their intelligence – or even, sometimes, fill a real function. Nor do they derive much personal satisfaction from it – but it does fill time.

So, increasingly, in the new bedroom suburbs, the really interesting volunteer jobs – the leadership of the cooperative nurseries, the free libraries, the school board posts, the selectmenships and, in some suburbs, even the P.T.A. presidencies – are filled by men.[5] The housewife who doesn't 'have time' evades a serious commitment through which she might finally realize herself; she evades it by stepping up her domestic routine until she is truly trapped.

Is that domestic trap an illusion, despite its all-too-solid reality, an illusion created by the feminine mystique? Take, for instance, the open plan of the contemporary 'ranch' or split-level house, $14,990 to $54,990, which has been built in the millions from Roslyn Heights to the Pacific Palisades. They give the illusion of more space for less money. But the women to whom they are sold almost *have* to live the feminine mystique. There are no true walls or doors; the woman in the beautiful electronic kitchen is never separated from her children. In what is basically one free-flowing room, instead of many rooms separated by walls and stairs, continual messes continually need picking up. A man, of course, leaves the house for most of the day. But the feminine mystique forbids the woman this.

A friend of mine, an able writer turned full-time housewife, had her suburban dream house designed by an architect to her own specifications, during the period when she defined herself as housewife and no longer wrote. The house, which cost approximately $50,000, was almost literally one big kitchen. There was a separate studio for her husband, who was a photographer, and cubbyholes for sleeping, but there wasn't any place where she could get out of the kitchen, away from her children, during the working hours. The gorgeous mahogany and stainless steel of her custom-built kitchen cabinets and electric appliances were indeed a dream, but when I saw that house, I wondered where, if she ever wanted to write again, she would put her typewriter.

A sociologist's study of upper-income suburban wives who married young and woke, after fifteen years of child-living, P.T.A., do-it-yourself, garden-and-barbecue, to the realization that they wanted to do some real work themselves, found that the ones who did something about this often moved back to the city.[6] But among the women I talked to, this moment of personal truth was more likely to be marked by adding a room with a door to their open-plan house, or simply by putting a door on one room in the house, 'so I can have some place to myself, just a door to shut between me and the children when I want to think' – or work, study, be alone.

Most American housewives, however, do not shut that door. As another social scientist said, the American housewife's dilemma is that she does not have the privacy to follow real interests of her own, but even if she had more time and space to herself, she would not know what to do with it.[7]

For the very able woman, who has the ability to create culturally as well as biologically, the only possible rationalization is to convince herself – as the new mystique tries so hard to convince her – that the minute physical details of child care are indeed mystically creative; that her children will be tragically deprived if she is not there every minute; that the dinner she gives the boss's wife is as crucial to her husband's career as the case he fights in court or the problem he solves in the laboratory. And because husband and children are soon out of the house most of the day, she must keep on having new babies, or somehow make the minutiae of housework itself important enough, necessary enough, hard enough, creative enough to justify her very existence.

The most glaring proof that, no matter how elaborate,

'Occupation: housewife' is not an adequate substitute for truly challenging work, important enough to society to be paid for in its coin, arose from the comedy of 'togetherness'. The women acting in this little morality play were told that they had the starring roles, that their parts were just as important, perhaps even more important than the parts their husbands played in the world outside the home. Was it unnatural that, since they were doing such a vital job, women insisted that their husbands share in the housework? Surely it was an unspoken guilt, an unspoken realization of their wives' entrapment, that made so many men comply, with varying degrees of grace, to their wives' demands. But having their husbands share the housework didn't really compensate women for being shut out of the larger world. If anything, by removing still more of their functions, it increased their sense of individual emptiness. They needed to share vicariously more and more of their children's and husbands' lives. Togetherness was a poor substitute for equality; the glorification of women's role was a poor substitute for free participation in the world as an individual.

In Minneapolis recently a schoolteacher named Maurice K. Enghausen read a story in the local newspaper about the long work week of today's housewife. Declaring in a letter to the editor that 'any woman who puts in that many hours is awfully slow, a poor budgeter of time, or just plain inefficient', this thirty-six-year-old bachelor offered to take over any household and show how it could be done.

Scores of irate housewives dared him to prove it. He took over the household of Mr and Mrs Robert Dalton, with four children, aged two to seven, for three days. In a single day, he cleaned the first floor, washed three loads of clothes and hung them out to dry, ironed all the laundry including underwear and sheets, fixed a soup-and-sandwich lunch and a big backyard supper, baked two cakes, prepared two salads for the next day, dressed, undressed, and bathed the children, washed woodwork and scrubbed the kitchen floor. Mrs Dalton said he was even a better cook than she was. 'As for cleaning,' she said, 'I am more thorough, but perhaps that is unnecessary.'

Pointing out that he had kept house for himself for seven years and had earned money at college by housework, Enghausen said, 'I still wish that teaching 115 students were as easy as handling four children and a house.... I still maintain that housework is not the interminable chore that women claim it is.'[8]

This claim, periodically expressed by men privately and publicly, has been borne out by a recent time–motion study. Recording and analysing every movement made by a group of housewives, this study concluded that most of the energy expended in housework is superfluous. A series of intensive studies sponsored by the Michigan Heart Association at Wayne University disclosed that 'women were working more than twice as hard as they should', squandering energy through habit and tradition in wasted motion and unneeded steps.

The puzzling question of 'housewife's fatigue' sheds additional light. Doctors in many recent medical conventions report failure to cure it or get to its cause. At a meeting of the American College of Obstetricians and Gynaecologists, a Cleveland doctor stated that mothers, who 'cannot get over 'that tired feeling' and complain that their doctors are no help, are neither sick nor maladjusted, but actually tired. 'No psychoanalysis or deep probing is necessary,' said Dr Leonard Lovshin, of the Cleveland Clinic. 'She has a work day of sixteen hours, a work week of seven days. ... Being conscientious, she gets involved in Cubs, Brownies, P.T.A.s, heart drives, church work, hauling children to music and dancing.' But strangely enough, he remarked, neither the housewife's work load nor her fatigue seemed affected by how many children she had. Most of these patients had only one or two. 'A woman with one child just worries four times as much about the one as the woman with four children, and it all comes out even,' Dr Lovshin said.

Some doctors, finding nothing organically wrong with these chronically tired mothers, told them, 'It's all in your mind'; others gave them pills, vitamins, or injections for anaemia, low blood pressure, low metabolism, or put them on diets (the average housewife is twelve to fifteen pounds overweight), deprived them of drinking (there are approximately a million known alcoholic housewives in America), or gave them tranquillizers. All such treatments were futile, Dr Lovshin said, because these mothers were truly tired.[9]

Other doctors, finding that such mothers get as much or more sleep than they need, claimed the basic cause was not fatigue but boredom. This problem became so severe that the women's magazines treated it fulsomely – in the Pollyanna terms of the feminine mystique. In a spate of articles that appeared in the late 1950s, the 'cures' suggested were usually of the more-praise-and-appreciation-from-husband variety, even though the doctors interviewed in these articles indicated clearly enough that the cause was in the 'housewife–mother' role. But the magazines drew their usual conclusion: that is, and always will be, woman's lot, and she just has to make the best of it. Thus *Redbook* ('Why Young Mothers Are Always Tired', September 1959) reports the findings of the Baruch study of chronic-fatigue patients:

... Fatigue of any kind is a signal that something is wrong. Physical fatigue protects the organism from injury through too great activity of any part of the body. Nervous fatigue, on the other hand, is usually a warning of danger to the personality. This comes out very clearly in the woman patient who complains bitterly that she is 'just a housewife', that she is wasting her talents and education on household drudgery and losing her attractiveness, her intelligence, and indeed her very identity as a person, explains Dr Harley C. Sands, one of the co-heads of the Baruch project. In industry the most fatiguing jobs are those which only partially occupy the worker's attention, but at the same time prevent him from concentrating on anything else. Many young wives say that this mental grey-out is what bothers them most in caring for home and children. 'After a while your mind becomes a blank,' they say. 'You can't concentrate on anything. It's like sleepwalking.'

The magazine also quotes a Johns Hopkins psychiatrist to the effect that the major factor which produces chronic fatigue in patients was 'monotony unpunctuated by any major triumph or disaster', noting that this 'sums up the predicament of many a young mother'. It even cites the results of the

University of Michigan study in which of 524 women asked 'What are some of the things which make you feel "useful and important?"', almost none answered 'Housework'; among the women who had jobs, 'the overwhelming majority, married and single felt that the job was more satisfying than the housework'. At this point the magazine interjects editorially: 'This, of course, does not mean that a career is the alternative to fatigue for a young mother. If anything, the working mother may have more troubles than the housebound young matron.'

Since the demands of housework and child-rearing are not very flexible, there is no complete solution to chronic-fatigue problems. Many women, however, can cut down fatigue if they stop asking too much of themselves. By trying to understand realistically what she can – and, more important, what she cannot – do, a woman may, in the long run, be a better wife and mother, albeit a tired one.

Another such article ('Is Boredom Bad For You?' *McCall's*, April 1957) asked, 'Is the housewife's chronic fatigue really boredom?' and answers: 'Yes. The chronic fatigue of many housewives is brought on by the repetition of their jobs, the monotony of the setting, the isolation, and lack of stimulation. The heavy household chores, it's been found, aren't enough to explain the fatigue. ... The more your intelligence exceeds your job requirements, the greater your boredom.... It is this boredom plus, of course, the day-to-day frustrations which makes the average housewife's job more emotionally fatiguing than her husband's.' The cure: 'Honest enjoyment in some part of the job such as cooking or an incentive such as a party in the offing and, above all, male praise are good antidotes for domestic boredom.'

For the women I interviewed, the problem seemed to be not that too much was asked of them, but too little. 'A kind of torpor comes over me when I get home from the errands,' one woman told me.

It's as if there's nothing I really have to do, though there's plenty to do around the house. So I keep a bottle of martinis in the refrigerator, and I pour myself some so I'll feel more like doing something. Or just to get through till Don comes home.

Other women eat, as they stretch out the housework, just to fill the time available. Obesity and alcoholism, as neuroses, have often been related to personality patterns that stem from childhood. But does this explain why so many American housewives around forty have the same dull lifeless look; does it explain their lack of vitality, the deadly sameness of their lives, the furtive between-meal snacks, drinks, tranquillizers, sleeping pills? Even given the various personalities of these women, there must be something in the nature of their work, of the lives they lead, that drives them to these escapes.

This is no less true of the American housewife's work than it is of the work of most American men, on the assembly lines or in corporation offices: work that does not fully use a man's capacities leaves in him a vacant, empty need for escape – television, tranquillizers, alcohol, sex. But the husbands of the women I interviewed were often engaged in work that demanded ability, responsibility, and decision. I noticed that when these men were saddled with a domestic chore, they polished it off in much less time than it seemed to take their wives. But, of course, for them this was never the work that justified their lives. Whether they put more energy into it for this reason, just to get it over with, or whether housework did not have to take so much of their energy, they did it more quickly and sometimes even seemed to enjoy it more.

Social critics, during the togetherness era, often complained that men's careers suffered because of all this housework. But most husbands of the women I interviewed didn't seem to let housework interfere with their careers. When husbands did that bit of housework evenings and weekends because their wives had careers, or because their wives had made such a career of housework they could not get it done themselves, or because their wives were too passive, dependent, helpless to get it done, or even because the wives left housework for their husbands, for revenge – it did not expand.

But I noticed that housework did tend to expand to fill the time available with a few husbands who seemed to be using domestic chores as an excuse for not meeting the challenge of their own careers. 'I wish he wouldn't insist on vacuuming the whole house on Tuesday evenings. It doesn't need it and he could be working on his book,' the wife of a college professor told me. A capable social worker herself, she had managed all her professional life to work out ways of caring for her house and children without hiring servants. With her daughter's help, she did her own thorough housecleaning on Saturday; it didn't need vacuuming on Tuesday.

To do the work that you are capable of doing is the mark of maturity. It is not the demands of housework and children, or the absence of servants, that keep most American women from growing up to do the work of which they are capable. In an earlier era when servants were plentiful, most of the middle-class women who hired them did not use their freedom to take a more active part in society; they were confined by 'woman's role' to leisure. In countries like Israel and Russia, where women are expected to be more than just housewives, servants scarcely exist, and yet home and children and love are evidently not neglected.

It is the mystique of feminine fulfilment, and the immaturity it breeds, that prevents women from doing the work of which they are capable.

For fifteen years and longer, there has been a propaganda campaign, as unanimous in this democratic nation as in the most efficient of dictatorships, to give women 'prestige' as housewives. But can the sense of self in woman, which once rested on necessary work and achievement in the home, be recreated by housework that is no longer really necessary or really uses much ability – in a country and at a time when women can be free, finally, to move on to something more? It is wrong for a woman, for whatever reason, to spend her days in work that is not moving as the world around her is moving, in work that does not truly use her creative energy. Women themselves are discovering that though there is always 'some way you can get rid of it', they can have no peace until they begin to *use* their abilities.

Surely there are many women in America who are happy at the moment as housewives, and some whose abilities are fully used in the housewife role. But happiness is not the same thing as the aliveness of being fully used. Nor is human intelligence, human ability, a static thing. Housework, no matter how it is expanded to fill the time available, can hardly use the abilities of a woman of average or normal human intelligence, much less the fifty per cent of the female population whose intelligence, in childhood, was above average.

Some decades ago, certain institutions concerned with the mentally retarded discovered that housework was peculiarly suited to the capacities of feeble-minded girls. In many towns, inmates of institutions for the mentally retarded were in great demand as houseworkers, and housework was much more difficult then than it is now.

Basic decisions as to the upbringing of children, interior decoration, menu-planning, budget, education, and recreation do involve intelligence, of course. But, as it was put by one of the few home-and-family experts who saw the real absurdity of the feminine mystique, most housework, and the part that still takes the most time, 'can be capably handled by an eight-year-old child'.

The role of the housewife is, therefore, analogous to that of the president of a corporation who would not only determine policies and make over-all plans but also spend the major part of his time and energy in such activities as sweeping the plant and oiling machines. Industry, of course, is too thrifty of the capacities of its personnel to waste them in such fashion.

The true satisfaction of 'creating a home', the personal relationship with husband and children, the atmosphere of hospitality, serenity, culture, warmth, or security a woman gives to the home comes by way of her personality, not her broom, stove, or dishpan. For a woman to get a rewarding sense of total creation by way of the multiple monotonous chores that are her daily lot would be as irrational as for an assembly line worker to rejoice that he had created an automobile because he tightened a bolt.[10]

No matter how much the 'home-and-family career' is rationalized to justify such appalling waste of able womanpower; no matter how ingeniously the manipulators coin new scientific-sounding words, 'lubrilator' and the like, to give the illusion that dumping the clothes in the washing machines is an act akin to deciphering the genetic code; no matter how much housework is expanded to fill the time available, it still presents little challenge to the adult mind. Into this mental vacuum have flooded an endless line of books on gourmet cooking, scientific treatises on child care, and above all, advice on the techniques of 'married love', sexual intercourse. These, too, offer little challenge to the adult mind. The results could almost have been predicted. To the great dismay of men, their wives suddenly became 'experts', know-it-alls, whose unshakable superiority at home, a domain they both occupied, was impossible to compete with, and very hard to live with. As Russell Lynes put it, wives began to treat their husbands as part-time servants – or the latest new appliance.[11] With a snap course in home economics or marriage and family under her belt and copies of Dr Spock and Dr Van de Velde side by side on the shelf; with all that time, energy, and intelligence directed on husband, children, and house, the young American wife – easily, inevitably, disastrously – began to dominate the family even more completely than her 'mom'.

CHAPTER II

The Sex-Seekers

I DID not do a Kinsey study. But when I was on the trail of the problem that has no name, the suburban housewives I interviewed would often give me an explicitly sexual answer to a question that was not sexual at all. I would ask about their personal interests, ambitions, what they did, or would like to do, not necessarily as wives or mothers, but when they were not occupied with their husbands or their children or their housework. The question might even be what they were doing with their education. But some of these women simply assumed that I was asking about sex. Was the problem that has no name a sexual problem, after all? I might have thought so, except that when these women spoke of sex, there was a false note, a strange quality about their words. They made mysterious allusions or broad hints; they were eager to be asked about sex; even if I did not ask, they often took pride in recounting the explicit details of some sexual adventure. They were not making them up; these adventures were real enough. But what made them sound unsexual, so unreal?

A thirty-eight-year-old mother of four told me sex was the only thing that made her 'feel alive'. But something had gone wrong; her husband did not give her that feeling any more. She was beginning to feel contemptuous of him in bed. 'I need sex to feel alive, but I never really feel him,' she said.

In a flat, matter-of-fact tone that added to the unreality, a thirty-year-old mother of five, calmly knitting a sweater, said she was thinking of going away, to Mexico perhaps, to live with a man with whom she was having an affair. She did not love him, but she thought if she gave herself to him 'completely' she might find the feeling that she knew now was 'the only important thing in life'. What about the children?

226

Vaguely, she guessed she would take them along – he wouldn't mind. What was the feeling she was looking for? She had found it at first with her husband, she supposed. At least she remembered that when she married him – she was eighteen – she had 'felt so happy I wanted to die'. But he did not 'give himself completely' to her; he gave so much of himself to his work. So she found that feeling for a while, she thought, with her children. Shortly after she weaned her fifth baby from the breast, at three, she had her first affair. She discovered 'it gave me that wonderful feeling again, to give my whole self to someone else'. But that affair could not last; he had too many children, so did she. He said when they broke up, 'You've given me such a feeling of identity.' And she wondered, 'What about my own identity?' So she went off by herself for a month that summer, leaving the children with her husband. 'I was looking for something, I'm not sure what, but the only way I get that feeling is when I'm in love with someone.' She had another affair, but that time the feeling did not appear. So with this new one, she wanted to go away completely. 'Now that I know how to get that feeling,' she said, knitting calmly, 'I will simply keep trying until I find it again.'

She did take off for Mexico with that shadowy, faceless man, taking her five children with her; but six months later, she was back, children and all. Evidently she did not find her phantom 'feeling'. And whatever happened, it was not real enough to affect her marriage, which went on as before. Just what was the feeling she expected to get from sex? And why was it, somehow, always out of reach? Does sex become un-real, a fantasy, when a person needs it to feel 'alive', to feel 'my own identity'?

In another suburb, I spoke to an attractive woman in her late thirties who had 'cultural' interests, though they were rather vague and unfocused. She started paintings which she did not finish, raised money for concerts she did not listen to, said she had not 'found her medium yet'. I discovered that she engaged in a sort of sexual status-seeking which had the same vague, unfocused pretentions as her cultural dabblings, and, in fact, was part of it. She boasted of the intellectual prowess, the professional distinction, of the man who, she hinted, wanted to sleep with her. 'It makes you feel proud, like an achievement. You don't want to hide it. You want everyone to know, when it's a man of his stature,' she told me. How much she really wanted to sleep with this man, professional stature or no, was another question. I later learned from her neighbours that she was a community joke. Everyone did indeed 'know', but her sexual offerings were so impersonal and predictable that only a newcomer husband would take them seriously enough to respond.

Just as college girls used the sexual fantasy of married life to protect them from the conflicts and growing pains and work of a personal commitment to science, or art, or society, are these married women putting into their insatiable sexual search the aggressive energies which the feminine mystique forbids then to use for larger human purposes? Are they using sex or sexual fantasy to fill needs that are not sexual? Is that why their sex, even when it is real, seems like fantasy? Is that why, even when they experience orgasm, they feel 'unfulfilled'? Are they driven to this never-satisfied sexual seeking because, in their marriages, they have not found the sexual fulfilment which the feminine mystique promises? Or is that feeling of personal identity, of fulfilment, they seek in sex something that sex alone cannot give?

Sex is the only frontier open to women who have always lived within the confines of the feminine mystique. In the past fifteen years, the sexual frontier has been forced to expand perhaps beyond the limits of possibility, to fill the time available, to fill the vacuum created by denial of larger goals and purposes for American women. The mounting sex-hunger of American women has been documented *ad nauseam* – by Kinsey, by the sociologists and novelists of suburbia, by the mass media, ads, television, movies, and women's magazines that pander to the voracious female appetite for sex fantasy. It is not an exaggeration to say that several generations of able American women have been successfully reduced to sex creatures, sex-seekers. But something has evidently gone wrong.

Instead of fulfilling the promise of infinite orgastic bliss, sex in the America of the feminine mystique is becoming a strangely joyless national compulsion, if not a contemptuous mockery. The sex-glutted novels become increasingly explicit and increasingly dull; the sex kick of the women's magazines has a sickly sadness; the endless flow of manuals describing new sex techniques hint at an endless lack of excitement. This sexual boredom is betrayed by the ever-growing size of the Hollywood starlet's breasts, by the sudden emergence of the male phallus as an advertising 'gimmick'. Sex has become depersonalized, seen in terms of these exaggerated symbols. But of all the strange sexual phenomena that have appeared in the era of the feminine mystique, the most ironic are these – the frustrated sexual hunger of American women has increased, and their conflicts over femininity have intensified, as they have reverted from independent activity to search for their sole fulfilment through their sexual role in the home. And as American women have turned their attention to the exclusive, explicit, and aggressive pursuit of sexual fulfilment, or the acting-out of sexual fantasy, the sexual disinterest of American men, and their hostility towards women, have also increased.

According to Kinsey, there has been no increase in sexual 'outlet' in recent decades. But in the past decade there has been an enormous increase in the American preoccupation with sex and sexual fantasy.[1]

In January 1950, and again in January 1960, a psychologist studied every reference to sex in American newspapers, magazines, television and radio programmes, plays, popular songs, best-selling novels, and non-fiction books. He found an enormous increase in explicit references to sexual desires and expressions (including 'nudity, sex organs, scatology, "obscenity", lasciviousness, and sexual intercourse'). These constituted over fifty per cent of the observed references to human sexuality, with 'extramarital coitus' (including 'fornication, adultery, sexual promiscuity, prostitution, and venereal disease') in second place. In American media there were more than $2\frac{1}{2}$ times as many references to sex in 1960 as in 1950, an increase from 509 to 1,341 'permissive' sex references in the

THE FEMININE MYSTIQUE

200 media studied. The so-called 'men's magazines' not only reached new excesses in their preoccupation with specific female sex organs, but a rash of magazines blossomed frankly geared to homosexuality. The most striking new sexual phenomenon, however, was the increased and evidently 'insatiable' lasciviousness of best-selling novels and periodical fiction, whose audience is primarily women.

Despite his professional approval of the 'permissive' attitude to sex compared to its previous hypocritical denial, the psychologist was moved to speculate:

> Descriptions of sex organs ... are so frequent in modern novels that one wonders whether they have become requisite for sending a work of fiction into the best-selling lists. Since the old, mild depictions of intercourse have seemingly lost their ability to excite, and even sex deviations have now become commonplace in modern fiction, the current logical step seems to be detailed descriptions of the sex organs themselves. It is difficult to imagine what the next step in salaciousness will be.[2]

From 1950 to 1960 the interest of men in the details of intercourse paled before the avidity of women – both as depicted in these media, and as its audience. Already by 1950 the salacious details of the sex act to be found in men's magazines were outnumbered by those in fiction best-sellers sold mainly to women.

During this same period, the women's magazines displayed an increased preoccupation with sex in a rather sickly disguise.[3] Such 'health' features as 'Making Marriage Work', 'Can This Marriage Be Saved?', 'Tell Me, Doctor', described the most intimate sexual details in moralistic guise as 'problems', and women read about them in much the same spirit as they had read the case histories in their psychology texts.

At the same time one could see, almost in parallel step, human sexuality reduced to its narrowest physiological limits in the numberless sociological studies of sex in the suburbs and in the Kinsey investigations. The two Kinsey reports, in 1948 and 1953, treated human sexuality as a status-seeking game in which the goal was the greatest number of 'outlets', orgasms achieved equally by masturbation, nocturnal emissions during dreams, intercourse with animals, and in various postures with the other sex, pre-, extra-, or post-marital. What the Kinsey investigators reported and the way they reported it, no less than the sex-glutted novels, magazines, plays and novels, were all symptoms of the increasing depersonalization, immaturity, joylessness, and spurious senselessness of our sexual overpreoccupation.

That this spiral of sexual 'lust, luridness, and lasciviousness' was not exactly a sign of healthy affirmation of human intercourse became apparent as the image of males lusting after women gave way to the new image of women lusting after males. Exaggerated, perverted extremes of the sex situations seemed to be necessary to excite hero and audience alike. Perhaps the best example of this perverse reversal was the Italian movie *La Dolce Vita*, which, with all its artistic and symbolic pretentions, was a hit in America because of its much-advertised sexual titillation. Though a comment on Italian sex and society, this particular movie was in the chief characteristics of its sexual preoccupation devastatingly pertinent to the American scene.

As is increasingly the case in American novels, plays, and movies, the sex-seekers were mainly the women, who were shown as mindless over- or under-dressed sex creatures (the Hollywood star) and hysterical parasites (the journalist's girlfriend). In addition, there was the promiscuous rich girl who needed the perverse stimulation of the borrowed prostitute's bed, the aggressively sex-hungry women in the candlelit 'hide and seek' castle orgy, and finally the divorcée who performed her writhing striptease to a lonely, bored, and indifferent audience.

All the men, in fact, were too bored or too busy to be bothered. The indifferent, passive hero drifted from one sex-seeking woman to another – a Don Juan, an implied homosexual, drawn in fantasy to the asexual little girl, just out of reach across the water. The exaggerated extremes of the sex situations end finally in a depersonalization that creates a bloated boredom – in hero and audience alike.

The image of the aggressive female sex-seeker also comes

across in novels like *Peyton Place* and *The Chapman Report* – which consciously cater to the female hunger for sexual fantasy. Whether or not this fictional picture of the over-lusting female means that American women have become avid sex-seekers in real life, at least they have an insatiable appetite for books dealing with the sexual act – an appetite that, in fiction and real life, does not always seem to be shared by the men. This discrepancy between the sexual preoccupation of American men and women – in fiction or reality – may have a simple explanation. Suburban housewives, in particular, are more often sex-seekers than sex-finders, not only because of the problems posed by children coming home from school, cars parked overtime in driveways, and gossiping servants, but because, quite simply, men are not all that available. So, from teen age to late middle age, American women are doomed to spend most of their lives in sexual fantasy.

But what happens when a woman bases her whole identity on her sexual role; when sex is necessary to make her 'feel alive'? To state it quite simply, she puts impossible demands on her own body, her 'femaleness', as well as on her husband and his 'maleness'. A marriage counsellor told me that many of the young suburban wives he dealt with make 'such heavy demands on love and marriage, but there is no excitement, no mystery, sometimes almost literally nothing happens'.

A psychiatrist states that he has often seen sex 'die a slow, withering death' when women, or men, use the family 'to make up in closeness and affection for failure to achieve goals and satisfactions in the wider community'.[4] Sometimes, he told me, 'there is so little real life that finally even the sex deteriorates, and gradually dies, and months go by without any desire, though they are young people'. The sexual act 'tends to become mechanized and depersonalized, a physical release that leaves the partners even lonelier after the act than before'.

Even though they find no satisfaction in sex, these women continue their endless search. For the woman who lives according to the feminine mystique, there is no road to achievement, or status, or identity, except the sexual one: the achievement of sexual conquest, status as a desirable sex object, identity as a sexually successful wife and mother. And yet because sex does not really satisfy these needs, she seeks to buttress her nothingness with things, until often even sex itself, and the husband and the children on whom the sexual identity rests, become possessions, things. A woman who is herself only a sexual object, lives finally in a world of objects, unable to touch in others the individual identity she lacks herself.

Kinsey, from his interviews of 5,940 women, found that American wives, especially of the middle class, after ten or fifteen years of marriage, reported greater sexual desire than their husbands seemed to satisfy. One out of four, by the age of forty, had engaged in some extramarital activity – usually quite sporadic. Some seemed insatiably capable of 'multiple orgasms'. A growing number engaged in the 'extramarital petting' more characteristic of adolescence. Kinsey also found that the sexual desire of American husbands, especially in the middle-class educated groups, seemed to wane as their wives' increased.[5]

But even more disturbing than the signs of increased sexual hunger are the signs of increased conflict over their own femaleness. There is evidence that the signs of feminine sexual conflict, often referred to by the euphemism of 'female troubles', occur earlier than ever, and in intensified form, in this era when women have sought to fulfil themselves so early and exclusively in sexual terms.

The chief of the gynaecological service of a famous hospital said:

The question is whether these young mothers will be pathologically blown apart when they lose their reproductive function. I see plenty of women with these menopausal difficulties which are activated, I'm sure, by the emptiness of their lives. And by simply having spent the last twenty-eight years hanging on to the last child until there's nothing left to hang on to. In contrast, women who've had children, sexual relations, but who somehow have much more whole-hearted personalities, without continually having to rationalize themselves as female by having one more baby and holding on to it, have very few hot flashes, insomnia, nervousness, jitteriness. The ones with female troubles are the ones who have denied their femininity, or are pathologically female. But we see these symptoms now in more and more young wives, in their twenties, young women who are fatally invested in their children, who have not developed resources other than their children – coming in with the same impairments of the ovarian cycle, menstrual difficulties, characteristic of the menopause. A woman twenty-two years old, who's had three children, with symptoms more frequently seen with menopause ... I say to her, 'the only trouble with you is that you've had too many babies too fast' and reserve to myself the opinion 'your personality has not developed far enough.'

At this same hospital, studies have been made of women recovering from hysterectomy, women with menstrual complaints, and women with difficult pregnancies. The ones who suffered the most pain, nausea, vomiting, physical and emotional distress, depression, apathy, anxiety, were women 'whose lives revolved almost exclusively around the reproductive function and its gratification in motherhood. A prototype of this attitude was expressed by one woman who said, "In order to be a woman, I have to be able to have children."'[6] The ones who suffered least had 'well-integrated egos', had resources of the intellect and were directed outward in their interests, even in the hospital, rather than preoccupied with themselves and their sufferings.

Obstetricians have seen this too. One told me:

It's a funny thing. The women who have the backaches, the bleeding, the difficult pregnancy and delivery, are the ones who think their whole purpose in life is to have babies. Women who have other interests than just being reproductive machines have less trouble having babies. Don't ask me to explain it. I'm no psychiatrist. But we've all noticed it.

Another gynaecologist spoke of many patients in this era of 'femaleness fulfilled' to whom neither having babies nor sexual intercourse brought 'fulfilment'. They were, in his words:

Women who feel very unsure about their sex and need to have children again and again to prove that they are feminine; women who have the fourth or fifth child because they can't think of anything else to do; women who are dominant and this is something else to dominate; and then I have hundreds of patients who are college girls who don't know what to do with themselves, their mothers bring them in for diaphragms. Because they are immature, going to bed means nothing – it is like taking medicine, no orgasm, nothing. For them getting married is an evasion.

The high incidence of cramps with menstruation, nausea, and vomiting during pregnancy, depression with childbirth, and severe physiological and psychological distress at menopause have come to be accepted as a 'normal' part of feminine biology.[7] When a woman is a 'sex creature', does she see unconsciously in each step of her feminine sexual cycle a giving up, a kind of death, of her very reason for existence?

The air of unreality that hovered over my interviews with suburban housewife sex-seekers, the unreality that pervades the sex-preoccupied novels, plays, and movies – as it pervades the ritualistic sex talk at suburban parties – I suddenly saw for what it was, on an island ostensibly far removed from suburbia, where sex-seeking is omnipresent, in pure fantasy. During the week, this island is an exaggeration of a suburb, for it is utterly removed from outside stimuli, from the world of work and politics; the men do not even come home at night. The women who were spending the summer there were extremely attractive young housewives. They had married early; they lived through their husbands and children; they had no interest in the world outside the home. Here on this island, they found a new diversion that killed two birds with one stone, a diversion that gave them a spurious sense of sexual status, but relieved them of the frightening necessity to prove it. On this island, there was a colony of 'boys' right out of the world of Tennessee Williams. During the week when their husbands were working in the city, the young housewives had 'wild' orgies, all-night parties, with these sexless boys. In a sort of humorous puzzlement, a husband who took the boat over unexpectedly one midweek to console his bored and lonely wife, speculated: 'Why do they do it? Maybe it has something to do with this place being a matriarchy.'

Perhaps, too, it had something to do with boredom – there

just was not anything else to do. But it looked like sex; that's what made it so exciting, even though there was, of course, no sexual contact. Perhaps, these housewives and their boyfriends recognized themselves in each other. For like the call girl in Truman Capote's *Breakfast at Tiffany's* who spends the sexless night with the passive homosexual, they were equally child-like in their retreat from life. And in each other, they sought the same non-sexual reassurance.

But in the suburbs where most hours of the day there are virtually no men at all – to give even the appearance of sex – women who have no identity other than sex creatures must ultimately seek their reassurance through the possession of 'things'. As long as woman's needs for achievement and identity can be channelled into this search for sexual status, she is easy prey for any product which presumably promises her that status – a status that cannot be achieved by effort or achievement of her own. And since that endless search for status as a desirable sexual object is seldom satisfied in reality for most American housewives (who at best can only try to *look* like Elizabeth Taylor), it is very easily translated into a search for status through the possession of objects.

Thus women are aggressors in suburban status-seeking and their search has the same falseness and unreality as their sex-seeking. Status, after all, is what men seek and acquire through their work in society. A woman's work – housework – cannot give her status; it has the lowliest status of almost any work in society. A woman must acquire her status vicariously through her husband's work. The husband himself, and even the children, become symbols of status, for when a woman defines herself as a housewife, the house and the things in it are, in a sense, her identity. If her husband is unable to provide the things she needs for status, he becomes an object of contempt, just as she is contemptuous of him if he cannot fill her sexual needs. Her very dissatisfaction with herself she feels as dissatisfaction with her husband and their sexual relations. As a psychiatrist put it: 'She demands too much satisfaction from her marital relations. Her husband resents it and becomes unable to function sexually with her at all.'

Could this be the reason for the rising tide of resentment among the new young husbands at the girls whose only ambition was to be their wives? The old hostility against domineering 'moms' and aggressive career girls may, in the long run, pale before the new male hostility for the girls whose active pursuit of the 'home career' has resulted in a new kind of domination and aggression. To be the tool, the sex-instrument, the 'man around the house', is evidently no dream-come-true for a man.

Four years ago, I interviewed a number of wives on a certain pseudo-rural road in a fashionable suburb. They had everything they wanted: lovely houses, a number of children, attentive husbands. Today, on that same road, there are a growing spate of dream-houses in which, for various and sometimes unaccountable reasons, the wives now live alone with the children, while the husbands – doctors, lawyers, account chiefs – have moved to the city. Divorce, in America, according to the sociologists, is in almost every instance sought by the husband, even if the wife ostensibly gets it.[8] There are, of course, many reasons for divorce, but chief among them seems to be the growing aversion and hostility that men have for the feminine millstones hanging around their necks, a hostility that is not always directed at their wives, but at their mothers, the women they work with – in fact, women in general.

According to Kinsey, the majority of the American middle-class males' sexual outlets are not in relations with their wives after the fifteenth year of marriage; at fifty-five, one out of two American men is engaging in extramarital sex.[9] This male sex-seeking – the office romance, the casual or intense affair, even the depersonalized sex-for-sex's-sake satirized in the recent movie *The Apartment* – is, as often as not, motivated simply by the need to escape from the devouring wife. Sometimes the man seeks the human relationship that got lost when he became merely an appendage to his wife's aggressive 'home career'. Sometimes his aversion to his wife finally makes him seek in sex an object totally divorced from any human relationship. Sometimes, in fantasy more often than in fact, he seeks a girl-child, a Lolita, as sexual object – to escape that grown-up woman who is devoting all her aggressive energies, as well as her sexual energies, to living through him. There is no doubt that male outrage against women – and inevitably, against sex – has increased enormously in the era of the feminine mystique.[10] As a man wrote in a letter to the *Village Voice*, New York's Greenwich Village newspaper, in February 1962: 'It isn't a problem any more of whether White is too good to marry Black, or vice versa, but whether women are good enough to marry men, since women are on the way out.'

The public symbol of this male hostility is the retreat of American playwrights and novelists from the problems of the world to an obsession with images of the predatory female, the passive martyred male hero (in homo- or heterosexual clothes), the promiscuous childlike heroine, and the physical details of arrested sexual development. It is a special world, but not so special that millions of men and women, boys and girls cannot identify with it.

All of these plays and novels are an agonized shout of obsessed love-hate against women. Significantly, a great many are written by Southern writers, where the 'femininity' which the mystique enshrines remains most intact.

This male outrage is the result, surely, of an implacable hatred for the parasitic women who keep their husbands and sons from growing up, who keep them immersed at that sickly level of sexual fantasy.

Is there, after all, a link between what is happening to the women in America and increasingly overt male homosexuality? According to the feminine mystique, the 'masculinization' of American women which was caused by emancipation, education, equal rights, careers, is producing a breed of increasingly 'feminine' men. But is this the real explanation? As a matter of fact, the Kinsey figures showed no increase in homosexuality in the generations which saw the emancipation of women. The Kinsey report revealed in 1948 that 37 per cent of American men had had at least some homosexual experience, that 13 per cent were predominantly homosexual (for at least three years between 16 and 55), and 4 per cent exclusively homosexual – some 2,000,000 men. But there was 'no evidence that the homosexual group involved more males or fewer males today than it did among older generations'.[11]

Whether or not there has been an increase in homosexuality in America, there has certainly been in recent years an increase in its overt manifestations.[12] I do not think that this is unrelated to the national embrace of the feminine mystique. Male homosexuals – and the male Don Juans, whose compulsion to test their potency is often caused by unconscious homosexuality – are, no less than the female sex-seekers, Peter Pans, for ever childlike, afraid of age, grasping at youth in their continual search for reassurance in some sexual magic.

The role of the mother in homosexuality was pinpointed by Freud and the psychoanalysts. But the mother whose son becomes homosexual is usually not the 'emancipated' woman who competes with men in the world, but the very paradigm of the feminine mystique – a woman who lives through her son, whose femininity is used in virtual seduction of her son, who attaches her son to her with such dependence that he can never mature to love a woman, nor can he, often, cope as an adult with life on his own. The love of men masks his forbidden excessive love for his mother; his hatred and revulsion for all women is a reaction to the one woman who kept him from becoming a man. The conditions of this excessive mother–son love are complex. Freud wrote:

In all the cases examined we have ascertained that the later inverts go through in their childhood a phase of very intense but short-lived fixation on the woman (usually the mother) and after overcoming it, they identify themselves with the woman and take themselves as the sexual object; that is, proceeding on a narcissistic basis, they look for young men resembling themselves in persons whom they wish to love as their mother loved them.[13]

Extrapolating from Freud's insights, one could say that such an excess of love–hate is almost implicit in the relationship of mother and son – when her exclusive role as wife and mother, her relegation to the home, force her to live through her son. Male homosexuality was and is far more common than female homosexuality. The father is not as often tempted or forced by society to live through or seduce his daughter. Not many men become overt homosexuals, but a great many have suppressed enough of this love–hate to feel not only a deep repugnance for homosexuality, but a general and sublimated revulsion for women.

But the homosexuality that is spreading like a murky smog over the American scene is no less ominous than the restless, immature sex-seeking of the young women who are the aggressors in the early marriages that have become the rule rather than the exception. Nor is it any less frightening than the passivity of the young males who acquiesce to early marriage rather than face the world alone. These victims of the feminine mystique start their search for the solace of sex at an earlier and earlier age. In recent years, I have interviewed a number of sexually promiscuous girls from comfortable suburban families, including a number – and this number is growing[14] – of girls who marry in their early teens because they are pregnant. Talking to these girls, and to the professional workers who are trying to help them, one quickly sees that sex, for them, is not sex at all. They have not even begun to experience a sexual response, much less 'fulfilment'. They use sex – pseudo-sex – to erase their lack of identity; it seldom matters who the boy is; the girl almost literally does not 'see' him when she has as yet no sense of herself.

Early sex, early marriage, has always been a characteristic of underdeveloped civilizations and, in America, of rural and city slums. One of the most striking of Kinsey's findings, however, was that a delay in sexual activity was less a characteristic of socio-economic origin than of the ultimate destination – as measured, for instance, by education. A boy from a slum background, who put himself through college and became a scientist or judge, showed the same postponement of sexual activity in adolescence as others who later became scientists or judges, not as others from the same slum background. Boys from the right side of the tracks, however, who did not finish college showed more of that earlier sexual activity that was characteristic of the slum.[15] Whatever this indicates about the relationship between sex and the intellect, a certain postponement of sexual activity seemed to accompany the growth in mental activity required and resulting from higher education, and the achievement of the professions of highest value to society.

Among the girls in the Kinsey survey, there even seemed to be a relationship between the ultimate level of mental or intellectual growth as measured by education, and sexual satisfaction. Girls who married in their teens – who, in Kinsey's cases, usually stopped education with high school – started having sexual intercourse five or six years earlier than girls who continued their education through college or into professional training. This earlier sexual activity did not, however, usually lead to orgasm; these girls were still experiencing less sexual fulfilment, in terms of orgasm, five, ten, and fifteen years after marriage than those who had continued their education.[16] As with the promiscuous girls in the suburbs, early sexual preoccupation seemed to indicate a weak core of self which even marriage did not strengthen.

Psychiatrists have explained that the key problem in promiscuity is usually 'low self-esteem', which often seems to stem from an excessive mother–child attachment; the type of sex-seeking is relatively irrelevant. As Clara Thompson, speaking of homosexuality, says:

Overt homosexuality may express fear of the opposite sex, fear of adult responsibility ... it may represent a flight from reality into absorption in bodily stimulation very similar to the auto-erotic activities of the schizophrenic, or it may be a symptom of destructiveness of oneself or others. ... People who have a low self-esteem ... have a tendency to cling to their own sex because it is less frightening.... However, the above considerations do not invariably produce homosexuality, for the fear of disapproval from the culture and the need to conform often drive these very people into marriage. The fact that one is married by no means proves that one is a mature person.... The mother-child attachment is sometimes found to be the important part of the picture.... Promiscuity is possibly more frequent among homosexuals than heterosexuals, but its significance in the personality structure is very similar in the two. In both, the chief interest is in genitals and body stimulation.

The person chosen to share the experience is not important. The sexual activity is compulsive and is the sole interest.[17]

Compulsive sexual activity, homosexual or heterosexual, usually veils a lack of potency in other spheres of life. Contrary to the feminine mystique, sexual satisfaction is not necessarily a mark of fulfilment, in woman or man. According to Erich Fromm:

> Often psychoanalysts see patients whose ability to love and so be close to others is damaged and yet who function very well sexually and indeed make sexual satisfaction a substitute for love because their sexual potency is their only power in which they have confidence. Their inability to be productive in all other spheres of life and the resulting unhappiness is counterbalanced and veiled by their sexual activities.[18]

There is a similar undertone to the sex-seeking in colleges, even though the potential ability to be 'productive in all other spheres of life' is high. A psychiatrist consultant for Harvard–Radcliffe students recently pointed out that college girls often seek 'security' in these intense sexual relationships because of their own feelings of inadequacy, when, probably for the first time in their lives, they have to work hard, face real competition, think actively instead of passively – which is 'not only a strange experience, but almost akin to physical pain'.

The significant facts are the lowered self-esteem and the diminution in zest, energy, and capacity to function in a creative way. The depression seems to be a kind of declaration of dependence, of helplessness, and a muted cry for help as well. And it occurs at some time and in varying intensity in practically every girl during her career at college.[19]

All this may simply represent 'the first response of a sensitive, naïve adolescent to a new, frighteningly complicated and sophisticated environment', the psychiatrist said. But if the adolescent is a girl, she evidently should not, like the boy, be expected to face the challenge, master the painful work, meet the competition. The psychiatrist considers it 'normal' that the girl seeks her 'security' in 'love', even though the boy himself may be 'strikingly immature, adolescent, and dependent' – 'a slender reed, at least from the point of view of the girl's needs'. The feminine mystique hides the fact that this early sex-seeking, harmless enough for the boy or girl who looks for no more than it offers, cannot give these young women that 'clearer image of themselves' – the self-esteem they need and 'the vigour to lead satisfying and creative lives'. But the mystique does not always hide from the boy the fact that the girl's dependence on him is not really sexual, and that it may stifle his growth. Hence the boy's hostility – even as he helplessly succumbs to the sexual invitation.

A Radcliffe student recently wrote a sensitive account of a boy's growing bitterness at the girl who cannot study without him – a bitterness not even stilled by the sex with which they nightly evade study together.

She was bending down the corner of a page and he wanted to tell her to stop; the little mechanical action irritated him out of all proportion, and he wondered if he was so tense because they hadn't made love for four days.... I bet she needs it now, he thought, that's why she's so quivery, close to tears, and maybe that's why I loused up the exam. But he knew it was not an excuse; he felt his resentment heating as he wondered why he had not really reviewed. ... The clock would never let him forget the amount of time he was wasting ... he slammed his books closed and began to stack them together. Eleanor looked up and he saw the terror in her eyes....

'Look, I'm going to walk you back now,' he said.... 'I've got to get something done tonight' ... He remembered that he had a long walk back, but as he bent hurriedly to kiss her she slipped her arms around him and he had to pull back hard in order to get away. She let go at last, and no longer smiling, she whispered: 'Hal, don't go.' He hesitated. 'Please, don't go, please ...' She strained up to kiss him and when she opened her mouth he felt tricked, for if he put his tongue between her lips, he would not be able to leave. He kissed her, beginning half-consciously to forget that he should go ... he pulled her against him, hearing her moan with pain and excitation. Then he drew back and said, his voice already laboured: 'Isn't there anywhere we can go?' ... She was looking around eagerly and hopefully and he wondered again, how much of her desire was passion and how much grasping: girls used sex to get a hold on you, he knew – it was so easy for them to pretend to be excited.[20]

These are, of course, the first of the children who grew up under the feminine mystique. Why is it so difficult for these youngsters to endure discomfort, to make an effort, to postpone present pleasure for future long-term goals? Sex and early marriage are the easiest way out; playing house at nineteen evades the responsibility of growing up alone. And even if a father tried to get his son to be 'masculine', to be independent, active, strong, both mother and father encouraged their daughter in that passive, weak, grasping dependence known as 'femininity', expecting her, of course, to find 'security' in a boy, never expecting her to live her own life.

And so the circle tightens. The million married before the age of nineteen, in earlier and earlier travesty of sex-seeking, betray an increased immaturity, emotional dependence, and passivity on the part of the newest victims of the feminine mystique. The shadow of sex without self may be dispelled momentarily in a sunny suburban dream house. But what will these childlike mothers and immature fathers do to their children, in that fantasy paradise where the pursuit of pleasure and things hides the loosening links to complex modern reality? What kind of sons and daughters are raised by girls who became mothers before they have ever faced that reality, or sever their links to it by becoming mothers?

There are frightening implications for the future of our nation in the parasitical softening that is being passed on to the new generation of children as a result of our stubborn embrace of the feminine mystique. The tragedy of children acting out the sexual fantasies of their housewife–mothers is only one sign of the progressive dehumanization that is taking place. And in this 'acting out' by the children, the feminine mystique can finally be seen in all its sick and dangerous obsolescence.

CHAPTER 12

Progressive Dehumanization:
The Comfortable Concentration Camp

THE voices now deploring American women's retreat to home reassure us that the pendulum has begun to swing in the opposite direction. But has it? There are already signs that the daughters of the able and energetic women who went back home to live in the housewife image find it more difficult than their mothers to move forward in the world. Evidence of something similar to the housewife's problem that has no name in a more pathological form has been seen in her sons and daughters by many clinicians, analysts, and social scientists. The danger sign is not the competitiveness engendered by the Little League or the race to get into college, but a kind of infantilism that makes the children of the housewife–mothers incapable of the effort, the endurance of pain and frustration, the discipline needed to compete on the baseball field, or get into college.

In an eastern suburb in 1960, I heard a high-school sophomore stop a psychiatrist who had just given an assembly talk and ask him for 'the name of that pill that you can take to hypnotize yourself so you'll wake up knowing everything you need for the test without studying'. That same winter two college girls on a train to New York during the middle of mid year exam week told me they were going to some parties to 'clear their minds' instead of studying for the exams. 'Psychology has proved that when you're really motivated, you learn instantly,' one explained. 'If the professor can't make it interesting enough so that you know it without working, that's his fault, not yours.' A bright boy who had dropped out of college told me it was a waste of his time; 'intuition' was what counted, and they didn't teach that at college. He worked a few weeks at a gas station, a month at a bookstore.

245

Then he stopped work and spent his time literally doing nothing – getting up, eating, going to bed, not even reading.

I saw this same vacant sleepwalking quality in a thirteen-year-old girl I interviewed in a Westchester suburb in an investigation of teenage sexual promiscuity. She was barely passing in her school work even though she was intelligent; she 'couldn't apply herself', as the guidance counsellor put it. She seemed always bored, not interested, off in a daze. She also seemed not quite awake, like a puppet with someone else pulling the strings, when every afternoon she got into a car with a group of older boys who had all 'dropped out' of school in their search for 'kicks'.

The sense that these new kids are, for some reason, not growing up 'real' has been seen by many observers. A Texas educator, who was troubled because college boys were not really interested in the courses they were taking as an automatic passport to the right job, discovered they also were not really interested in anything they did outside of school either. Mostly, they just 'killed time'. A questionnaire revealed that there was literally nothing these kids felt strongly enough about to die for, as there was nothing they actually did in which they felt really alive. Ideas, the conceptual thought which is uniquely human, were completely absent from their minds or lives.[1]

A social critic, one or two perceptive psychoanalysts, tried to pinpoint this change in the younger generation as a basic change in the American character.[2] In the 1950s, David Riesman found no boy or girl with that emerging sense of his own self which used to mark human adolescence, 'though I searched for autonomous youngsters in several public schools and several private schools'.[3]

At Sarah Lawrence College, where students had taken a large responsibility for their own education and for the organization of their own affairs, it was discovered that the new generation of students was helpless, apathetic, incapable of handling such freedom. Harold Taylor, then president of Sarah Lawrence, described the change as follows:

Whereas in earlier years it had been possible to count on the strong motivation and initiative of students to conduct their own affairs, to form new organizations, to invent new projects either in social welfare, or in intellectual fields, it now became clear that for many students the responsibility for self-government was often a burden to bear rather than a right to be maintained. ... Students who were given complete freedom to manage their own lives and to make their own decisions often did not wish to do so.... Students in college seem to find it increasingly difficult to entertain themselves, having become accustomed to depend upon arranged entertainment in which their role is simply to participate in the arrangements already made. ... The students were unable to plan anything for themselves which they found interesting enough to engage in.[4]

The educators, at first, blamed this on the caution and conservatism of the McCarthy era, the helplessness engendered by the atom bomb; later, in the face of Soviet advances in the space race, the politicians and public opinion blamed the general 'softness' of the educators. But, whatever their own weaknesses, the best of the educators knew only too well that they were dealing with a passivity which the children brought with them to school, a frightening 'basic passivity which ... makes heroic demands on those who must daily cope with them in or out of school'.[5] The physical passivity of the younger generation showed itself in a muscular deterioration, finally alarming the White House. Juvenile delinquency ratios just as high as those in the city slums began to show up in the pleasant bedroom suburbs among the children of successful, educated, respected and self-respecting members of society, middle-class children who had all the 'advantages', all the 'opportunities'.

That this passivity was more than a question of boredom – that it signalled a deterioration of the human character – was felt by those who studied the behaviour of the American G.I.s who were prisoners of war in Korea in the 1950s. An Army doctor, Major Clarence Anderson, who was allowed to move freely among the prison camps to treat the prisoners, observed:

On the march, in the temporary camps, and in the permanent ones, the strong regularly took food from the weak. There was no discipline to prevent it. Many men were sick, and these men, instead of being helped and nursed by the others, were ignored, or worse. Dysentery was common, and it made some men too weak to walk. On winter nights, helpless men with dysentery were rolled outside the huts by their comrades and left to die in the cold.[6]

Some thirty-eight per cent of the prisoners died, a higher prisoner death rate than in any previous American war, including the Revolution. Most prisoners became inert, inactive, withdrawing into little shells they had erected against reality. They did nothing to get food, firewood, keep themselves clean, or communicate with each other. The Major was struck by the fact that these new American G.I.s almost universally 'lacked the old Yankee resourcefulness', an ability to cope with a new and primitive situation. He concluded: 'This was partly – but only partly, I believe – the result of the psychic shock of being captured. It was also, I think, the result of some new failure in the childhood and adolescent training of our young men – a new softness.' Discounting the Army's propaganda point, an educational psychologist commented: 'There was certainly something terribly wrong with these young men; not softness, but hardness, slickness, and brittleness. I would call it ego-failure – a collapse of identity.... Adolescent growth can and should lead to a completely human adulthood, defined as the development of a stable sense of self....'[7]

The shocked recognition that this passive non-identity was 'something new in history' came, and only came, when it began to show up in the boys. But the apathetic, dependent, infantile, purposeless being, who seems so shockingly non-human when remarked as the emerging character of the new American man, is strangely reminiscent of the familiar 'feminine' personality as defined by the mystique.

What does it mean, this emergence now, in American boys as well as girls, of a personality arrested at the level of infantile fantasy and passivity? The boys and girls in whom I saw it were children of mothers who lived within the limits of the feminine mystique. Some had more than normal ability, and some had more than normal education, but they were alike in the intensity of their preoccupation with their children, who seemed to be their main and only interest.

I used to let them turn over all the furniture and build houses in the living-room that would stay up for days, so there was no place for me even to sit and read. I couldn't bear to make them do what they didn't want to do, even take medicine when they were sick. I couldn't bear for them to be unhappy, or fight, or be angry at me. I couldn't separate them from myself somehow. I was always understanding, patient. I felt guilty leaving them even for an afternoon. I worried over every page of their homework; I was always concentrating on being a good mother. I was proud that Steve didn't get in fights with other kids in the neighbourhood. I didn't even realize anything was wrong until he started doing so badly in school, and having nightmares about death, and didn't want to go to school because he was afraid of the other boys.

Another woman said:

I thought I had to be there every afternoon when they got home from school. I read all the books they were assigned so I could help them with their schoolwork. I haven't been as happy and excited for years as the weeks I was helping Mary get her clothes ready for college. But I was so upset when she wouldn't take art. That had been my dream, before I got married, of course. Maybe it's better to live your own dreams.

I do not think it is a coincidence that the increasing passivity – and dreamlike unreality – of today's children has become so widespread in the same years that the feminine mystique encouraged the great majority of American women – including the most able, and the growing numbers of the educated – to give up their own dreams, and even their own education, to live through their children. The 'absorption' of the child's personality by the middle-class mother – already apparent to a perceptive sociologist in the 1940s – has inevitably increased during these years. Without serious interests outside the home, and with housework routinized by appliances, women could devote themselves almost exclusively to the cult of the child from cradle to kindergarten. To many, their relationship with their children became a love affair, or a kind of symbiosis.

'Symbiosis' is a biological term; it refers to the process by which, to put it simply, two organisms live as one. There is a biological oneness in the beginning between mother and child, a wonderful and intricate process. But this relationship ends with the severing of the umbilical cord and the birth of the baby into the world as a separate human being.

At this point, child psychologists construe a psychological or emotional 'symbiosis' between mother and child in which mother love takes the place of the amniotic fluid which perpetually bathed and fed the foetus in the womb. This emotional symbiosis feeds the psyche of the child until he is ready to be psychologically born, as it were. Thus the psychological writers – like the literary and religious eulogists of mother-love before the psychological era – depict a state in which mother and baby still retain a mystical oneness; they are not really separate beings. 'Symbiosis', in the hands of the psychological popularizers, strongly implied that the constant loving care of the mother was absolutely necessary for the child's growth, for an indeterminate number of years.

But in recent years the 'symbiosis' concept has crept with increasing frequency into the case histories of disturbed children. More and more of the new child pathologies seem to stem from that very symbiotic relationship with the mother, which has somehow kept children from becoming separate selves. These disturbed children seem to be 'acting out' the mother's unconscious wishes or conflicts – infantile dreams she had not outgrown or given up, but was still trying to gratify for herself in the person of her child.

The term 'acting out' is used in psychotherapy to describe the behaviour of a patient which is not in accord with the reality of a given situation, but is the expression of unconscious infantile wishes or fantasy. Therapists can trace the actual steps whereby the mother, who is using the child to gratify her own infantile dreams, unconsciously pushes him into the behaviour which is destructive to his growth. The Westchester executive's wife who had pushed her daughter at thirteen into sexual promiscuity had not only been grooming her in the development of her sexual charms – in a way that completely ignored the child's own personality – but, even before her breasts began to develop, had implanted, by warnings and by a certain intensity of questioning, her expectation that the child would act out in real life her mother's fantasies of prostitution.

It has never been considered pathological for mothers or fathers to act out their dreams through their children, except when the dream ignores and distorts the reality of the child. If in recent years the process has begun to seem pathological, it is because the mothers' dreams which the children are acting out have become increasingly infantile. These mothers have themselves become more infantile, and because they are forced to seek more and more gratification through the child, they are incapable of finally separating themselves from the child. Thus, it would seem, it is the child who supports life in the mother in that 'symbiotic' relationship, and the child is virtually destroyed in the process.

This destructive symbiosis is literally built into the feminine mystique. And the process is progressive. It begins in one generation, and continues into the next. Mothers with infantile selves will have even more infantile children, who will retreat even earlier into fantasy from the tests of reality.

The signs of this pathological retreat will be more apparent in boys, since even in childhood boys are expect to commit themselves to tests of reality which the feminine mystique permits the girls to evade in sexual fantasy. But these very expectations ultimately make the boys grow further towards a strong self and make the girls the worst victims, as well as the 'typhoid Marys' of the progressive dehumanization of their own children.

From psychiatrists and suburban clinicians, I learned how this process works. One psychiatrist, Andras Angyal, describes it, not necessarily in relation to women, as 'neurotic evasion of growth'. There are two key methods of evading growth. One is 'noncommitment': a man lives his life – school, job, marriage – 'going through the motions without ever being wholeheartedly committed to any actions'. He vaguely experiences himself as 'playing a role'. On the surface, he may appear to be moving normally through life, but what he is actually doing is 'going through the motions'.

The other method of evading growth Angyal called the method of 'vicarious living'. It consists in a systematic denial and repression of one's own personality, and an attempt to substitute some other personality, an 'idealized conception, a standard of absolute goodness by which one tries to live, suppressing all those genuine impulses that are incompatible with the exaggerated and unrealistic standard', or simply taking the personality that is 'the popular cliché of the time'.

The most frequent manifestation of vicarious living is a particularly structured dependence on another person, which is often mistaken for love. Such extremely intense and tenacious attachments, however, lack all the essentials of genuine love – devotion, intuitive understanding, and delight in the being of the other person in his own right and in his own way. On the contrary, these attachments are extremely possessive and tend to deprive the partner of a 'life of his own'. .... The other person is needed not as someone to relate oneself to; he is needed for filling out one's inner emptiness, one's nothingness. This nothingness originally was only a phantasy, but with the persistent self-repression it approaches the state of being actual.

All these attempts at gaining a substitute personality by vicarious living fail to free the person from a vague feeling of emptiness. The repression of genuine, spontaneous impulses leaves the person with a painful emotional vacuousness, almost with a sense of non-existence ... [8]

'Noncommitment' and 'vicarious living', Angyal concludes, 'can be understood as attempted solutions of the conflict between the impulse to grow and the fear of facing new situations' – but, though they may temporarily lessen the pressure, they do not actually resolve the problem; 'their result, even if not their intent, is always an evasion of personal growth'.

Noncommitment and vicarious living are, however, at the very heart of our conventional definition of femininity. But if the human organism has an innate urge to grow, to expand, and become all it can be, it is not surprising that the bodies and the minds of healthy women begin to rebel as they try to adjust to a role that does not permit this growth. Their symptoms which so puzzle the doctors and the analysts are a warning sign that they cannot forfeit their own existence, evade their own growth, without a battle.

I have seen this battle being fought by women I interviewed and by women of my own community, and unfortunately, it is often a losing battle. One young girl, first in high school and later in college, gave up all her serious interests and ambitions in order to be 'popular'. Married early, she played the role of the conventional housewife, in much the same way as she played the part of a popular college girl. I don't know at what point she lost track of what was real and what was façade, but when she became a mother, she would sometimes lie down on the floor and kick her feet in the kind of tantrum she was not able to handle in her three-year-old daughter. At the age of thirty-eight, she slashed her wrists in attempted suicide.

Another extremely intelligent woman, who gave up a challenging career as a cancer researcher to become a housewife, suffered a severe depression just before her baby was born. After she recovered she was so 'close' to him that she had to stay with him at nursery school every morning for four months, or else he went into a violent frenzy of tears and tantrums. In first grade, he often vomited in the morning when he had to leave her. His violence on the playground approached danger to himself and others. When a neighbour took away from him a baseball bat with which he was about to hit a child on the head, his mother objected violently to the 'frustration' of her child. She found it extremely difficult to discipline him herself.

Over a ten-year period, as she went correctly through all the motions of motherhood in suburbia, except for this inability to deal firmly with her children, she seemed visibly less and less alive, less and less sure of her own worth. The day before she hung herself in the basement of her spotless split-level house, she took her three children for a checkup by the pediatrician, and made arrangements for her daughter's birthday party.

Few suburban housewives resort to suicide, and yet there is other evidence that women pay a high emotional and physical price for evading their own growth. They are not, as we now know, the biologically weaker of the species. In every age group, fewer women die than men. But in America, from the time when women assume their feminine sexual role as housewives, they no longer live with the zest, the enjoyment, the sense of purpose that is characteristic of true human health.

During the 1950s, psychiatrists, analysts, and doctors in all fields noted that the housewife's syndrome seemed to become increasingly pathological. The mild undiagnosable symptoms – bleeding blisters, malaise, nervousness, and fatigue of young housewives – became heart attacks, bleeding ulcers, hypertension, broncho-pneumonia; the nameless emotional distress became a psychotic breakdown. Among the new housewife-mothers, in certain sunlit suburbs, this single decade saw a fantastic increase in 'maternal psychoses', mild-to-suicidal depressions or hallucinations over childbirth. According to medical records compiled by Dr Richard Gordon and his wife Katherine (psychiatrist and social psychologist, respectively) in the suburbs of Bergen County, N.J., during the 1950s, approximately one out of three young mothers suffered depression or psychotic breakdown over childbirth. This compared to previous medical estimates of psychotic breakdown in one out of 400 pregnancies, and less severe depressions in one out of 80.

In Bergen County during 1953–7 one out of ten of the 746 adult psychiatric patients were young wives who broke down over childbirth. In fact, young housewives (18 to 44) suffering not only childbirth depression, but all psychiatric and psychosomatic disorders with increasing severity, became during the fifties by far the predominant group of adult psychiatric patients. The number of disturbed young wives was more than half again as big as the number of young husbands, and three times as big as any other group. (Other surveys of both private and public patients in the suburbs have turned up similar findings.) From the beginning to the end of the fifties, the young housewives also increasingly displaced men as the main sufferers of coronary attack, ulcers, hypertension and bronchial pneumonia. In the hospital serving this suburban county, women now make up 40 per cent of the ulcer patients.[9]

I went to see the Gordons, who had attributed the increased pathologies of these new young housewives – not found among women in comparable rural areas, or older suburbs and cities – to the 'mobility' of the new suburban population. But the 'mobile' husbands were not breaking down as were their wives and their children. Previous studies of childbirth depression had indicated that successful professional or career women sometimes suffered 'role-conflict' when they became housewife-mothers. But these new victims, whose rate of childbirth depression or breakdown was so much greater than all previous estimates, had never wanted to be anything more than housewife–mothers. The Gordons pointed out that their findings do not indicate that the young housewives are necessarily subjected to more stress than their husbands; for some reason, the women simply show an increased tendency to succumb to stress. Could that mean that the role of house-wife–mother was too much for them; or could it mean that it was not enough?

These women did not share the same childhood seeds of neurosis; some, in fact, showed none. But a striking similarity that emerged in their case histories was the fact that they had abandoned their education below the level of their ability. The sufferers were the ones who quit high school or college; more often than comparable women their age, they had started college – and left, usually after a year.[10] Many also had come from 'the more restrictive ethnic groups' (Italian or Jewish) or from small towns in the South where 'women were protected and kept dependent'. Most had not pursued either education or job, nor moved in the world on their own in any capacity. A few who broke down had held relatively unskilled jobs, or had the beginnings of interests which they gave up when they became suburban housewife–mothers. But most had had no ambition other than that of marrying an up-and-coming man; many were fulfilling not only their own dreams but also the frustrated status dreams of their mothers, in marrying ambitious, capable men. As Dr Gordon described them to me:

They were not capable women. They had never done anything. They couldn't even organize the committees which needed to be organized in these places. They had never been required to apply themselves, learn how to do a job and then do it. Many of them quit school. It's easier to have a baby than get an A. They never learned to take stresses, pain, hard work. As soon as the going was tough, they broke down.

Perhaps because these girls were more passive, more dependent than other women, walled up in the suburbs, they sometimes seemed to become as infantile as their children. And their children showed a passivity and infantilism that seemed pathological – very early in the sons. One finds in the suburban mental-health clinics today, the overwhelming majority of the child patients are boys, in dramatic and otherwise inexplicable reversal of the fact that most of the adult patients in all clinics and doctors' offices today are women – that is, housewives. Putting aside the theoretical terms of his profession a Boston analyst who has many women patients told me:

It is true, there are too many more women patients than men. Their complaints are varied, but if you look underneath, you find this underlying feeling of emptiness. It is not inferiority. It is almost like nothingness. The situation is that they are not pursuing any goals of their own.

Another doctor, in a suburban mental-health clinic, told me of the young mother of a sixteen-year-old girl who, since their move to the suburb seven years ago, has been completely preoccupied with her children except for a little 'do good' work in the community. Despite this mother's constant anxiety about her daughter ('I think about her all day – she doesn't have any friends and will she get into college?'), she *forgot* the day her daughter was to take her college entrance exams.

Her anxiousness about her daughter and what she was doing was her own anxiety about herself, and what she wasn't doing. When these women suffer with the preoccupation of what they aren't doing with themselves, the children actually get very little real contact with them. I think of another child, two years old, with very severe symptoms because he has almost no actual contact with his mother. She is very much in the home, all day, every day. I have to teach her to have even physical contact with the child. But it won't be solved until the mother faces her own need for self-fulfilment. Being available to one's children has nothing to do with the amount of time – being able to be there for each child in terms of what he needs can happen in a split second. And a mother can be there all day, and not be there for the child, because of her preoccupation with herself. So he holds his breath in temper tantrums; he fights in anger; he refuses to let her leave him at nursery school; even at nine a boy still requires his mother to go to the bathroom with him, lie down with him or he can't go to sleep. Or he becomes withdrawn to the point of schizophrenia. And she is frantically trying to answer the child's needs and demands. But if she was really able to fulfil herself, she would be able to be there for her child. She has to be complete herself, and there herself, to help the child to grow, and learn to handle reality, even to know what his own real feelings are.

In another clinic, a therapist spoke of a mother who was panicky because her child could not learn to read at school, though his intelligence tested high. The mother had left college, thrown herself into the role of housewife, and had lived for the time when her son would go to school, and she would fulfil herself in his achievement. Until therapy made the mother 'separate' herself from the child, he had no sense of himself as a separate being at all. He could, would, do nothing, even in play, unless someone told him to. He could not even learn to read, which took a self of his own.

The strange thing was, the therapist said, like so many other women of this era of the 'feminine role', in her endeavour to be a 'real woman', a good wife and mother, 'she was really playing a very masculine role. ... She was pushing everyone around – dominating the children's lives, ruling the house with an iron hand, managing the carpentry, nagging her husband to do odd jobs he never finished, managing the finances, supervising the recreation and the education – and her husband was just the man who paid the bills.'

In a Westchester community whose school system is world

famous, it was recently discovered that graduates with excellent high-school records did very poorly in college and did not make much of themselves afterwards. An investigation revealed a simple psychological cause. All during high school, the mothers literally had been doing their children's homework and term papers. They had been cheating their sons and daughters out of their own mental growth.

Another analyst illuminates how juvenile delinquency is caused by the child's acting out of the mother's needs, when the mother's growth has been stunted.

Regularly the more important parent – usually the mother, although the father is always in some way involved – has been seen unconsciously to encourage the amoral or anti-social behaviour of the child. The neurotic needs of the parent ... are vicariously gratified by the behaviour of the child. Such neurotic needs of the parent exist either because of some current inability to satisfy them in the world of adults, or because of the stunting experiences in the parent's own childhood – or more commonly, because of a combination of both of these factors.[11]

The symbiotic love or permissiveness which has been the translation of mother love during the years of the feminine mystique is not enough to create a social conscience and strength of character in a child. For this it takes a mature mother with a firm core of self, whose own sexual, instinctual needs are integrated with social conscience. 'Firmness bespeaks a parent who has learned ... how all of his major goals may be reached in some creative course of action....'[12]

A therapist reported the case of a nine-year-old girl who stole. She will outgrow it, said her protective mother – with a 'permissiveness born of her own need for vicarious satisfaction'. At one point, the nine-year-old asked the therapist, 'When is my mother going to do her own stealing?'

At its most extreme, this pattern of progressive dehumanization can be seen in the cases of schizophrenic children: 'autistic' or 'atypical' children, as they are sometimes called. I visited a famous clinic which has been studying these children for almost twenty years. During this period, cases of these children, arrested at a very primitive, sub-infantile level, have seemed to some to be on the increase. The authorities differ as to the cause of this strange condition, and whether it is actually on the increase or only seems to be because it is now more often diagnosed. Until quite recently, most of these children were thought to be mentally retarded. But the condition is being seen more frequently now, in hospitals and clinics, by doctors and psychiatrists. And it is not the same as the irreversible, organic types of mental retardation. It can be treated, and sometimes cured.

These children often identify themselves with things, inanimate objects – cars, radios, etc., or with animals – pigs, dogs, cats. The crux of the problem seems to be that these children have not organized or developed strong enough selves to cope even with the child's reality; they cannot distinguish themselves as separate from the outside world; they live on the level of things or of instinctual biological impulse that has not been organized into a human framework at all. As for the causes, the authorities felt they 'must examine the personality of the mother, who is the medium through which the primitive infant transforms himself into a socialized human being'.[13]

At the clinic I visited (The James Jackson Putnam Children's Center in Boston) the workers were cautious about drawing conclusions about these profoundly disturbed children. But one of the doctors said, a bit impatiently, about the increasing stream of 'missing egos, fragile egos, poorly developed selves' that he has encountered – 'It's just the thing we've always known, if the parent has a fragile ego, the child will.'

Most of the mothers of the children who never developed a core of human self were 'extremely immature individuals' themselves, though on the surface they 'give the impression of being well-adjusted'. They were very dependent on their own mothers, fled this dependency into early marriage, and 'have struggled heroically to build and maintain the image they have created of a fine woman, wife and mother'.

The need to be a mother, the hope and expectation that through this experience she may become a real person, capable of true emotions, is so desperate that of itself it may create anxiety, ambivalence, fear of failure. Because she is so barren of spontaneous manifestations of maternal feelings, she studies vigilantly all the new methods of upbringing and reads treatises about physical and mental hygiene.[14]

When she discovers that she cannot really find her own ful-filment through the child:

she fights desperately for control, no longer of herself perhaps, but of the child. The struggles over toilet training and weaning are generally battles in which she tries to redeem herself. The child becomes the real victim – victim of the mother's helplessness which, in turn, creates an aggression in her that mounts to destruction. The only way for the child to survive is to retreat, to withdraw, not only from the dangerous mother, but from the whole world as well.[15]

In this clinic, the doctors were often able to trace a similar pattern back several generations. The dehumanization was indeed progressive.

In view of these clinical observations, we may assume that the conflict we have discovered in two generations may well have existed for generations before and will continue in those to come, unless the pattern is interrupted by therapeutic intervention or the child rescued by a masculine father-figure, a hope which our experience would not lead us to expect.[16]

I noticed this same pattern in many of the women I inter-viewed, women who dominated their daughters, or bred them into passive dependence and conformity or unconsciously pushed them into sexual activities. One of the most tragic women I interviewed was the mother of that 'sleepwalking' thirteen-year-old girl. A wealthy executive's wife whose life was filled with all the trappings, she lived the very image of suburban 'togetherness', except that it was only a shell. Her husband's real life was centred in his business; a life that he could not, or would not, share with his wife. She had sought to recapture her sense of life by unconsciously pushing her thirteen-year-old daughter into promiscuity. She lived in her daughter's pseudo-sex life, which for the girl was so devoid of actual feeling that she became in it merely a 'thing'.

Quite a few therapists and counsellors were trying to 'help' the mother and the father, on the premise, I suppose, that if the mother's sexual-emotional needs were filled in her marriage by her husband, she would not need to solve them through her daughter – and her daughter could grow out of the 'thingness' to womanhood herself. It was because the husband had so many problems of his own, and the prospects of the mother ever getting enough love from him looked dim, that the counsellors were trying to get the mother to develop some real interests in her own life.

But with other women I have encountered who have evaded their own growth in vicarious living and lack of personal purposes, not even the most loving of husbands have managed to stop the progressive damage to their own lives and the lives of their children. I have seen what happens when women unconsciously push their daughters into too early sexuality, because the sexual adventure was the only real adventure – or means of achieving status or identity – in their own lives. Today these daughters, who acted out their mothers' dreams or frustrated ambitions in the 'normal' feminine way and hitched their wagons to the rising stars of ambitious, able men, are, in too many cases, as frustrated and unfulfilled as their mothers.

But in suburbs like Bergen County, the rate of 'separations' increased a wild 100 per cent during the 1950s, as the able, ambitious men kept on growing in the city while their wives evaded growth in vicarious living or noncommitment, fulfilling their feminine role at home. As long as the children were home, as long as the husband was there, the wives suffered increasingly severe illnesses, but recovered. But in Bergen County, during this decade, there was a drastic increase in suicides of women over forty-five, and of hospitalized women psychiatric patients whose children had grown up and left home.[17] The housewives who had to be hospitalized and who did not recover quickly were, above all, those who had never developed their own abilities in work outside the home.[18]

The massive breakdown that may take place as more and more of these new young housewife–mothers who are the products of the feminine mystique reach their forties is still a matter of speculation. But the progressive infantilization of their sons and daughters, as it is mirrored in the rash of early marriages, has become an alarming fact. In March 1962, at the national conference of the Child Study Association, the new early marriages and parenthood, which had formerly been considered an indication of 'improved emotional maturity' in the younger generation, were at last recognized as a sign of increasing 'infantilization'. These infantile brides and grooms were diagnosed as the victims of this generation's 'sick, sad love-affair with their own children'.

Many girls will admit that they want to get married because they do not want to work any longer. They harbour dreams of being taken care of for the rest of their lives without worry, with just enough furnishing, to do little housework, interesting downtown shopping trips, happy children, and nice neighbours. The dream of a husband seems somehow less important but in the fantasies of girls about marriage, it usually concerns a man who has the strength of an indestructible, reliable, powerful father, and the gentleness, givingness, and self-sacrificing love of a good mother. Young men give as their reason for wanting to marry very often the desire to have a motherly woman in the house, and regular sex just for the asking without trouble and bother. ... In fact, what is supposed to secure maturity and independence is in reality a concealed hope to secure dependency, to prolong the child–parent relationship with the privileges of being a child, and with as little as possible of its limitations.[19]

And there were other ominous signs across the nation of mounting uncontrollable violence among young parents and their children trapped in that passive dependence. A psychiatrist reported that such wives were reacting to hostility from their husbands by becoming even more dependent and passive, until they sometimes became literally unable to move, to take a step, by themselves. This did not make their husbands treat them with more love, but more rage. And what was happening to the rage the wives did not dare to use against their husbands? Consider this recent news item (*Time*, 20 July 1962) about the 'Battered-Child Syndrome'.

To many doctors, the incident is becoming distressingly familiar.

A child, usually under three, is brought to the office with multiple fractures – often including a fractured skull. The parents express appropriate concern, report that the child fell out of bed, or tumbled down the stairs, or was injured by a playmate. But X-rays and experience lead the doctor to a different conclusion: the child has been beaten by his parents.

Gathering documentation from 71 hospitals, a University of Colorado team found 302 battered-child cases in a single year; 33 died, 85 suffered permanent brain damage. The parents, who were driven 'to kick and punch their children, twist their arms, beat them with hammers or the buckle end of belts, burn them with cigarettes or electric irons', were as likely to live in those suburban split-levels as in tenements. The A.M.A. predicted that when statistics on the battered-child syndrome are complete, 'it is likely that it will be found to be a more frequent cause of death than such well-recognized and thoroughly studied diseases as leukaemia, cystic fibrosis, and muscular dystrophy'.

The 'parent' with the most opportunity to beat that battered child was, of course, the mother. As one young mother of four said to the doctor, as she confessed to the wish to kill herself:

There doesn't seem any reason for me to go on living. I don't have anything to look forward to. Jim and I don't even talk to each other any more except about the bills and things that need to be fixed in the house. I know he resents being so old and tied down when he's still young, and he blames it on me because it was I that wanted us to get married then. But the worst thing is, I feel so envious of my own children. I almost hate them, because they have their lives ahead, and mine is over.

It may or may not be a symbolic coincidence but the same week the child-and-family profession recognized the real significance of the early marriages, the *New York Times Book Review* (Sunday, 18 March 1962) recorded a new and unprecedented popularity among American adults of books about 'love' affairs between human beings and animals. In half a century, there have not been as many books about animals on the American best-seller lists as in the last three years (1959–

62). While animals have always dominated the literature for small children, with maturity human beings become more interested in other human beings. (It is only a symbol, but in the Rorschach test a preponderance of animal over human images is a sign of infantilism). And so progressive dehumanization has carried the American mind in the last fifteen years from youth worship to that 'sick love-affair' with our own children; from preoccupation with the physical details of sex, divorced from a human framework, to a love affair between man and animal. Where will it end?

I think it will not end, as long as the feminine mystique masks the emptiness of the housewife role, encouraging girls to evade their own growth by vicarious living, by non-commitment. We have gone on too long blaming or pitying the mothers who devour their children, who sow the seeds of progressive dehumanization, because they have never grown to full humanity themselves. If the mother is at fault, why isn't it time to break the pattern by urging all these Sleeping Beauties to grow up and live their own lives? There never will be enough Prince Charmings, or enough therapists to break that pattern now. It is society's job, and finally that of each woman alone. For it is not the strength of the mothers that is at fault but their weakness, their passive childlike dependency and immaturity that is mistaken for 'femininity'. Our society forces boys, in so far as it can, to grow up, to endure the pains of growth, to educate themselves to work, to move on. Why aren't girls forced to grow up – to achieve somehow the core of self that will end the unnecessary dilemma, the mistaken choice between femaleness and humanness that is implied in the feminine mystique?

It is urgent to understand how the very condition of being a housewife can create a sense of emptiness, non-existence, nothingness, in women. There are aspects of the housewife role that make it almost impossible for a woman of adult intelligence to retain a sense of human identity, the firm core of self or 'I' without which a human being, man or woman, is not truly alive. For women of ability, in America today, I am convinced there is something about the housewife state itself that is dangerous. In a sense that is not as far-fetched as it sounds, the women who 'adjust' as housewives, who grow up wanting to be 'just a housewife', are in as much danger as the millions who walked to their own death in the concentration camps – and the millions more who refused to believe that the concentration camps existed.

In fact, there is an uncanny, uncomfortable insight into why a woman can so easily lose her sense of self as a housewife in certain psychological observations made of the behaviour of prisoners in Nazi concentration camps. In these settings, purposely contrived for the dehumanization of man, the prisoners literally became 'walking corpses'. Those who 'adjusted' to the conditions of the camps surrendered their human identity and went almost indifferently to their deaths. Strangely enough, the conditions which destroyed the human identity of so many prisoners were not the torture and the brutality, but conditions similar to those which destroy the identity of the American housewife.

In the concentration camps the prisoners were forced to adopt childlike behaviour, forced to give up their individuality and merge themselves into an amorphous mass. Their capacity for self-determination, their ability to predict the future and to prepare for it, was systematically destroyed. It was a gradual process which occurred in virtually imperceptible stages – but at the end, with the destruction of adult self-respect, of an adult frame of reference, the dehumanizing process was complete. This was observed by Bruno Bettelheim, psychoanalyst and educational psychologist, when he was a prisoner at Dachau and Buchenwald in 1939.[20]

It was said, finally, that not the S.S. but the prisoners themselves became their own worst enemy. Because they could not bear to see their situation as it really was – because they denied the very reality of their problem, and finally 'adjusted' to the camp itself as if it were the only reality – they were caught in the prison of their own minds. The guns of the S.S. were not powerful enough to keep all those prisoners subdued. They were manipulated to trap themselves; they imprisoned themselves by making the concentration camp the whole world, by blinding themselves to the larger world of the past, their responsibility for the present, and their possibilities for the future. The ones who survived, who neither died nor were exterminated, were the ones who retained in some essential degree the adult values and interests which had been the essence of their past identity.

All this seems terribly remote from the easy life of the American suburban housewife. But is her house in reality a comfortable concentration camp? Have not women who live in the image of the feminine mystique trapped themselves within the narrow walls of their homes? They have learned to 'adjust' to their biological role. They have become dependent, passive, childlike; they have given up their adult frame of reference to live at the lower human level of food and things. The work they do does not require adult capabilities; it is endless, monotonous, unrewarding. American women are not, of course, being readied for mass extermination, but they are suffering a slow death of mind and spirit. Just as with the prisoners in the concentration camps, there are American women who have resisted that death, who have managed to retain a core of self, who have not lost touch with the outside world, who use their abilities to some creative purpose. They are women of spirit and intelligence who have refused to 'adjust' as housewives.

It has been said time and time again that education has kept American women from 'adjusting' to their role as housewives. But if education, which serves human growth, which distils what the human mind has discovered and created in the past, and gives man the ability to create his own future – if education has made more and more American women feel trapped, frustrated, guilty as housewives, surely this should be seen as a clear signal that *women have outgrown the housewife role*.

It is not possible to preserve one's identity by adjusting for any length of time to a frame of reference that is in itself destructive to it. It is very hard indeed for a human being to sustain such an 'inner' split – conforming outwardly to one reality, while trying to maintain inwardly the values it denies. The comfortable concentration camp that American women have walked into, or have been talked into by others, is just such a reality, a frame of reference that denies woman's adult human identity. By adjusting to it, a woman stunts her intelligence to become childlike, turns away from individual identity to become an anonymous biological robot in a docile mass. And yet in the comfortable concentration camp as in the real one, something very strong in a woman resists the death of herself.

Describing an unforgettable experience in a real concentration camp, Bettelheim tells of a group of naked prisoners – no longer human, merely docile robots – who were lined up to enter the gas chamber. The S.S. commanding officer, learning that one of the women prisoners had been a dancer, ordered her to dance for him. She did, and as she danced, she approached him, seized his gun and shot him down. She was immediately shot to death, but Bettelheim is moved to ask:

Isn't it probable that despite the grotesque setting in which she danced, dancing made her once again a person? Dancing, she was singled out as an individual, asked to perform in what had once been her chosen vocation. No longer was she a number, a nameless depersonalized prisoner, but the dancer she used to be. Transformed however momentarily, she responded like her old self, destroying the enemy bent on her destruction even if she had to die in the process.

Despite the hundreds of thousands of living dead men who moved quietly to their graves, this one example shows that in an instant, the old personality can be regained, its destruction undone, once we decide on our own that we wish to cease being units in a system. Exercising the lost freedom that not even the concentration camp could take away – to decide how one wishes to think and feel about the conditions of one's life – this dancer threw off her real prison. This she could do because she was willing to risk her life to achieve autonomy once more.[21]

The suburban house is not a German concentration camp, nor are American housewives on their way to the gas chamber. But they are in a trap, and to escape they must, like the dancer, finally exercise their human freedom, and recapture their sense of self. They must refuse to be nameless, depersonalized, manipulated, and live their own lives again according to a self-chosen purpose. They must begin to grow.

CHAPTER 13

The Forfeited Self

SCIENTISTS of human behaviour have become increasingly interested in the basic human need to grow, man's will to be all that is in him to be. Thinkers in many fields – from Bergson to Kurt Goldstein, Heinz Hartmann, Allport, Rogers, Jung, Adler, Rank, Horney, Angyal, Fromm, May, Maslow, Bettelheim, Riesman, Tillich, and the existentialists – all postulate some positive growth tendency within the organism, which, from within, drives it to fuller development, to self-realization.[1] Moreover, many of these thinkers have advanced a new concept of the psychologically healthy man – and of normality and pathology. Normality is considered to be the 'highest excellence of which we are capable'. The premise is that man is happy, self-accepting, healthy, without guilt, only when he is fulfilling himself and becoming what he can be.

In this new psychological thinking, which seeks to understand what makes men human, and defines neurosis in terms of that which destroys man's capacity to fulfil his own being, the significant tense is the future. It is not enough for an individual to be loved and accepted by others, to be 'adjusted' to his culture. He must take his existence seriously enough to make his own commitment to life, and to the future; he forfeits his existence by failing to fulfil his entire being.

For years, psychiatrists have tried to 'cure' their patients' conflicts by fitting them to the culture. But adjustment to a culture which does not permit the realization of one's entire being is not a cure at all, according to the new psychological thinkers.

Then the patient accepts a confined world without conflict, for now his world is identical with the culture. And since anxiety comes only with freedom, the patient naturally gets over his anxiety: he is relieved from his symptoms because he surrenders the possibilities which caused his anxiety. ... There is certainly a question how far this gaining of release from conflict by giving up being can proceed without generating in individuals and groups a submerged despair, a resentment which will later burst out in self-destructiveness, for history proclaims again and again that sooner or later man's need to be free will out.[2]

What they are describing as unseen self-destruction in man, is, I think, no less destructive in women who adjust to the feminine mystique, who never make a commitment of their own to society or to the future, who never realize their human potential. For the problem that has no name, from which so many women in America suffer today, is caused by adjustment to an image that does not permit them to become what they now can be. It is the growing despair of women who have forfeited their own existence, although by so doing they may also have evaded that lonely, frightened feeling that always comes with freedom.

Anxiety occurs at the point where some emerging potentiality or possibility faces the individual, some possibility of fulfilling his existence; but this very possibility involves the destroying of present security, which thereupon gives rise to the tendency to deny the new potentiality.[3]

The new thinking, which is by no means confined to existentialists, would not analyse 'away' a person's guilt over refusing to accept the intellectual and spiritual possibilities of his existence. Not all feelings of human guilt are unfounded; guilt over the murder of another is not to be analysed away, nor is guilt over the murder of oneself. As was said of a man: 'The patient was guilty because he had locked up some essential potentialities in himself.'[4]

The failure to realize the full possibilities of their existence has not been studied as a pathology in women. But one could apply to millions of women, adjusted to the housewife's role, the insights of neurologists and psychiatrists who have studied male patients with portions of their brain shot away and schizophrenics who have for other reasons forfeited their ability to relate to the real world. Such patients are seen now to have lost the unique mark of the human being: the capacity to transcend the present and to act in the light of the possible, the mysterious capacity to shape the future.[5]

It is precisely this unique human capacity that is the distinction between animal and human behaviour, or between the human being and the machine. In his study of soldiers who had sustained brain injuries, Dr Kurt Goldstein found that what they lost was no more nor less than the ability of abstract human thought: to think in terms of 'the possible', to order the chaos of concrete detail with an idea, to move according to a purpose. These men were tied to the immediate situation in which they found themselves; their sense of time and space was drastically curtailed; they had lost their human freedom.[6]

A similar 'dailyness' shrinks the world of a depressed schizophrenic, to whom 'each day was a separate island with no past and no future'. When such a patient has a terrifying delusion that his execution is imminent, it is 'the result, not the cause, of his own distorted attitude towards the future'.

There was no action or desire which, emanating from the present, reached out to the future, spanning the dull, similar days. As a result, each day kept an unusual independence; failing to be immersed in the perception of any life continuity, each day life began anew, like a solitary island in a grey sea of passing time. ... There seemed to be no wish to go further; every day was an exasperating monotony of the same words, the same complaints, until one felt that this being had lost all sense of necessary continuity. ... His attention was short-lived and he seemed unable to go beyond the most banal questions.[7]

Recent experimental work by various psychologists reveals that sheep can bind past and future into the present for a span of about fifteen minutes, and dogs for half an hour. But a human being can bring the past of thousands of years ago into the present as guide to his personal actions, and can project himself in imagination into the future, not only for half an hour, but for weeks and years. This capacity to 'transcend the immediate boundaries of time', to act and react, and see one's experience in the dimensions of both past and future, is the unique characteristic of human existence.[8] The brain-injured soldiers thus were doomed to the inhuman hell of eternal 'dailyness'.

American housewives have not had their brains shot away, nor are they schizophrenic in the clinical sense. But if this new thinking is right, and the fundamental human drive is not the urge for pleasure or the satisfaction of biological needs, but the need to grow and to realize one's full potential, their comfortable, empty, purposeless days are indeed cause for a nameless terror. In the name of femininity, they have evaded the choices that would have given them a personal purpose, a sense of their own being. For, as the existentialists say, the values of human life never come about automatically. 'The human being can lose his own being by his own choices, as a tree or stone cannot.'[9]

It is surely as true of women's whole human potential what earlier psychological theorists have only deemed true of her sexual potential – that if she is barred from realizing her true nature, she will be sick. The frustration not only of needs like sex, but of individual abilities, could result in neurosis. Her anxiety can be soothed by therapy, or tranquillized by pills, or evaded temporarily by busywork. But her unease, her desperation, is nonetheless a warning that her human existence is in danger.

Only recently have we come to accept the fact that there is an evolutionary scale or hierarchy of needs in man (and thus in woman), ranging from the needs usually called instincts because they are shared with animals, to needs that come later in human development. These later needs, the needs for knowledge, for self-realization, are as instinctive, in a human sense, as the needs shared with other animals of food, sex, survival. The clear emergence of the later needs seems to rest upon prior satisfaction of the physiological needs. The man who is extremely and dangerously hungry has no other interest but food. Capacities not useful for the satisfying of hunger are pushed into the background. 'But what happens to man's desires when there is plenty of food and his belly is chronically filled? At once, other (and higher) needs emerge and these, rather than the physiological hungers, dominate the organism.'[10]

In a sense, this evolving hierarchy of needs moves further and further away from the physiological level which depends on the material environment, and tends towards a level relatively independent of the environment, more and more self-determined. But the progress leading finally to the highest human level is easily blocked – blocked by deprivation of a lower need, as the need for food or sex; blocked also by channelling all existence into these lower needs and refusing to recognize that higher needs exist.

In our culture, the development of women has been blocked at the physiological level with, in many cases, no need recognized higher than the need for love or sexual satisfaction. Even the need for self-respect, for self-esteem, and for the esteem of others – 'the desire for strength, for achievement, for adequacy, for mastery and competence, for confidence in the face of the world, and for independence and freedom' – is not clearly recognized for women. Self-esteem in woman, as well as in man, can only be based on real capacity, competence, and achievement; on deserved respect from others rather than unwarranted adulation. Despite the glorification of 'Occupation: housewife', if that occupation does not demand, or permit, realization of woman's full abilities, it cannot provide adequate self-esteem, much less pave the way to a higher level of self-realization.

We are living through a period in which a great many of the higher human needs are reduced to, or are seen as, symbolic workings-out of the sexual need. A number of advanced thinkers now seriously question such 'explanations by reduction'. While every kind of sexual symbolism and emotional pathology can be found by those who explore, with this aim, the works and early life of a Shakespeare, a da Vinci, a Lincoln, an Einstein, a Freud, or a Tolstoy, these 'reductions' do not explain the work that lived beyond the man, the unique creation that was his, and not that of a man suffering a similar pathology. But the sexual symbol is easier to see than sex itself as a symbol. If woman's needs are not recognized by herself or others in our culture, she is forced to seek identity and self-esteem in the only channels open to her: the pursuit of sexual fulfilment, motherhood, and the possession of material things. And, chained to these pursuits, she is stunted at a lower level of living, blocked from the realization of her higher human needs.

It is a fact, documented by history, if not in the clinic or laboratory, that man has always searched for knowledge and truth, even in the face of the greatest danger. Further, recent studies of psychologically healthy people have shown that this search, this concern with great questions, is one of the defining characteristics of human health. There is something less than fully human in those who have never known a commitment to an idea, who have never risked an exploration of the unknown, who have never attempted the kind of creativity of which men and women are potentially capable. As A. H. Maslow puts it:

Capacities clamour to be used, and cease their clamour only when they are well used. That is, capacities are also needs. Not only is it fun to use our capacities, but it is also necessary. The unused capacity or organ can become a disease centre or else atrophy, thus diminishing the person.[11]

But women in America are not encouraged, or expected, to use their full capacities. In the name of femininity, they are encouraged to evade human growth.

Growth has not only rewards and pleasure, but also many intrinsic pains and always will have. Each step forward is a step into the unfamiliar and is thought of as possibly dangerous. It also frequently means giving up something familiar and good and satisfying. It frequently means a parting and a separation with consequent nostalgia, loneliness and mourning. It also often means giving up a simpler and easier and less effortful life in exchange for a more demanding, more difficult life. Growth forward is in spite of these losses and therefore requires courage, strength in the individual, as well as protection, permission and encouragement from the environment, especially for the child.[12]

What happens if the environment frowns on that courage and strength – sometimes virtually forbids, and seldom actually encourages, that growth in the child who is a girl? What happens if human growth is considered antagonistic to femininity, to fulfilment as a woman, to woman's sexuality? The feminine mystique implies a choice between 'being a woman' or risking the pains of human growth. Thousands of women, reduced to biological living by their environment, lulled into a false sense of anonymous security in their comfortable concentration camps, have made a wrong choice. The irony of their mistaken choice is this: the mystique holds out 'feminine fulfilment' as the prize for being only a wife and mother. But it is no accident that thousands of suburban housewives have not found that prize. The simple truth would seem to be that women will never know sexual fulfilment and the peak experience of human love until they are allowed and encouraged to grow to their full strength as human beings. For according to the new psychological theorists, self-realization, far from preventing the highest sexual fulfilment, is inextricably linked to it. And there is more than theoretical reason to believe that this is as true for women as for men.

In the late thirties, Professor Maslow began to study the relationship between sexuality and what he called 'dominance feeling' or 'self-esteem' or 'ego level' in women – 130 women, of college education or of comparable intelligence, between twenty and twenty-eight, most of whom were married, of Protestant middle-class city background.[13] He found, contrary to what one might expect from the psychoanalytical theories and the conventional images of femininity, that the more 'dominant' the woman, the greater her enjoyment of sexuality – and the greater her ability to 'submit' in a psychological sense, to give herself freely in love, to have orgasm. It was not that these women higher in 'dominance' were more 'highly sexed', but they were, above all, more completely themselves, more free to be themselves – and this seemed inextricably linked with a greater freedom to give themselves in love.

I have never seen the implications of this research discussed in popular psychological literature about femininity or women's sexuality. It was, perhaps, not noticed at the time, even by the theorists, as a major landmark. But its findings are thought-provoking for American women today. Remember that this study was done in the late 1930s, before the mystique became all-powerful. For these strong, spirited, educated women, evidently there was no conflict between the driving force to be themselves and to love. Here is the way Professor Maslow contrasted these women with their more 'feminine' sisters – in terms of themselves, and in terms of their sexuality:

High dominance feeling involves good self-confidence, self-assurance, high evaluation of the self, feelings of general capability or superiority, and lack of shyness, timidity, self-consciousness or embarrassment. Low dominance feeling involves lack of self-confidence, self-assurance and self-esteem; instead there are extensive feelings of general and specific inferiority, shyness, timidity, fearfulness, self-consciousness. ... The person who describes herself as completely lacking in what she may call 'self-confidence in general' will describe herself as self-confident in her home, cooking, sewing or being a mother ... but almost always underestimates to a greater or lesser degree her specific abilities and endowments; the high dominance person usually gauges her abilities accurately and realistically.[14]

These high-dominance women were not 'feminine' in the conventional sense, partly because they felt free to choose rather than be bound by convention, and partly because they were stronger as individuals than most women.

Such women prefer to be treated 'Like a person, not like a woman'. They prefer to be independent, stand on their own two feet, and generally do not care for concessions that imply they are inferior, weak or that they need special attention and cannot take care of themselves. This is not to imply that they cannot behave conventionally. They do when it is necessary or desirable for any reason, but they do not take the ordinary conventions seriously. A common phrase is 'I can be nice and sweet and clinging-vine as anyone else, but my tongue is in my cheek'.... Rules per se generally mean nothing to these women. It is only when they approve of the rules and can see and approve of the purpose behind them that they will obey them.... They are strong, purposeful and do live by rules, but these rules are autonomous and personally arrived at. ...

Low dominance women are very different. They ... usually do not dare to break rules, even when they (rarely) disapprove of them. ... Their morality and ethics are usually entirely conventional. That is, they do what they have been taught to do by their parents, their teachers, or their religion. The dictum of authority is usually not questioned openly, and they are more apt to approve of the status quo in every field of life, religious, economic, educational and political.[15]

Professor Maslow found that the higher the dominance, or strength of self in a woman, the less she was self-centred and the more her concern was directed outward to other people and to problems of the world. On the other hand, the main preoccupation of the more conventionally feminine low-dominance women was themselves and their own inferiorities. From a psychological point of view, a high-dominance woman was more like a high-dominance man than she was like a low-dominance woman. Thus Professor Maslow suggested that either you have to describe as 'masculine' both high-dominance men and women or drop the terms 'masculine' and 'feminine' altogether because they are so 'misleading'.

Our high-dominance women feel more akin to men than to women in tastes, attitudes, prejudices, aptitudes, philosophy, and inner personality in general. ... Many of the qualities that are considered in our culture to be 'manly' are seen in them in high degree, e.g., leadership, strength of character, strong social purpose, emancipation from trivialities, lack of fear, shyness, etc. They do not ordinarily care to be housewives or cooks alone, but wish to combine marriage with a career. ... Their salary may come to no more than the salary of a housekeeper, but they feel other work to be more important than sewing, cooking, etc.[16]

Above all, the high-dominance woman was more psychologically free – more autonomous. The low-dominance woman was not free to be herself, she was other-directed. Such women 'usually admire and respect others more than they do themselves'; and along with this 'tremendous respect for authority', with idolization and imitation of others, with the complete 'voluntary subordination to others' and the great respect for others, went 'hatred, and resentment, envy, jealousy, suspicion, distrust'.

Where the high-dominance women were freely angry, the

low-dominance women did not 'have "nerve" enough to say what they think and courage enough to show anger when it is necessary'. Thus, their 'feminine' quietness was a concomitant of 'shyness, inferiority feelings, and a general feeling that anything they could say would be stupid and would be laughed at'. Such a woman 'does not want to be a leader except in her fantasies, for she is afraid of being in the forefront, she is afraid of responsibility, and she feels that she would be incompetent'.

And again Professor Maslow found an evident link between strength of self and sexuality, the freedom to be oneself and the freedom to 'submit'.

It would seem as if every sexual impulse or desire that has ever been spoken of may emerge freely and without inhibition in these women. ... Generally the sexual act is apt to be taken not as a serious rite with fearful aspects, and differing in fundamental quality from all other acts, but as a game, as fun, as a highly pleasurable animal act.[17]

Moreover, Maslow found that, even in dreams and fantasies, women of above-average dominance enjoyed sexuality, while in low-dominance women the sexual dreams are always 'of the romantic sort, or else are anxious, distorted, symbolized and concealed'.

Did the makers of the mystique overlook such strong and sexually joyous women when they defined passivity and renunciation of personal achievement and activity in the world as the price of feminine sexual fulfilment? Perhaps the strength of self which Maslow found in the cases he studied was a new phenomenon in women.

The mystique kept even the behavioural scientists from exploring the relationship between sex and self in women in the ensuing era. But, quite aside from questions of women, in recent years behavioural scientists have become increasingly uneasy about basing their image of human nature on a study of its diseased or stunted specimens – patients in the clinic. In this context, Professor Maslow later set about to study people, dead and alive, who showed no evidence of neurosis, psychosis, or psychopathic personality; people who, in his view, showed positive evidence of 'self-actualization', which he defined as 'the full use and exploitation of talents, capacities, potentialities. Such people seem to be fulfilling themselves and to be doing the best that they are capable of doing. . . . They are people who have developed or are developing to the full stature of which they are capable.'[18]

There are many things that emerged from this study which bear directly on the problem of women in America today. For one thing, among the public figures included in his study, Professor Maslow was able to find only two women who had actually fulfilled themselves – Eleanor Roosevelt and Jane Addams. (The men included Lincoln, Jefferson, Einstein, Freud, G. W. Carver, Debs, Schweitzer, Kreisler, Goethe, Thoreau, William James, Spinoza, Whitman, Franklin Roosevelt, Beethoven.) Apart from public and historical figures, he studied at close range a small number of unnamed subjects who met his criteria – all in their 50s and 60s – and he screened 3,000 college students, finding only twenty who seemed to be developing in the direction of self-actualization; here also, there were very few women. As a matter of fact, his findings implied that self-actualization, or the full realization of human potential, was hardly possible at all for women in our society.

Professor Maslow found in his study that self-actualizing people invariably have a commitment, a sense of mission in life that makes them live in a very large human world, a frame of reference beyond privatism and preoccupation with the petty details of daily life.

Further, he saw that self-actualizing people, who live in a larger world, somehow thereby never stale, in their enjoyment of the day-to-day living, the trivialities which can become unbearably chafing to those for whom they are the only world. They '. . . have the wonderful capacity to appreciate again and again, freshly and naïvely, the basic goods of life with awe, pleasure, wonder, and even ecstasy, however stale these experiences may have become to others'.[19]

He also reported 'the very strong impression that the sexual pleasures are found in their most intense and ecstatic perfection in self-actualizing people'. It seemed as if fulfilment of personal capacity in this larger world opened new vistas of sexual ecstasy. And yet sex, or even love, was not the driving purpose in their lives.

In self-actualizing people, the orgasm is simultaneously more important and less important than in average people. It is often a profound and almost mystical experience, and yet the absence of sexuality is more easily tolerated by these people. ... Loving at a higher need level makes the lower needs and their frustrations and satisfactions less important, less central, more easily neglected. But it also makes them more wholeheartedly enjoyed when gratified. ... Food is simultaneously enjoyed and yet regarded as relatively unimportant in the total scheme of life. ... Sex can be wholeheartedly enjoyed, enjoyed far beyond the possibility of the average person, even at the same time that it does not play a central role in the philosophy of life. It is something to be enjoyed, something to be taken for granted, something to build upon, something that is very basically important like water or food, and that can be enjoyed as much as these; but gratification should be taken for granted.[20]

He also found, in contradiction both to the conventional view and to esoteric theorists of sex, that in self-actualizing people the quality of both love and sexual satisfaction improves with the age of the relationship. ('It is a very common report from these individuals that sex is better than it used to be and seems to be improving all the time.') For such a person, with the years, becomes more and more himself, and truer to himself.

What we see is a fusion of great ability to love and at the same time great respect for the other and great respect for oneself. ... Throughout the most intense and ecstatic love affairs, these people remain themselves and remain ultimately masters of themselves as well, living by their own standards, even though enjoying each other intensely.[21]

In our society, love has customarily been defined, at least for women, as a complete merging of egos and a loss of separateness – 'togetherness', a giving up of individuality rather than a strengthening of it. But in the love of self-actualizing people, Maslow found that the individuality is strengthened, that 'the ego is in one sense merged with another, but yet in another sense remains separate and strong as always. The two tendencies, to transcend individuality and to sharpen and strengthen it, must be seen as partners and not as contradictory.'

He also found in the love of self-actualizing people the tendency to more and more complete spontaneity, the dropping of defences, growing intimacy, honesty, and self-expression. These people found it possible to be themselves, to feel natural; they could be psychologically (as well as physically) naked and still feel loved and wanted and secure; they could let their faults, weaknesses, physical and psychological shortcomings be freely seen. They did not always have to put their best foot forward, to hide false teeth, grey hairs, signs of age; they did not have to 'work' continually at their relationships; there was much less mystery and glamour, much less reserve and concealment and secrecy. In such people, there did not seem to be hostility between the sexes. In fact, he found that such people 'made no really sharp differentiation between the roles and personalities of the two sexes'.

That is, they did not assume that the female was passive and the male active, whether in sex or love or anything else. These people were all so certain of their maleness or femaleness that they did not mind taking on some of the cultural aspects of the opposite sex role. It was especially noteworthy that they could be both active and passive lovers, and this was the clearest in the sexual act and in physical lovemaking. Kissing and being kissed, being above or below in the sexual act, taking the initiative, being quiet and receiving love, teasing and being teased – these were all found in both sexes.[22]

And thus, while in the conventional and even in the sophisticated view, masculine and feminine love, active and passive, seem to be at opposite poles, in self-actualizing people 'the dichotomies are resolved and the individual becomes both active and passive, both selfish and unselfish, both masculine and feminine, both self-interested and self-effacing'.

Love for self-actualizing people differed from the conventional definition of love in yet another way; it was not motivated by need, to make up a deficiency in the self; it was more purely 'gift' love, a kind of 'spontaneous admiration'.[23]

Such disinterested admiration and love used to be considered a superhuman ability, not a natural human one. But as Maslow says, 'human beings at their best, fully grown, show many characteristics one thought, in an earlier era, to be supernatural prerogatives'.

And there, in the words 'fully grown', is the clue to the mystery of the problem that has no name. The transcendence of self, in sexual orgasm, as in creative experience, can only be attained by one who is himself, or herself, complete, by one who has realized his or her own identity. The theorists know this is true for man, though they have never thought through the implications for women. The suburban doctors, gynaecologists, obstetricians, child-guidance clinicians, pediatricians, marriage counsellors, and ministers who treat women's problems have all seen it, without putting a name to it, or even reporting it as a phenomenon. What they have seen confirms that for woman, as for man, the need for self-fulfilment – autonomy, self-realization, independence, individuality, self-actualization – is as important as the sexual need, with as serious consequences when it is thwarted. Woman's sexual problems are, in this sense, by-products of the suppression of her basic need to grow and fulfil her potentialities as a human being, potentialities which the mystique of feminine fulfilment ignores.

Psychoanalysts have long suspected that woman's intelligence does not fully flower when she denies her sexual nature; but by the same token can her sexual nature fully flower when she must deny her intelligence, her highest human potential? All the words that have been written criticizing American women for castrating their husbands and sons, for dominating their children, for their material greediness, for their sexual frigidity or denial of femininity may simply mask this one underlying fact: that woman, no more than man, can live by sex alone; that her struggle for identity, autonomy – that 'personally productive orientation based on the human need for active participation in a creative task' – is inextricably linked with her sexual fulfilment, as a condition of her maturity.

Professor Maslow told me that he thought self-actualization is only possible for women today in America if one person can grow through another – that is, if the woman can realize her own potential through her husband and children. 'We do not know if this is possible or not,' he said.

The new theorists of the self, who are men, have usually evaded the question of self-realization for a woman. Bemused themselves by the feminine mystique, they assume that there must be some strange 'difference' which permits a woman to find self-realization by living through her husband and children, while men must grow to theirs. It is still very difficult, even for the most advanced psychological theorist, to see woman as a separate self, a human being who, in that respect, is no different in her need to grow than is a man. Most of the conventional theories about women, as well as the feminine mystique, are based on this 'difference'. But the actual basis for this 'difference' is the fact that the possibility for true self-realization has not existed for women until now.

Many psychologists, including Freud, have made the mistake of assuming, from observations of women who did not have the education and the freedom to play their full part in the world, that it was woman's essential nature to be passive, conformist, dependent, fearful, childlike – just as Aristotle, basing his picture of human nature on his own culture and particular period of time, made the mistake of assuming that just because a man was a slave, this was his essential nature and therefore 'it was good for him to be a slave'.

Now that education, freedom, the right to work on the great human frontiers – all the roads by which men have realized themselves – are open to women, only the shadow of the past enshrined in the mystique of feminine fulfilment keeps women from finding their road. The mystique promises women sexual fulfilment through abdication of self. But there is massive statistical evidence that the very opening to American women of those roads to their own identity in society brought a real and dramatic increase in woman's capacity for sexual fulfilment: the orgasm. In the years between the 'emancipation' of women won by the feminists and the sexual counter-revolution of the feminine mystique, American women enjoyed a decade-by-decade increase in sexual orgasm. And the women who enjoyed this the most fully were, above all, the women who went furthest on the road to self-realization, women who were educated for active participation in the world outside the home.

This evidence is found in two famous studies, generally not cited for this pupose. The first of these, the Kinsey report, was based on interviews with 5,940 women who grew up in the various decades of the twentieth century during which the emancipation of women was won, and before the era of the feminine mystique. Even according to Kinsey's measure of sexual fulfilment, the orgasm (which many psychologists, sociologists, and analysts have criticized for its narrow, mechanistic, over-physiological emphasis, and its disregard of basic psychological nuances), his study shows a dramatic increase in sexual fulfilment during these decades. The increase began with the generation born between 1900 and 1909, who were maturing and marrying in the 1920s – the era of feminism, the winning of the vote and the great emphasis on women's rights, independence, careers, and equality with men, including the right to sexual fulfilment. The increase in wives reaching orgasm and the decrease in frigid women continued in each succeeding generation down to the youngest generation in the Kinsey sample which was marrying in the 1940s.[24]

And the most 'emancipated' women, women educated beyond college for professional careers, showed a far greater capacity for complete sexual enjoyment, full orgasm, than the rest. The Kinsey figures also showed that women who married before twenty were least likely to experience sexual orgasm, and were likely to enjoy it less frequently in or out of marriage, though they started sexual intercourse five or six years earlier than women who finished college or graduate school.

While the Kinsey data showed that over the years 'a distinctly higher proportion of the better educated females, in contrast to the grade school and high school females, had actually reached orgasm in a higher percentage of their marital coitus', the increased enjoyment of sex did not, for the most part, mean an increased incidence of it, in the woman's life. On the whole, there was a slight trend in the opposite direction. And that increase in extramarital sex was less marked with professionally trained women.[25]

Perhaps something about the supposedly 'unfeminine' strength, or self-realization achieved by women educated for professional careers enabled them to enjoy greater sexual fulfilment in their marriages than other women – as measured by the orgasm – and thus less likely to seek it outside of marriage. Or perhaps they simply had less need to seek status, achievement, or identity in sex. The relationship between woman's sexual fulfilment and self-realization indicated by Kinsey's findings is underlined by the fact that, as many critics have pointed out, Kinsey's sample was over-representative of professional women, college graduates, women with unusually high 'dominance' or strength of self. Kinsey's sample under-represented the 'typical' American housewife who devotes her life to husband, home, and children; it under-represented women with little education; because of its use of volunteers, it under-represented the kind of passive, submissive, conformist women whom Maslow found to be incapable of sexual enjoyment.[26] The increase in sexual fulfilment and decrease in frigidity which Kinsey found during the decades after women's emancipation may not have been felt by the 'average' American housewife as much as by this minority of women who directly experienced emancipation through education and participation in the professions. Nevertheless, the decrease in frigidity was so dramatic in that large, if unrepresentative, sample of nearly 6,000 women that even Kinsey's critics found it significant.

It was hardly an accident that this increase in woman's sexual fulfilment accompanied her progress to equal participation in the rights, education, work, and decisions of American society. The coincidental sexual emancipation of American men – the lifting of the veil of contempt and degradation from sexual intercourse – was surely related to the American male's new regard for the American woman as an equal, a person like himself, and not just a sexual object. Evidently, the further women progressed from that state, the more sex became an act of human intercourse rather than a dirty joke to men; and the more women were able to love men, rather than submit, in passive distaste, to their sexual desire. In fact, the feminine mystique itself – with its acknowledgement of woman as subject and not just object of the sexual act, and its assumption that her active, willing participation was essential to man's pleasure – could not have come without the emancipation of women to human equality. As the early feminists foresaw, women's rights did indeed promote greater sexual fulfilment, for men and women.

Other studies also showed that education and independence increased the American woman's ability to enjoy a sexual relationship with a man, and thus to affirm more fully her own sexual nature as a woman. Repeated reports, before and after Kinsey, showed college-educated women to have a much lower than average divorce rate. More specifically, a massive and famous sociological study by Ernest W. Burgess and Leonard S. Cottrell indicated that women's chances of happiness in marriage increased as their career preparation increased – with teachers, professional nurses, women doctors, and lawyers showing fewer unhappy marriages than any other group of women. These women were more likely to enjoy happiness in marriage than women who held skilled office positions, who, in turn, had happier marriages than women who had not worked before marriage or who had no vocational ambition or who worked at a job that was not in accordance with their own ambitions, or whose only work training or experience was domestic or unskilled. In fact, the higher the woman's income at the time of her marriage, the more probable her married happiness. As the sociologists put it:

Apparently in the case of wives, the traits that make for success in the business world as measured by monthly income are the traits that make for success in marriage. The point, of course, may be made that income indirectly measures education since the amount of educational training influences income.[27]

Among 526 couples, less than ten per cent showed 'low' marital adjustment where the wife had been employed seven or more years, had completed college or professional training, and had not married before twenty-two. Where wives had been educated *beyond college*, less than 5 per cent of marriages scored 'low' in happiness. The following table shows the relationship between the marriage and the educational achievement of the wife.

MARRIAGE ADJUSTMENT SCORES
AT DIFFERENT EDUCATIONAL LEVELS

Wife's educational level	Marital adjustment score			
	Very low	*Low*	*High*	*Very high*
Graduate work	0.0	4.6	38.7	56.5
College	9.2	18.9	22.9	48.9
High school	14.4	16.3	32.2	37.1
Grades only	33.3	25.9	25.9	14.8

One might have predicted from such evidence a relatively poor chance of married happiness, or of sexual fulfilment, or even of orgasm, for the women whom the mystique encouraged to marry before twenty, to forgo higher education, careers, independence, and equality with men in favour of femininity. And, as a matter of fact, the youngest group of wives studied by Kinsey – the generation born between 1920 and 1929 who met the feminine mystique head-on in the 1940s when the race back home began – showed, by the fifth year of marriage, a sharp reversal of that trend towards increased sexual fulfilment in marriage which had been manifest in every decade since women's emancipation in the 1920s.

The percentage of women enjoying orgasm in all or nearly all of their married sex life in the fifth year of marriage had risen from 37 per cent of women in the generation born before 1900 to 42 per cent in the generations born in the next two decades. The youngest group, whose fifth year of marriage was in the late 1940s, enjoyed full orgasm in even less cases (36 per cent) than women born before 1900.[28]

Would a new Kinsey study find the young wives who are products of the feminine mystique enjoying even less sexual fulfilment than their more emancipated, more independent, more educated, more grownup-when-married forebears? Only fourteen per cent of Kinsey's women had married by twenty; a bare majority – fifty-three per cent – had married by twenty-five, though most did marry. This is quite a difference from the America of the 1960s, when fifty per cent of women marry in their teens.

Recently, Helene Deutsch, the eminent psychoanalyst who went even further than Freud in equating femininity with masochistic passivity and, in warning women that 'outward-directed activity' and 'masculinizing' intellectuality might interfere with a fully feminine orgasm, threw a psychoanalytic conference into an uproar by suggesting that perhaps too much emphasis had been put on 'the orgasm' for women. In the 1960s, she was suddenly not so sure that women had to have, or could have, a real orgasm. Perhaps a more 'diffuse' fulfilment was all that could be expected. After all, she had women patients who were absolutely psychotic who seemed to have orgasms; but most women she saw now did not seem to have them at all.

What did it mean? Could women, then, not experience orgasm? Or had something happened, during this time when so much emphasis has been placed on sexual fulfilment, to keep women from experiencing orgasm? The experts did not all agree. But in other contexts, not concerned with women, analysts reported that passive people who 'psychologically feel empty' – who fail to 'develop adequate egos', have 'little sense of their own identity' – cannot submit to the experience of sexual orgasm for fear of their own non-existence.[29] Fanned into an all-consuming sexual search by the popularizers of Freudian 'femininity', many women had, in effect, renounced everything for the orgasm that was supposed to be at the end of the rainbow. To say the least, they directed quite a lot of their emotional energies and needs towards the sexual act. As somebody said about a truly beautiful woman in America, her image has been so over-exposed, in the ads, television, movies, that when you see the real thing, you're disappointed. Without even delving into the murky depths of the unconscious, one might assume it was asking a lot of the beautiful orgasm, not only to live up to its overadvertised claims, but to constitute the equivalent of an A in sex, a salary raise, a good review on opening night, promotion to senior editor or associate professor, much less the basic 'experience of oneself', the sense of identity.[30] As one psychotherapist reported:

One of the major reasons, ironically, why so many women are not achieving full-flowering sexuality today is because they are so over determined to achieve it. They are so ashamed if they do not reach the heights of expressive sensuality that they tragically sabotage their own desires. That is to say, instead of focusing clearly on the real problem at hand, these women are focusing on quite a different problem, namely, 'Oh, what an idiot and an incompetent person I am for not being able to achieve satisfaction without difficulty'. Today's women are often obsessed with the notion of *how*, rather than *what*, they are doing when they are having marital relations. That is fatal.

If sex itself, as another psychoanalyst put it, is beginning to have a 'depressive' quality in America, it is perhaps because too many Americans – especially the women sex-seekers – are putting into the sexual search all their frustrated needs for self-realization. American women are suffering, quite simply, a massive sickness of sex without self. No one has warned them that sex can never be a substitute for personal identity; that sex itself cannot give identity to a woman, any more than to a man; that there may be no sexual fulfilment at all for the woman who seeks her self in sex.

The question of how a person can most fully realize his own capacities and thus achieve identity has become an important concern of the philosophers and the social and psychological thinkers of our time – and for good reason. Thinkers of other times put forth the idea that people were, to a great extent, defined by the work they did. The work that a man had to do to eat, to stay alive, to meet the physical necessities of his environment, dictated his identity. And in this sense, when work is seen merely as a means of survival, human identity was dictated by biology.

But today the problem of human identity has changed. For the work that defined man's place in society and his sense of himself has also changed man's world. Work, and the advance of knowledge, has lessened man's dependence on his environment; his biology and the work he must do for biological survival are no longer sufficient to define his identity. This can be most clearly seen in our own abundant society; men no longer need to work all day to eat. They have an unprecedented freedom to choose the kind of work they will do; they also have an unprecedented amount of time apart from the hours and days that must actually be spent in making a living. And suddenly one realizes the significance of today's identity crisis – for women, and increasingly, for men. One sees the human significance of work – not merely as the means of biological survival, but as the giver of self and the transcender of self, as the creator of human identity and human evolution.

For 'self-realization' or 'self-fulfilment' or 'identity' does not come from looking into a mirror in rapt contemplation of one's own image. Those who have most fully realized themselves, in a sense that can be recognized by the human mind even though it cannot be clearly defined, have done so in the service of a human purpose larger than themselves. Men from varying disciplines have used different words for this mysterious process from which comes the sense of self. The religious mystics, the philosophers, Marx, Freud, all had different names for it: man finds himself by losing himself; man is defined by his relation to the means of production; the ego, the self, grows through understanding and mastering reality – through work and love.

The identity crisis, which has been noted by Erik Erikson and others in recent years in the American man, seems to occur for lack of, and be cured by finding, the work, or cause, or purpose that evokes his own creativity.[31] Some never find it, for it does not come from busywork or punching a time clock. It does not come from just making a living, working by formula, finding a secure spot as an organization man. The very argument, by Riesman and others, that man no longer finds identity in the work defined as a pay-cheque job, assumes that identity for man comes through creative work of his own that contributes to the human community: the core of the self becomes aware, becomes real, and grows, through work that carries forward human society.

Work, the shopworn staple of the economists, has become the new frontier of psychology. Psychiatrists have long used 'occupational therapy' with patients in mental hospitals; they have recently discovered that to be of real psychological value, it must be not just 'therapy', but real work, serving a real purpose in the community. And work can now be seen as the key to the problem that has no name. The identity crisis of American women began a century ago, as more and more of the work important to the world, more and more of the work that used their human abilities and through which they were able to find self-realization, was taken from them.

Until, and even into, the last century, strong, capable women were needed to pioneer our new land; with their husbands, they ran the farms and plantations and Western homesteads. These women were respected and self-respecting members of a society whose pioneering purpose centred in the home. Strength and independence, responsibility and self-confidence, self-discipline and courage, freedom and equality were part of the American character for both men and women, in all the first generations. The women who came by steerage from Ireland, Italy, Russia, and Poland worked beside their husbands in the sweatshops and the laundries, learned the new language, and saved to send their sons and daughters to college. Women were never quite as 'feminine', or held in as much contempt, in America as they were in Europe. American women seemed to European travellers, long before our time, less passive, childlike, and feminine than their own wives in France or Germany or England. By an accident of history, American women shared in the work of society longer, and grew with the men. Grade- and high-school education for boys and girls alike was almost always the rule; and in the West, where women shared the pioneering work the longest, even the universities were co-educational from the beginning.

The identity crisis for women did not begin in America until the fire and strength and ability of the pioneer women were no longer needed, no longer used, in the middle-class homes of the Eastern and Midwestern cities, when the pioneering was done and men began to build the new society in industries and professions outside the home. But the daughters of the pioneer women had grown too used to freedom and work to be content with leisure and passive femininity.[32]

It was not an American, but a South African woman, Mrs Olive Schreiner, who warned at the turn of the century that the quality and quantity of women's functions in the social universe were decreasing as fast as civilization was advancing; that if women did not win back their right to a full share of honoured and useful work, woman's mind and muscle would weaken in a parasitic state; her offspring, male and female, would weaken progressively, and civilization itself would deteriorate.[33]

The feminists saw clearly that education and the right to participate in the more advanced work of society were women's greatest needs. They fought for and won the rights to new, fully human identity for women. But how very few of their daughters and granddaughters have chosen to use their education and their abilities for any large creative purpose, for responsible work in society? How many of them have been deceived, or have deceived themselves, into clinging to the outgrown, childlike femininity of 'Occupation: housewife'?

It was not a minor matter, their mistaken choice. We now know that the same range of potential ability exists for women as for men. Women, as well as men, can only find their identity in work that uses their full capacities.

'We measure ourselves by many standards,' said the great American psychologist William James, nearly a century ago. 'Our strength and our intelligence, our wealth and even our good luck, are things which warm our heart and make us feel ourselves a match for life. But deeper than all such things, and able to suffice unto itself without them, is the sense of the amount of effort which we can put forth.'[34]

A woman today who has no goal, no purpose, no ambition patterning her days into the future, making her stretch and grow beyond that small score of years in which her body can fill its biological function, is committing a kind of suicide. For that future half-century after the child-bearing years are over is a fact that an American woman cannot deny. Nor can she deny that as a housewife, the world is indeed rushing past her door while she just sits and watches. The terror she feels is real, if she has no place in that world.

The feminine mystique has succeeded in burying millions of American women alive. There is no way for these women to break out of their comfortable concentration camps except by finally putting forth an effort — that human effort which reaches beyond biology, beyond the narrow walls of home, to help shape the future.

CHAPTER 14

A New Life Plan for Women

'EASY enough to say,' the woman inside the housewife's trap remarks, 'but what can I do, alone in the house, with the children yelling and the laundry to sort and no grandmother to baby-sit?' It is easier to live through someone else than to become complete yourself. The freedom to lead and plan your own life is frightening if you have never faced it before. It is frightening when a woman finally realizes that there is no answer to the question 'Who am I?' except the voice inside herself. She may spend years on the analyst's couch, working out her 'adjustment to the feminine role', her blocks to 'fulfilment as a wife and mother'. And still the voice inside her may say, 'That's not it.' Even the best psychoanalyst can only give her the courage to listen to her own voice.

To face the problem is not to solve it. But once a woman faces it, as women are doing today all over America without much help from the experts, once she asks herself 'What do I want to do?' she begins to find her own answers. Once she begins to see through the delusions of the feminine mystique – and realizes that neither her husband nor her children, nor the things in her house, nor sex, nor being like all the other women, can give her a self – she often finds the solution much easier than she anticipated.

Of the many women I talked to in the suburbs and cities, some were just beginning to face the problem, others were well on their way to solving it, and for still others it was no longer a problem. In the stillness of an April afternoon with all her children in school, a woman told me:

I put all my energies into the children, carting them around, worrying about them, teaching them things. Suddenly, there was this terrible feeling of emptiness. All that volunteer work I'd taken on – Scouts, P.T.A., the League, just didn't seem worth doing all of a sudden. As a girl, I wanted to be an actress. It was too late to go back to that. I stayed in the house all day, cleaning things I hadn't cleaned in years. I spent a lot of time just crying. My husband and I talked about its being an American woman's problem, how you give up a career for the children, and then you reach a point where you can't go back. I felt so envious of the few women I know who had a definite skill and kept working at it. My dream of being an actress wasn't real – I didn't work at it. Did I have to throw my whole self into the children? I've spent my whole life just immersed in other people, and never even knew what kind of a person I was myself. Now I think even having another baby wouldn't solve that emptiness long. You can't go back – you have to go on. There must be some real way I can go on myself.

This woman was just beginning her search for identity. Another woman had made it to the other side, and could look back now and see the problem clearly. Her home was colour-ful, casual, but technically she was no longer 'just a house-wife'. She was paid for her work as a professional painter. She told me that when she stopped conforming to the conven-tional picture of femininity she finally began to *enjoy* being a woman. She said:

I used to work so hard to maintain this beautiful picture of myself as a wife and mother. I had all of my children by natural childbirth. I breastfed them all. I got mad once at an older woman at a party when I said childbirth is the most important thing in life, the basic animal, and she said, 'Don't you want to be more than an animal?'

You do want something more, only you don't know what it is. So you put even more into housekeeping. It's not challenging enough, just ironing dresses for your little girls, so you go in for ruffly dresses that need more ironing, and bake your own bread, and refuse to get a dishwasher. You think if you make a big enough chal-lenge out of it, then somehow it will be satisfying. And still it wasn't.

I almost had an affair. I used to feel so discontented with my husband. I used to feel outraged if he didn't help with the house-work. I insisted that he do dishes, scrub floors, everything. We wouldn't quarrel, but you can't deceive yourself sometimes in the middle of the night.

I couldn't seem to control this feeling that I wanted something more from life. So I went to a psychiatrist. He kept trying to make me enjoy being feminine, but it didn't help. And then I went to one who seemed to make me find out who I was, and forget about this beautiful feminine picture. I realized I was furious at myself, furious at my husband, because I'd left school.

I used to put the kids in the car and just drive because I couldn't bear to be alone in the house. I kept wanting to do something, but I was afraid to try. One day on a back road I saw an artist painting, and it was like a voice I couldn't control saying 'Do you give lessons?'

I'd take care of the house and kids all day, and after I finished the dishes at night, I'd paint. Then I took the bedroom we were going to use for another baby – five children was part of my beautiful picture – and used it for a studio for myself. I remember one night working and working and suddenly it was 2 a.m. and I was finished. I looked at the picture, and it was like finding myself.

I can't think what I was trying to do with my life before, trying to fit some picture of an old-time woman pioneer. I don't have to prove I'm a woman by sewing my own clothes. I am a woman, and I am myself, and I buy clothes and love them. I'm not such a darned patient, loving, perfect mother any more. I don't change the kids' clothes top to bottom every day, and no more ruffles. But I seem to have more time to enjoy them. I don't spend much time on housework now, but it's done before my husband gets home. We bought a dishwasher.

The longer it takes to wash dishes, the less time you have for anything else. It's not creative, doing the same thing over and over. Why should a woman feel guilty at getting rid of this repetitive work? There's no virtue in dishwashing, scrubbing floors. Dacron, dishwashers, drip dry – this is fine, this is the direction physical life should take. This is our time, our only time on earth. We can't keep throwing it away. My time is all I've got, and this is what I want to do with it.

I don't need to make such a production of my marriage now because it's real. Somehow, once I began to have the sense of myself, I became aware of my husband. Before, it was like he was part of me, not a separate human being. I guess it wasn't till I stopped trying to be feminine that I began to enjoy being a woman.

A young Ohio woman told me:

Lately, I've felt this need. I felt we simply had to have a bigger house, put on an addition, or move to a better neighbourhood. I went on a frantic round of entertaining but that was like living for the interruptions of your life.

My husband thinks that being a good mother is the most important career there is. I think it's even more important than a career. But I don't think most women are all mother. I enjoy my kids, but I don't like spending all my time with them. I'm just not their age. I could make housework take up more of my time. But the floors don't need vacuuming more than twice a week. My mother swept them every day.

I always wanted to play the violin. When I went to college, girls who took music seriously were peculiar. Suddenly, it was as if some voice inside me said, now is the time, you'll never get another chance. I felt embarrassed, practising at forty. It exhausts me and hurts my shoulder, but it makes me feel at one with something larger than myself. The universe suddenly becomes real, and you're part of it. You feel as if you really exist.

It would be quite wrong for me to offer any woman easy how-to answers to this problem. There are no easy answers, in America today; it is difficult, painful, and takes perhaps a long time for each woman to find her own answer. First, she must unequivocally say 'no' to the housewife image. This does not mean, of course, that she must divorce her husband, abandon her children, give up her home. She does not have to choose between marriage and career; that was the mistaken choice of the feminine mystique. In actual fact, it is not as difficult as the feminine mystique implies, to combine marriage and motherhood and even the kind of lifelong personal purpose that once was called 'career'. It merely takes a new life plan – in terms of one's whole life as a woman.

The first step in that plan is to see housework for what it is – not a career, but something that must be done as quickly and efficiently as possible. Once a woman stops trying to make cooking, cleaning, washing, ironing, 'something more', she can say 'no, I don't want a stove with rounded corners, I don't want four different kinds of soap'. She can say 'no' to those mass day-dreams of the women's magazines and television, 'no' to the depth researchers and manipulators who are trying to run her life. Then, she can use the vacuum cleaner and the dishwasher and all the automatic appliances, and even the instant mashed potatoes for what they are truly worth – to save time that can be used in more creative ways.

The second step, and perhaps the most difficult for the products of sex-directed education, is to see marriage as it really is, brushing aside the veil of over-glorification imposed by the feminine mystique. Many women I talked to felt strangely discontented with their husbands, continually irritated with their children, when they saw marriage and motherhood as the final fulfilment of their lives. But when they began to use their various abilities with a purpose of their own in society, they not only spoke of a new feeling of 'aliveness' or 'completeness' in themselves, but of a new, though hard to define, difference in the way they felt about their husbands and children. Many echoed this woman's words:

> The funny thing is, I enjoy my children more now that I've made room for myself. Before, when I was putting my whole self into the children, it was as if I was always looking for something through them. I couldn't just enjoy them as I do now, as though they were a sunset, something outside me, separate. Before, I felt so tied down by them, I'd try to get away in my mind. Maybe a woman has to be *by herself* to be really *with* her children.

A New England lawyer's wife told me:

> I thought I had finished. I had come to the end of childhood, had married, had a baby, and I was happy with my marriage. But somehow I was disconsolate, because I assumed this was the end. I would take up upholstery one week, Sunday painting the next. My house was spotless. I devoted entirely too much time to entertaining my child. He didn't need all that adult companionship. A grown woman playing with a child all day, disintegrating herself in a hundred directions to fill the time, cooking fancy food when no one needs it, and then furious if they don't eat it – you lose your adult common sense, your whole sense of yourself as a human being.
>
> Now I'm studying history, one course a year. It's work, but I haven't missed a night in two and a half years. Soon I'll be teaching. I love being a wife and mother, but I know now that when marriage is the end of your life, because you have no other mission, it becomes a miserable, tawdry thing. Who said women have to be happy, to be amused, to be entertained? You have to work. You

don't have to have a job. But you have to tackle something yourself, and see it through, to feel alive.

An hour a day, a weekend, or even a week off from motherhood is not the answer to the problem that has no name. That 'mother's hour off',[1] as advised by child-and-family experts or puzzled doctors as the antidote for the housewife's fatigue or trapped feeling, assumes automatically that a woman is 'just a housewife', now and forever a mother. A person fully used by his work can enjoy 'time off'. But the mothers I talked to did not find any magical relief in an 'hour off'; in fact, they often gave it up on the slightest pretext, either from guilt or from boredom. A woman who has no purpose of her own in society, a woman who cannot let herself think about the future because she is doing nothing to give herself a real identity in it, will continue to feel a desperation in the present – no matter how many 'hours off' she takes. Even a very young woman today must think of herself as a human being first, not as a mother with time on her hands, and make a life plan in terms of her own abilities, a commitment of her own to society, with which her commitments as wife and mother can be integrated.

A woman I interviewed, a mental-health educator who was for many years 'just a housewife' in her suburban community, sums it up: 'I remember my own feeling that life wasn't full enough for me. I wasn't using myself in terms of my capacities. It wasn't enough making a home. You can't put the genie back in the bottle. You can't just deny your intelligent mind; you need to be part of the social scheme.'

And looking over the trees of her garden to the quiet, empty suburban street, she said:

If you knock on any of these doors, how many women would you find whose abilities are being used? You'd find them drinking, or sitting around talking to other women and watching children play because they can't bear to be alone, or watching TV or reading a book. Society hasn't caught up with women yet, hasn't found a way yet to use the skills and energies of women except to bear children. Over the last fifteen years, I think women have been running away from themselves. The reason the young ones have swallowed this feminine business is because they think if they go back and look for all their satisfaction in the home, it will be easier. But it won't be. Somewhere along the line a woman, if she is going to come to terms with herself, has to find herself as a person.

But a job, any job, is not the answer – in fact, it can be part of the trap. Women who do not look for jobs equal to their actual capacity, who do not let themselves develop the lifetime interests and goals which require serious education and training, who take a job at twenty or forty to 'help out at home' or just to kill extra time, are walking, almost as surely as the ones who stay inside the housewife trap, to a nonexistent future.

If a job is to be the way out of the trap for a woman, it must be a job that she can take seriously as part of a life plan, work in which she can grow as part of society. Suburban communities, particularly the new communities where social, cultural, educational, political, and recreational patterns are not as yet firmly established, offer numerous opportunities for the able, intelligent woman. But such work is not necessarily a 'job'. In Westchester, on Long Island, in the Philadelphia suburbs, women have started mental-health clinics, art centres, day camps. In big cities and small towns, women all the way from New England to California have pioneered new movements in politics and education.

In some suburbs and communities there is now little work left for the non-professional that requires intelligence – except for the few positions of leadership which most women, these days, lack the independence, the strength, the self-confidence to take. If the community has a high proportion of educated women, there simply are not enough such posts to go around. As a result, community work often expands in a kind of self-serving structure of committees and red tape, in the purest sense of Parkinson's law, until its real purpose seems to be just to keep women busy. Such busywork is not satisfying to mature women, nor does it help the immature to grow. This is not to say that being a den mother, or serving on a P.T.A. committee, or organizing a covered-dish supper is not useful work; for a woman of intelligence and ability, it is simply not enough.

Because of the feminine mystique (and perhaps because of the simple human fear of failure, when one does compete, without sexual privilege or excuse), it is the jump from amateur to professional that is often hardest for a woman on her way out of the trap. But even if a woman does not have to work to eat, she can find identity only in work that is of real value to society[2] – work for which, usually, our society pays. Being paid is, of course, more than a reward – it implies a definite commitment. For fear of that commitment, hundreds of able, educated suburban housewives today fool themselves about the writer or actress they might have been, or dabble at art or music in the dilettante's limbo of 'self-enrichment', or apply for jobs as receptionists or saleswomen, jobs well below their actual abilities. These are also ways of evading growth.

The growing boredom of American women with volunteer work, and their preference for paid jobs, no matter how low-level, has been attributed to the fact that professionals have taken over most of the posts in the community requiring intelligence. But the fact that women did not become professionals themselves, the reluctance of women in the last twenty years to commit themselves to work, paid or unpaid, requiring initiative, leadership and responsibility is due to the feminine mystique. This attitude of noncommitment among young housewives was confirmed by a recent study done in Westchester County.[3] In an upper-income suburb, more than 50 per cent of a group of housewives between 25 and 35, with husbands in the over-$25,000-a-year income group, wanted to go to work: 13 per cent immediately, the rest in 5 to 15 years. Of those who planned to go to work, 3 out of 4 felt inadequately prepared. (All of these women had some college education but only one a graduate degree; a third had married at twenty or before.) These women were not driven to go to work by economic need but by what the anthropologist who made the survey called 'the psychological need to be economically productive'. Evidently, volunteer work did not meet this need; though 62 per cent of these women were doing volunteer work, it was of the 'one day and under' variety. And though they wanted jobs and felt inadequately prepared, of the 45 per cent taking courses, very few were working towards a degree. The element of fantasy in their work plans was witnessed by 'the small businesses that open and close with sad regularity'. When an alumnae association sponsored a two-session forum in the suburb on 'How Women in the Middle Years Can Return to Work', twenty-five women attended. As a beginning step, each woman was asked to come to the second meeting with a résumé. The résumé took some thought, and, as the researcher put it, 'sincerity of purpose'. Only one woman was serious enough to write the résumé.

In another suburb, there is a guidance centre which in the early years of the mental-health movement gave real scope to the intelligence of college-educated women of the community. They never did therapy, of course, but in the early years they administered the centre and led the educational parent-discussion groups. Now that 'education for family living' has become professionalized, the centre is administered and the discussion groups led by professionals, often brought in from the city, who have M.A.s or doctorates in the field. In only a very few cases did the women who 'found themselves' in the work of the guidance centre go on in the new profession, and get their own M.A.s and Ph.D.s. Most backed off when to continue would have meant breaking away from the house-wife role, and becoming seriously committed to a profession.

Ironically, the only kind of work which permits an able woman to realize her abilities fully, to achieve identity in society in a life plan that can encompass marriage and mother-hood, is the kind that was forbidden by the feminine mystique: the lifelong commitment to an art or science, to politics or profession. Such a commitment is not tied to a specific job or locality. It permits year-to-year variation – a full-time paid job in one community, part-time in another, exercise of the professional skill in serious volunteer work or a period of study during pregnancy or early motherhood when a full-time job is not feasible. It is a continuous thread, kept alive by work and study and contacts in the field, in any part of the country.

The women I found who had made and kept alive such

long-term commitments did not suffer the problem that has no name. Nor did they live in the housewife image. But music or art or politics offered no magic solution for the women who did not, or could not, commit themselves seriously. The 'arts' seem, at first glance, to be the ideal answer for a woman. They can, after all, be practised in the home. They do not necessarily imply that dreaded professionalism, they are suitably feminine, and seem to offer endless room for personal growth and identity, with no need to compete in society for pay. But I have noticed that when women do not take up painting or ceramics seriously enough to become professionals – to be paid for their work, or for teaching it to others, and to be recognized as a peer by other professionals – sooner or later, they cease dabbling; the Sunday painting, the idle ceramics do not bring that needed sense of self when they are of no value to anyone else.

There are, of course, a number of practical problems involved in making a serious professional commitment. But somehow those problems only seem insurmountable when a woman is still half-submerged in the false dilemmas and guilts of the feminine mystique – or when her desire for 'something more' is only fantasy, and she is unwilling to make the necessary effort. Over and over, women told me that the crucial step for them was simply to take the first trip to the alumnae employment agency, or to send for the application for teacher certification, or to make appointments with former job contacts in the city. It is amazing how many obstacles and rationalizations the feminine mystique can throw up to keep a woman from making that trip or writing that letter.

Some women take the jobs but do not make the necessary new life plan. I interviewed two women of ability, both of whom were bored as housewives and both of whom got jobs in the same research institute. They loved the increasingly challenging work, and were quickly promoted. But, in their thirties, after ten years as housewives, they earned very little money. The first woman, clearly recognizing the future this work held for her, spent virtually her entire salary on a three-day-a-week cleaning woman. The second woman, who felt her work was justified only if it 'helped out with family expenses', would not spend any money for cleaning help. Nor did she consider asking her husband and children to help out with household chores, or save time by ordering groceries by phone and sending the laundry out. She quit her job after a year from sheer exhaustion. The first woman, who made the necessary household changes and sacrifices, today, at thirty-eight, has one of the leading jobs at the institute and makes a substantial contribution to her family's income, over and above what she pays for her part-time household help. The second, after two weeks of 'rest', began to suffer the old desperation. But she persuaded herself that she will 'cheat' her husband and children less by finding work she can do at home.

The picture of the happy housewife doing creative work at home – painting, sculpting, writing – is one of the semi-delusions of the feminine mystique. There are men and women who can do it; but when a man works at home, his wife keeps the children strictly out of the way, or else. It is not so easy for a woman; if she is serious about her work she often must find some place away from home to do it, or risk becoming an ogre to her children in her impatient demands for privacy. Her attention is divided and her concentration interrupted, on the job and as a mother. A no-nonsense nine-to-five job, with a clear division between professional work and housework, requires much less discipline and is usually less lonely. Some of the stimulation and the new friendships that come from being part of the professional world can be lost by the woman who tries to fit her career into the physical confines of her housewife life.

A woman must say 'no' to the feminine mystique very clearly indeed to sustain the discipline and effort that any professional commitment requires. For the mystique is no mere intellectual construct. A great many people have, or think they have, a vested interest in 'Occupation: housewife'. However long it may take for women's magazines, sociologists, educators, and psychoanalysts to correct the mistakes that perpetuate the feminine mystique, a woman must deal

with them now, in the prejudices, mistaken fears, and unnecessary dilemmas voiced by her husband; her friends and
neighbours; perhaps her minister, priest, or rabbi; or her
child's kindergarten teacher; or the well-meaning social
worker at the guidance clinic; or her own innocent little
children. But resistance, from whatever source, is better seen
for what it is.

Even the traditional resistance of religious orthodoxy is
masked today with the manipulative techniques of psychotherapy. Women of orthodox Catholic or Jewish origin do not
easily break through the housewife image; it is enshrined in
the canons of their religion, in the assumptions of their own
and their husbands' childhoods, and in their church's dogmatic
definitions of marriage and motherhood. The ease with which
dogma can be dressed in the psychological tenets of the mystique can be seen in this 'Suggested Outline for Married
Couples' Discussions' from the Family Life Bureau of the
Archdiocese of New York. A panel of three or four married
couples, after rehearsal by a 'priest-moderator', are instructed
to raise the question: 'Can a working wife be a challenge to
the authority of the husband?'

Most of the engaged couples are convinced that there is nothing
unusual or wrong in the wife working. ... Don't antagonize. Be
suggestive, rather than dogmatic. ... The panel couples should
point out that the bride who is happy at a 9-to-5 o'clock job has this
to think about:
a. She may be subtly undermining her husband's sense of vocation
as the bread-winner and head of the house. The competitive
business world can inculcate in the working bride attitudes and
habits which may make it difficult for her to adjust to her husband's leadership. ...
b. At the end of a working day, she presents her husband with a
tired mind and body at a time when he looks forward to the
cheerful encouragement and fresh enthusiasm of his spouse. ...
c. For some brides, the tension of doubling as business woman and
part-time housewife may be one of several factors contributing to
sterility. ...

One Catholic woman I interviewed withdrew from the state

board of the League of Woman Voters when, in addition to the displeasure of the priest and her own husband, the school psychologist claimed that her daughter's difficulties at school were due to her political activity. 'It is more difficult for a Catholic woman to stay emancipated,' she told me. 'I have retired. It will be better for everyone concerned if I am just a housewife.' At this point the telephone rang, and I eavesdropped with interest on half an hour of high political strategy, evidently not of the League but of the local Democratic Party. The 'retired' politician came back into the kitchen to finish preparing dinner, and confessed that she now hid her political activity at home 'like an alcoholic or a drug addict, but I don't seem to be able to give it up'.

Another woman, of Jewish tradition, gave up her profession as a doctor when she became a doctor's wife, devoting herself to bringing up their four children. Her husband was not overjoyed when she began brushing up to retake her medical exams after her youngest reached school age. An unassertive, quiet woman, she exerted almost unbelievable effort to obtain her licence after fifteen years of inactivity. She told me apologetically: 'You just can't stop being interested. I tried to make myself, but I couldn't.' And she confessed that when she gets a night call, she sneaks out as guiltily as if she were meeting a lover.

Even to a woman of less orthodox tradition, the most powerful weapon of the feminine mystique is the argument that she rejects her husband and her children by working outside the home. If, for any reason, her child becomes ill or her husband has troubles of his own, the feminine mystique, insidious voices in the community, and even the woman's own inner voice, will blame her 'rejection' of the housewife role. It is then that many a woman's commitment to herself and society dies aborning or takes a serious detour.

One woman told me that she gave up her job in television to become 'just a housewife' because her husband suddenly decided his troubles in his own profession were caused by her failure to 'play the feminine role'; she was trying to 'compete' with him; she wanted to 'wear the pants'. She, like most women today, was vulnerable to such charges – one psychiatrist calls it the 'career woman's guilt syndrome'. And so she began to devote all the energies she had once put into her work to running her family – and to a nagging critical interest in her husband's career.

In her spare time in the suburbs, however, she rather absent-mindedly achieved flamboyant local success as the director of a little-theatre group. This, on top of her critical attention to her husband's career, was far more destructive to his ego and a much more constant irritation to him and to her children than her professional work in which she had competed impersonally with other professionals in a world far away from home. One day, when she was directing a little-theatre rehearsal, her son was hit by a car. She blamed herself for the accident, and so she gave up the little-theatre group, resolving this time, cross her heart, that she would be 'just a housewife'.

She suffered, almost immediately, a severe case of the problem that has no name; her depression and dependence made her husband's life hell. She sought analytic help, and in a departure from the non-directive approach of orthodox analysts, her therapist virtually ordered her to get back to work. She started writing a serious novel with finally the kind of commitment she had evaded, even when she had a job. In her absorption, she stopped worrying about her husband's career; imperceptibly, she stopped fantasying another accident every time her son was out of her sight. And still, though she was too far along to retreat, she sometimes wondered if she were putting her marriage on the chopping block.

Contrary to the mystique, her husband – reacting either to the contagious example of her commitment, or to the breathing space afforded by the cessation of her hysterical dependence, or for independent reasons of his own – buckled down to the equivalent of that novel in his own career. There were still problems, of course, but not the old ones; when they broke out of their own traps, somehow their relationship with each other began growing again.

Still, with every kind of growth, there are risks. I encountered one woman in my interviews whose husband divorced her shortly after she went to work. Their marriage had become extremely destructive. The sense of identity that the woman achieved from her work may have made her less willing to accept the destructiveness, and perhaps precipitated the divorce; but it also made her more able to survive it.

In other instances, however, women told me that the violent objections of their husbands disappeared when they finally made up their own minds and went to work. Had they magnified their husband's objections to evade decision themselves? Husbands I have interviewed in this same context were sometimes surprised to find it 'a relief' to be no longer the only sun and moon in their wives' world; they were the object of less nagging and fewer insatiable demands and they no longer had to feel guilt over their wives' discontent. As one man put it: 'Not only is the financial burden lighter – and frankly, that is a relief – but the whole burden of living seems easier since Margaret went to work.'

There are husbands, however, whose resistance is not so easily dispelled. The husband who is unable to bear his wife's saying 'no' to the feminine mystique often has been seduced himself by the infantile fantasy of having an ever-present mother, or is trying to relive that fantasy through his children. It is difficult for a woman to tell such a husband that she is not his mother and that their children will be better off without her constant attention. Perhaps if she becomes more truly herself and refuses to act out his fantasy any longer, he will suddenly wake up and see *her* again. And then again, perhaps he will look for another mother.

Another hazard a woman faces on her way out of the housewife trap is the hostility of other housewives. Just as the man evading growth in his own work resents his wife's growth, so women who are living vicariously through their husbands and children resent the woman who has a life of her own. At dinner parties, the nursery school affair, the P.T.A. open house, a woman who is more than just a housewife can expect a few barbs from her suburban neighbours. She no longer has the time for idle gossip over endless cups of coffee in the breakfast nook; she can no longer share with other wives that cosy 'we're all in the same boat' illusion; her very presence rocks that boat. And she can expect her home, her husband, and her children to be scrutinized with more than the usual curiosity for the slightest sign of a 'problem'. This kind of hostility, however, sometimes masks a secret envy. The most hostile of the 'happy housewives' may be the first to ask her neighbour with the new career for advice about moving on herself.

For the woman who moves on, there is always the sense of loss that accompanies change: old friends, familiar and reassuring routines lost, the new ones not yet clear. It is so much easier for a woman to say 'yes' to the feminine mystique, and not risk the pains of moving on, that the will to make the effort – 'ambition' – is as necessary as ability itself, if she is going to move out of the housewife trap. 'Ambition', like 'career', has been made a dirty word by the feminine mystique. When Polly Weaver, 'College and Careers' editor of *Mademoiselle*, surveyed 400 women in 1956 on the subject of 'ambition' and 'competition',[4] most of them had 'guilty feelings' about being ambitious. They tried, in Miss Weaver's words, to

... make it uplifting, not worldly and selfish like eating. We were surprised ... at the number of women who drive themselves from morning to night for a job or the community or church, for example, but don't want a nickel's worth out of it for themselves. They don't want money, social position, power, influence, recognition. ... Are these women fooling themselves?

The mystique would have women renounce ambition for themselves. Marriage and motherhood is the end; after that, women are supposed to be ambitious only for their husbands and their children. Many women who indeed 'fool themselves' push husband and children to fulfil that unadmitted ambition of their own. There were, however, many frankly ambitious women among those who responded to the *Mademoiselle* survey – and they did not seem to suffer from it.

The ambitious women who answered our questionnaire had few

regrets over sacrifices of sweet old friends, family picnics, and time for reading books no one talks about. They got more than they gave up, they said, and cited new friends, the larger world they move in, the great spurts of growth they had when they worked with the brilliant and talented – and most of all the satisfaction of working at full steam, putt-putting along like a pressure cooker. In fact, some happy ambitious women make the people around them happy – their husbands, children, their colleagues.... A very ambitious woman is not happy, either, leaving her prestige entirely to her husband's success.... To the active, ambitious woman, ambition is the thread that runs through her life from beginning to end, holding it together and enabling her to think of her life as a work of art instead of a collection of fragments. ...

For the women I interviewed who had suffered and solved the problem that has no name, to fulfil an ambition of their own, long buried or brand-new, to work at top capacity, to have a sense of achievement, was like finding a missing piece in the puzzle of their lives. The money they earned often made life easier for the whole family, but none of them pretended this was the only reason they worked, or the main thing they got out of it. That sense of being complete and fully a part of the world – 'no longer an island, part of the mainland' – had come back. They knew that it did not come from the work alone, but from the whole – their marriage, homes, children, work, their changing, growing links with the community. They were once again human beings, not 'just housewives'. Such women are the lucky ones. Some may have been driven to that ambition by childhood rejection, by an ugly-duckling adolescence, by unhappiness in marriage, by divorce or widowhood. It is both an irony and an indictment of the feminine mystique that it often forced the unhappy ones, the ugly ducklings, to find themselves, while girls who fitted the image became adjusted 'happy' housewives and have never found out who they are. But to say that 'frustration' can be good for a girl would be to miss the point; such frustration should not have to be the price of identity for a woman, nor is it in itself the key. The mystique has kept both pretty girls and ugly ones, who might have written poems like Edith Sitwell, from discovering their own gifts; kept happy wives and unhappy ones, who might have found themselves as Ruth Benedict did in anthropology, from even discovering their own field. And suddenly the final piece of the puzzle fits into place.

The key to the trap is, of course, education. The feminine mystique has made higher education for women seem suspect, unnecessary, and even dangerous. But I think that education, and only education, has saved, and can continue to save, American women from the greater dangers of the feminine mystique.

In 1957 when I was asked to do an alumnae questionnaire of my own college classmates fifteen years after their graduation from Smith, I seized on the chance, thinking that I could disprove the growing belief that education made women 'masculine', hampered their sexual fulfilment, caused unnecessary conflicts and frustrations. I discovered that the critics were half-right; education was dangerous and frustrating – but only when women did not use it.

Of the 200 women who answered that questionnaire in 1957, 89 per cent were housewives. They had lived through all the possible frustrations that education can cause in housewives. But when they were asked, 'What difficulties have you found in working out your role as a woman? ... What are the chief satisfactions and frustrations of your life today? ... How have you changed inside? ... How do you feel about getting older? ... What do you wish you had done differently? ...' it was discovered that their real problems, as women, were not caused by their education. In general, they regretted only one thing – that they had not taken their education seriously enough, that they had not planned to put it to serious use.

Of the 97 per cent of these women who married – usually about three years after college – only 3 per cent had been divorced; of 20 per cent who had been interested in another man since marriage, most 'did nothing about it'. As mothers, 86 per cent planned their children's births and enjoyed their pregnancies; 70 per cent breastfed their babies from one to nine months. They had more children than their mothers (average: 2.94), but only 10 per cent had ever felt 'martyred' as mothers. Though 99 per cent reported that sex was only 'one factor among many' in their lives, they neither felt over and done with sexually, nor were they just beginning to feel the sexual satisfaction of being a woman. Some 85 per cent reported that sex 'gets better with the years', but they also found it 'less important than it used to be'. They shared life with their husbands 'as fully as one can with another human being', but 75 per cent admitted readily that they could not share all of it.

Most of them (60 per cent) could not honestly say, in reporting their main occupation as homemaker, that they found it 'totally fulfilling'. They only spent an average of four hours a day on housework and they did not 'enjoy' it. It was perhaps true that their education made them frustrated in their role as housewives. Educated before the era of the feminine mystique, many of them had faced a sharp break from their emerging identity in that housewife role. And yet most of these women continued to grow within the framework of suburban housewifery – perhaps because of the autonomy, the sense of purpose, the commitment to larger values which their education had given them.

Some 79 per cent had found some way to pursue the goals that education had given them, for the most part within the physical confines of their communities. The old Helen Hokinson caricatures notwithstanding, their assumption of community responsibility was, in general, an act of maturity, a commitment that used and renewed strength of self. For these women, community activity almost always had the stamp of innovation and individuality, rather than the stamp of conformity, status-seeking, or escape. They set up cooperative nursery schools in suburbs where none existed; they started teen-age canteens and libraries in schools where Johnny wasn't reading because, quite simply, there were no good books. They innovated new educational programmes that finally became a part of the curriculum. One was personally instrumental in getting 13,000 signatures for a popular referendum to get politics out of the school system. One publicly spoke out for desegregation of schools in the South. One got white children to attend a *de facto* segregated school in the North. One pushed an appropriation for mental-health clinics through a Western state legislature. One set up museum art programmes for school children in each of three cities she had lived in since marriage. Others started or led suburban choral groups, civic theatres, foreign-policy study groups. Thirty per cent were active in local party politics, from the committee level to the state assembly. Over 90 per cent reported that they read the newspaper thoroughly every day and voted regularly. They evidently never watched a daytime television programme and seemed almost never to play bridge, or read women's magazines. Of the fifteen to three hundred books apiece they had read in that one year, half were not bestsellers.

Facing forty, most of these women could report quite frankly that their hair was greying, and their 'skin looks faded and tired', and yet say, with not much regret for lost youth, 'I have a growing sense of self-realization, inner serenity and strength'; 'I have become more my real self.'

'How do you visualize your life after your children are grown?' they were asked on the questionnaire. Most of them (60 per cent) had concrete plans for work or study. They planned to finish their education finally, for many who had no career ambitions in college had them now. A few had reached 'the depths of bitterness', 'the verge of disillusion and despair', trying to live just as housewives. A few confessed longingly that 'running my house and raising four children does not really use my education or the ability I once seemed to have. If only it were possible to combine motherhood and a career.' And the most bitter were those who said: 'Never have found out what kind of a person I am. I wasted college trying to find myself in social life. I wish now that I had gone into something deeply enough to have a creative life of my own.' But most did know, now, who they were and what they wanted to do; and 80 per cent regretted not having planned, seriously, to *use* their education in professional work. Passive appreciation and even active participation in community affairs would no longer be enough when their children were a little older. Many women reported that they were planning to teach; fortunately for them, the great need for teachers gave them a chance to get back in the stream. Others anticipated years of further study before they would be qualified in their chosen fields.

These 200 Smith graduates have their counterparts in women all over the country, women of intelligence and ability, fighting their way out of the housewife trap, or never really trapped at all because of their education. But these graduates of 1942 were among the last American women educated before the feminine mystique.

In another questionnaire answered by almost 10,000 graduates of Mount Holyoke in 1962 – its 125th anniversary year – one sees the effect of the mystique on women educated in the last two decades. The Mount Holyoke alumnae showed a similar high marriage and low divorce rate (2 per cent overall). But before 1942, most were married at twenty-five or older; after 1942, the marriage age showed a dramatic drop, and the percentage having four or more children showed a dramatic rise. Before 1942, two thirds or more of the graduates went on to further study; that proportion has steadily declined. Few, in recent classes, have won advanced degrees in the arts, sciences, law, medicine, education, compared to the 40 per cent in 1937. A drastically decreasing number also seem to share the larger vistas of national or international commitment; participation in local political clubs had dropped to 12 per cent by the class of 1952. From 1942 on, few graduates had any professional affiliation. Half of all the Mount Holyoke alumnae had worked at one time but were no longer working, primarily because they had chosen 'the role of housewife'. Some had returned to work – both to supplement income and because they liked to work. But in the classes from 1942 on, where most of the women were now housewives, nearly half did not intend to return to work.

The declining area of commitment to the world outside the home from 1942 on is a clear indication of the effect of the feminine mystique on educated women. Having seen the desperate emptiness, the 'trapped' feeling of many young women who were educated under the mystique to be 'just a housewife', I realize the significance of my classmates' experience. Because of their education many of them were able to combine serious commitments of their own with marriage and family. They could participate in community activities that required intelligence and responsibility, and move on, with a few years' preparation, into professional social work or teaching. They could get jobs as substitute teachers or part-time social workers to finance the courses needed for certification. They had often grown to the point where they did not want to return to the fields they had worked in after college, and they could even get into a new field with the core of autonomy that their education had given them.

But what of the young women today who have never had a taste of higher education, who quit college to marry or marked time in their classrooms waiting for the 'right man'? What will they be at forty? Housewives in every suburb and city are seeking more education today, as if a course, any course, will give them the identity they are groping towards. But the courses they take, and the courses they are offered, are seldom intended for real use in society. Even more than the education she evaded at eighteen in sexual fantasy, the education a woman can get at forty is permeated, contaminated, diluted by the feminine mystique.

Courses in golf, bridge, rug-hooking, gourmet cooking, sewing are intended, I suppose, for real use, by women who stay in the housewife trap. The so-called intellectual courses offered in the usual adult education centres – art appreciation, ceramics, short-story writing, conversational French, Great Books, astronomy in the Space Age – are intended only as 'self-enrichment'.

Actually, many women who take these courses desperately need serious education; but if they have never had a taste of it, they do not know how and where to look for it, nor do they even understand that so many adult education courses are unsatisfactory simply because they are not serious. The dimension of reality essential even to 'self-enrichment' is barred, almost by definition, in a course specifically designed for 'housewives'. This is true, even where the institution giving the course has the highest standards. Recently, Radcliffe announced an 'Institute for Executives' Wives' (to be followed presumably by an 'Institute for Scientists' Wives', or an 'Institute for Artists' Wives', or an 'Institute for College Professors' Wives'). The executive's wife or the scientist's wife, at thirty-five or forty, whose children are all at school is hardly going to be helped to the new identity she needs by learning to take a more detailed, vicarious share of her husband's world. What she needs is training for creative work of her own.

Among the women I interviewed, education was the key to the problem that has no name only when it was part of a new life plan, and meant for serious use in society – amateur or professional. They were able to find such education only in the regular colleges and universities. Despite the wishful thinking engendered by the feminine mystique in girls and in their educators, an education evaded at eighteen or twenty-one is insuperably harder to obtain at thirty-one or thirty-eight or forty-one, by a woman who has a husband and three or four children and a home. She faces, in the college or university, the prejudices created by the feminine mystique. No matter how brief her absence from the academic proving-ground, she will have to demonstrate her seriousness of purpose over and over again to be readmitted. She must then compete with the teeming hordes of children she and others like her have overproduced in this era. It is not easy for a grown woman to sit through courses geared to teenagers, to be treated as a teenager again, to have to prove that she deserves to be taken as seriously as a teenager. A woman has to exercise great ingenuity, endure many rebuffs and disappointments, to find an education that fits her need, and also make it fit her other commitments as wife and mother.

One woman I interviewed who had never gone to college, decided, after psychotherapy, to take two courses a year at a nearby university which, fortunately, had an evening school. At first, she had no idea where it was leading her, but after two years, she decided to major in history and prepare to teach it in high school. She maintained a good record, even though she was often impatient with the slow pace and the busywork. But, at least, studying with some purpose made her feel better than when she used to read mystery stories or magazines at the playground. Above all, it was leading to something real for the future. But at the rate of two courses a year (which then cost $420, and two evenings a week in class), it would have taken her ten years to get a B.A. The second year, money was scarce, and she could only take one course. She could not apply for a student loan unless she went full time, which she could not do until her youngest was in first grade. In spite of it all, she stuck it out that way for four years – noticing that more and more of the other housewives in her classes dropped out because of money, or because 'the whole thing was going to take too long'.

Then, with her youngest in first grade, she became a full-time student in the regular college, where the pace was even slower because the students were 'less serious'. She couldn't endure the thought of all the years ahead to get an M.A. (which she would need to teach high-school history in that state), so she switched to an education major. She certainly would not have continued this expensive, tortuous education if, by now, she had not had a clear life plan to use it, a plan that required it. Committed to elementary teaching, she was able to get a government loan for part of her full-time tuition (now exceeding $1,000 a year), and in another two years she would be finished.

Even against such enormous obstacles, more and more women, with virtually no help from society and with belated and begrudging encouragement from educators themselves, are going back to school to get the education they need. Their determination betrays women's underestimated human strength and their urgent need to use it. But only the strongest, after nearly twenty years of the feminine mystique, can move on by themselves. For this is not just the private problem of each individual woman. There are implications of the feminine mystique that must be faced on a national scale.

The problem that has no name – which is simply the fact that American women are kept from growing to their full human capacities – is taking a far greater toll on the physical and mental health of our country than any known disease. Consider the high incidence of emotional breakdown of women in the 'role crises' of their twenties and thirties; the alcoholism and suicides in their forties and fifties; the housewives' monopolization of all doctors' time. Consider the prevalence of teenage marriages, the growing rate of illegitimate pregnancies, and even more seriously, the pathology of mother–child symbiosis. Consider the alarming passivity of American teenagers. If we continue to produce millions of young mothers who stop their growth and education short of identity, without a strong core of human values to pass on to their children, we are committing, quite simply, genocide, starting with the mass burial of American women and ending with the progressive dehumanization of their sons and daughters.

These problems cannot be solved by medicine, or even by psychotherapy. We need a drastic reshaping of the cultural image of femininity that will permit women to reach maturity, identity, completeness of self, without conflict with sexual fulfilment. A massive attempt must be made by educators and parents – and ministers, magazine editors, manipulators, guidance counsellors – to stop the early-marriage movement, stop girls from growing up wanting to be 'just a housewife', stop it by insisting, with the same attention from childhood on that parents and educators give to boys, that girls develop the resources of self, goals that will permit them to find their own identity.

It is, of course, no easier for an educator to say 'no' to the feminine mystique than for an individual girl or woman. Even the most advanced of educators, seriously concerned with the desperate need of housewives with left-over lives on their hands, hesitate to buck the tide of early marriage. They have been browbeaten by the oracles of popularized psychoanalysis and still tremble with guilt at the thought of interfering with a woman's sexual fulfilment. The rearguard argument offered by the oracles who are, in some cases, right on college campuses themselves is that since the primary road to identity for a woman is marriage and motherhood, serious educational interests or commitments which may cause conflicts in her role as wife and mother should be postponed until the child-bearing years are over. Such a warning was made in 1962 by a psychiatric consultant to Yale University – which had been considering admitting women as undergraduates for the same serious education it gives men.

Many young women – if not the majority – seem to be incapable of dealing with future long-range intellectual interests until they have proceeded through the more basic phases of their own healthy growth as women. ... To be well done, the mother's job in training children and shaping the life of her family should draw on all a woman's resources, emotional and intellectual, and upon all her skills. The better her training, the better chance she will have to do the job well, provided that emotional road-blocks do not stand in her way: provided, that is, that she has established a good basis for the development of adult femininity, and that during the course of her higher education, she is not subjected to pressures which adversely affect that development. ... To urge upon her conflicting goals, to stress that a career and a profession in the man's world should be the first consideration in planning her life, can adversely affect the full development of her identity. ... Of all the social freedoms won by her grandmothers, she prizes first the freedom to be a healthy, fulfilled woman, and she wants to be free of guilt and conflict about it. ... This means that though jobs are often possible within the framework of marriage, 'careers' rarely are ...[5]

The fact remains that the girl who wastes – as waste she does – her college years without acquiring serious interests, and wastes her early job years marking time until she finds a man, gambles with the possibilities for an identity of her own, as well as the possibilities for sexual fulfilment and wholly affirmed motherhood. The educators who encourage a woman to postpone larger interests until her children are grown make it virtually impossible for her ever to acquire them. It is not that easy for a woman who has defined herself wholly as wife and mother for ten or fifteen or twenty years to find new identity at thirty-five or forty or fifty. The ones who are able to do it are, quite frankly, the ones who made serious commitments to their earlier education, the ones who wanted and once worked at careers, the ones who bring to marriage and motherhood a sense of their own identity – not those who somehow hope to acquire it later on. A recent study of fifty women college graduates in an eastern suburb and city, the year after the oldest child had left home, showed that, with very few exceptions, the only women who had any interests to pursue – in work, in community activities, or in the arts – had acquired them in college. The ones who lacked such interests were not acquiring them now; they slept late, in their 'empty nests', and looked forward only to death.[6]

Educators at every women's college, at every university, junior college, and community college, must see to it that women make a lifetime commitment (call it a 'life plan', a 'vocation', a 'life purpose' if that dirty word *career* has too many celibate connotations) to a field of thought, to work of serious importance to society. They must expect the girl as well as the boy to take some field seriously enough to want to pursue it for life. This does not mean abandoning liberal education for women in favour of 'how to' vocational courses. Liberal education, as it is given at the best of colleges and universities, not only trains the mind but provides an ineradicable core of human values. But liberal education must be planned for serious use, not merely dilettantism or passive appreciation. As boys at Harvard or Yale or Columbia or Chicago go on from the liberal arts core to study architecture, medicine, law, science, girls must be encouraged to go on, to make a life plan. It has been shown that girls with this kind of a commitment are less eager to rush into early marriage, less panicky about finding a man, more responsible for their sexual behaviour.[7] Most of them marry, of course, but on a much more mature basis. Their marriages then are not an escape but a commitment shared by two people that becomes part of their commitment to themselves and society. If, in fact, girls are educated to make such commitments, the question of sex and when they marry will lose its overwhelming importance.[8]

In the face of the feminine mystique with its powerful

hidden deterrents, educators must realize that they cannot inspire young women to commit themselves seriously to their education without taking some extraordinary measures. The few so far attempted barely come to grips with the problem. Mary Bunting's new Institute for Independent Study at Radcliffe is fine for women who already know what they want to do, who have pursued their studies to the Ph.D. or are already active in the arts, and merely need some respite from motherhood to get back in the mainstream. Even more important, the presence of these women on the campus, women who have babies and husbands and who are still deeply committed to their own work, will undoubtedly help dispel the image of the celibate career woman and fire some of those Radcliffe sophomores out of the 'climate of unexpectation' that permits them to meet the nation's highest standard of educational excellence to use it later only in marriage and motherhood. This is what Mary Bunting had in mind. And it can be done elsewhere, in even simpler ways.

It would pay every college and university that wants to encourage women to take education seriously to recruit for their faculties all the women they can find who have combined marriage and motherhood with the life of the mind – even if it means concessions for pregnancies or breaking the old rule about hiring the wife of the male associate professor who has her own perfectly respectable M.A. or Ph.D. As for the unmarried woman scholars, they must no longer be treated like lepers. The simple truth is that they have taken their existence seriously, and have fulfilled their human potential. They might well be, and often are, envied by women who live the very image of opulent togetherness, but have forfeited themselves. Women, as well as men, who are rooted in human work are rooted in life.

It is essential, above all, for educators themselves to say 'no' to the feminine mystique and face the fact that the only point in educating women is to educate them to the limit of their ability. Women do not need courses in 'marriage and the family' to marry and raise families; they do not need courses in homemaking to make homes. But they must study science –

to discover in science; study the thought of the past – to create new thought; study society – to pioneer in society. Educators must also give up these 'one thing at a time' compromises. That separate layering of 'education', 'sex', 'marriage', 'motherhood', 'interests for the last third of life', will not solve the role crisis. Women must be educated to a new integration of roles. The more they are encouraged to make that new life plan – integrating a serious, lifelong commitment to society with marriage and motherhood – the less conflicts and unnecessary frustrations they will feel as wives and mothers, and the less their daughters will make mistaken choices for lack of a full image of woman's identity.

I could see this in investigating college girls' rush to early marriage. The few who were not in such a desperate hurry to 'get a man' and who committed themselves to serious long-range interests – evidently not worried that they would thereby lose their 'femininity' – almost all had mothers, or other private images of women, who were committed to some serious purpose. ('My mother happens to be a teacher.' 'My best friend's mother is a doctor; she always seems so busy and happy.')

Education itself can help provide that new image – and the spark in girls to create their own – as soon as it stops compromising and temporizing with the old image of 'woman's role'. For women as well as men, education is and must be the matrix of human evolution. If today American women are finally breaking out of the housewife trap in search of new identity, it is quite simply because so many women have had a taste of higher education – unfinished, unfocused, but still powerful enough to force them on.

For that last and most important battle *can* be fought in the mind and spirit of woman herself. Even without a private image, many girls in America who have been educated simply as people were given a strong enough sense of their human possibility to carry them past the old femininity, past that search for security in man's love, to find a new self. A Swarthmore graduate, entering her internship, told me that at first, as she felt herself getting more and more 'independent' in college, she worried a lot about having dates and getting married, wanted to 'latch on to a boy'. 'I tried to beat myself down to be feminine. Then I got interested in what I was doing and stopped worrying,' she said.

It's as if you've made some kind of shift. You begin to feel your competence in doing things. Like a baby learning to walk. Your mind begins to expand. You find your own field. And that's a wonderful thing. The love of doing the work and the feeling there's something there and you can trust it. It's worth the unhappiness. They say a man has to suffer to grow, maybe something like that has to happen to women too. You begin not to be afraid to be yourself.

Drastic steps must now be taken to re-educate the women who were deluded or cheated by the feminine mystique. Many of the women I interviewed who felt 'trapped' as housewives have in the last few years started to move out of the trap. But there are as many others who are sinking back again, because they did not find out in time what they wanted to do, or because they were not able to find a way to do it. In almost every case, it took too much time, too much money, using existing educational facilities. Few housewives can afford full-time study. Even if colleges admit them on a part-time basis – and many will not – few women can endure the slow-motion pace of usual undergraduate college education stretched over ten or more years. Some institutions are now willing to gamble on housewives, but will they be as willing when the flood of their college-bound offspring reaches its full height? The pilot programmes that have been started at Sarah Lawrence and the University of Minnesota begin to show the way, but they do not face the time–money problem which is, for so many women, the insurmountable one.

What is needed now is a national educational programme, similar to the G.I. bill, for women who seriously want to continue or resume their education – and who are willing to commit themselves to its use in a profession. The bill would provide properly qualified women with tuition fees, plus an additional subsidy to defray other expenses – books, travel, even, if necessary, some household help. Such a measure would cost far less than the G.I. bill. It would permit mothers to use existing educational facilities on a part-time basis and carry on individual study and research projects at home during the years when regular classroom attendance is impossible. The whole concept of women's education would be re-geared from four-year college to a life plan under which a woman could continue her education, without conflict with her marriage, her husband, and her children.

The G.I.s, matured by war, needed education to find their identity in society. In no mood for time-wasting, they astonished their teachers and themselves by their scholastic performance. Women who have matured during the housewife moratorium can be counted on for similar performance. Their desperate need for education and the desperate need of this nation for the untapped reserves of women's intelligence in all the professions justify these emergency measures.[9]

For those women who did not go to college, or quit too soon, for those who are no longer interested in their former field, or who never took their education seriously, I would suggest first of all an intensive concentrated re-immersion in, quite simply, the humanities – not abridgements and selections like the usual freshman or sophomore survey, but an intensive study like the educational experiments attempted by the Bell Telephone Company or the Ford Foundation for young executives who had conformed so completely to the role of organization man that they were not capable of the initiative and vision required in top executive ranks. For women, this could be done by a national programme, along the lines of the Danish Folk-High-School movement, which would first bring the housewife back into the mainstream of thought with a concentrated six-week summer course, a sort of intellectual 'shock therapy'. She would be subsidized so that she could leave home and go to a resident college, which is not otherwise used during the summer. Or she could go to a metro-politan centre on an equally intensive basis, five days a week for six or eight weeks during the summer, with a day camp provided for the children.

Assume that this educational shock treatment awakens able

women to purposes requiring the equivalent of a four-year college programme for further professional training. That college programme could be completed in four years or less, without full-time classroom attendance, by a combination of these summer institutes, plus prescribed reading, papers, and projects that could be done during the winter at home. Courses taken on television, or at local community colleges and universities on an extension basis, could be combined with tutorial conferences at mid year or every month. The courses would be taken for credit, and the customary degrees would be earned. Some system of 'equivalents' would have to be worked out, not to give a woman credit for work that does not meet requirements, but to give her credit for truly serious work, even if it is done at times, places, and in ways that violate conventional academic standards.

A number of universities automatically bar housewives by barring part-time undergraduate or graduate work. Perhaps they have been burned by dilettantes. But part-time college work, graduate or undergraduate, geared to a serious plan, is the only kind of education that can prevent a housewife from becoming a dilettante; it is the only way a woman with husband and children can get, or continue, an education. It could also be the most practical arrangement from the university's point of view. With their facilities already overtaxed by population pressures, universities and women alike would benefit from a study programme that does not require regular classroom attendance. While it makes a great deal of sense for the University of Minnesota to work out its excellent Plan for Women's Continuing Education[10] in terms of the regular university facilities, such a plan will not help the woman who must begin her education all over again to find out what she wants to do. But existing facilities, in any institution, can be used to fill in the gaps once a woman is under way on her life plan.

Colleges and universities also need a new life plan – to become lifetime institutions for their students; offer them guidance, take care of their records, and keep track of their advanced work or refresher courses, no matter where they are taken. How much greater that allegiance and financial support from their alumnae if, instead of the tea parties to raise funds and a sentimental reunion every fifth June, a woman could look to her college for continuing education and guidance! Barnard alumnae can, and do, come back and take, free, any course at any time, if they meet the qualifications for it. All colleges could conduct summer institutes to keep alumnae abreast of developments in their fields during the years of young motherhood. They could accept part-time students and offer extension courses for the housewife who could not attend classes regularly. They could advise her on reading programmes, papers, or projects that could be done at home. They could also work out a system whereby projects done by their alumnae in education, mental health, sociology, political science in their own communities could be counted as equivalent credits towards a degree. Instead of collecting dimes, let women volunteers serve supervised professional apprenticeships and collect the credits that are recognized in lieu of pay for medical interns. Similarly, when a woman has taken courses at a number of different institutions, perhaps due to her husband's geographical itinerary, and has earned her community credits from agency, hospital, library, or laboratory, her college of origin, or some national centre set up by several colleges, could give her the orals, the comprehensives, and the appropriate examinations for a degree. The concept of 'continuing education' is already a reality for men in many fields. Why not for women? Not education for careers instead of motherhood, not education for temporary careers before motherhood, not education to make them 'better wives and mothers', but an education they will use as full members of society.

'But how many American women really want to do more with their lives?' the cynic asks. A fantastic number of New Jersey housewives responded to an offer of intensive retraining in mathematics for former college women willing to commit themselves to becoming mathematics teachers. In January 1962, a simple news story in the *New York Times* announced that Sarah Lawrence's Esther Raushenbush had obtained a grant to help mature women finish their education or work for graduate degrees on a part-time basis that could be fitted in with their obligations as mothers. The response literally put the small Sarah Lawrence switchboard out of commission. Within twenty-four hours, Mrs Raushenbush had taken over 100 telephone calls. 'It was like bank night,' the operator said. 'As if they had to get in there right away, or they might miss the chance.' Interviewing the women who applied for the programme, Mrs Raushenbush, like Virginia Senders at Minnesota, was convinced of the reality of their need. They were not 'neurotically rejecting' their husbands and children; they did not need psychotherapy, but they did need more education – in a hurry – and in a form they could get without neglecting their husbands and families.

Education and re-education of American women for a serious purpose cannot be effected by one or two far-sighted institutions; it must be accomplished on a much wider scale. And no one serves this end who repeats, even for expedience or tact, the clichés of the feminine mystique. It is quite wrong to say, as some of the leading women educators are saying today, that women must of course use their education, but not, heaven forbid, in careers that will compete with men.[11] When women take their education and their abilities seriously and put them to use, ultimately they have to compete with men. It is better for a woman to compete impersonally in society, as men do, than to compete for dominance in her own home with her husband, compete with her neighbours for empty status, and so smother her son that he cannot compete at all. Consider this recent news item about America's latest occupational therapy for the pent-up feminine need to compete:

It is a typical weekday in Dallas. Daddy is at work. Baby is having his morning nap. In an adjoining room, Brother (age 3) is riding a new rocking horse and Sis (5) is watching TV cartoons. And Mommy? Mommy is just a few feet away, crouching over the foul line on Lane 53, her hip twisted sharply to the left to steer the blue-white-marbled ball into the strike pocket between the one and three pins. Mommy is bowling. Whether in Dallas or Cleveland or Albuquerque or Spokane, energetic housewives have dropped dustcloth and vacuum and hauled the children off to the new alleys, where full-time nurses stand ready to baby-sit in the fully equipped nurseries.

Said the manager of Albuquerque's Bowl-a-Drome: 'Where else can a woman compete after she gets married? They need competition just like men do. ... It sure beats going home to do the dishes!'[12]

It is perhaps beside the point to remark that bowling alleys and supermarkets have nursery facilities, while schools and colleges and scientific laboratories and government offices do not. But it is very much to the point to say that if an able American woman does not use her human energy and ability in some meaningful pursuit (which necessarily means competition, for there is competition in every serious pursuit of our society), she will fritter away her energy in neurotic symptoms, or unproductive exercise, or destructive 'love'.

It also is time to stop giving lip service to the idea that there are no battles left to be fought for women in America. In almost every professional field, in business and in the arts and sciences, women are still treated as second-class citizens. It would be a great service to tell girls who plan to work in society to expect this subtle, uncomfortable discrimination – tell them not to be quiet, and hope it will go away, but fight it. A girl should not expect special privileges because of her sex, but neither should she 'adjust' to prejudice and discrimination.

She must learn to compete then, not as a woman, but as a human being. Not until a great many women move out of the fringes into the mainstream will society itself provide the arrangements for their new life plan. But every girl who manages to stick it out through law school or medical school, who finishes her M.A. or Ph.D. and goes on to use it, helps others move on. The very existence of the President's Commission on the Status of Women, under Eleanor Roosevelt's leadership, creates a climate where it is possible to recognize and do something about discrimination against women, in terms not only of pay but of the subtle barriers to opportunity. Even in politics, women must make their contribution not as 'housewives' but as citizens. It is, perhaps, a step in the right direction when a woman protests nuclear testing under the banner of 'Women Strike for Peace'. But why does the professional illustrator who heads the movement say she is 'just a housewife', and her followers insist that once the testing stops, they will stay happily at home with their children? Even in the city strongholds of the big political party machines, women can – and are beginning to – change the insidious unwritten rules which let them do the political housework while the men make.the decisions.¹³

When enough women make life plans geared to their real abilities, and speak out for maternity leaves or even maternity sabbaticals, professionally run nurseries, and other changes in the rules that may be necessary, they will not have to sacrifice the right to honourable competition and contribution any more than they will have to sacrifice marriage and motherhood. It is wrong to keep spelling out unnecessary choices that make women unconsciously resist either commitment or motherhood¹⁴ – and that hold back recognition of the needed social changes. It is not a question of women having their cake and eating it, too. A woman is handicapped by her sex, and handicaps society, either by slavishly copying the pattern of man's advance in the professions, or by refusing to compete with man at all. But with the vision to make a new life plan of her own, she can fulfil a commitment to profession and politics, and to marriage and motherhood with equal seriousness.

Women who have done this, in spite of the dire warnings of the feminine mystique, are in a sense 'mutations', the image of what the American woman can be. When they did not or could not work full time for a living, they spent part-time hours on work which truly interested them. Because time was of the essence, they often skipped the time-wasting, self-serving details of both housewifery and professional busywork.

Whether they knew it or not, they were following a life plan. They had their babies before or after internship, between fellowships. If good full-time help was not available in the children's early years, they gave up their jobs and took a part-time post that may not have paid handsomely, but kept them moving ahead in their profession. The teachers innovated in P.T.A., and substituted; the doctors took clinical or research jobs close to home; the editors and writers started free-lancing. Even if the money they made was not needed for groceries or household help (and usually it was), they earned tangible proof of their ability to contribute. They did not consider themselves 'lucky' to be housewives; they competed in society. They knew that marriage and motherhood are an essential part of life, but not the whole of it.

These 'mutations' suffered – and surmounted – the 'cultural discontinuity in role conditioning', the 'role crisis', and the identity crisis. They had problems, of course, tough ones – juggling their pregnancies, finding nurses and housekeepers, having to give up good assignments when their husbands were transferred. They also had to take a lot of hostility from other women – and many had to live with the active resentment of their husbands. And, because of the mystique, many suffered unnecessary pains of guilt. It took, and still takes, extraordinary strength of purpose for women to pursue their own life plans when society does not expect it of them. However, unlike the trapped housewives whose problems multiply with the years, these women solved their problems and moved on. And they know quite surely now who they are.

The identity crisis in men and women cannot be solved by one generation for the next; in our rapidly changing society, it must be faced continually, solved only to be faced again in the span of a single lifetime. A life plan must be open to change, as new possibilities open, in society and in oneself.

In the light of woman's long battle for emancipation, the recent sexual counter-revolution in America has been perhaps a final crisis, a strange breath-holding interval before the larva breaks out of the shell into maturity – a moratorium during which many millions of women put themselves on ice and stopped growing. American women lately have been living much longer than men – walking through their left-over lives like living dead women. Perhaps men may live longer in America when women carry more of the burden of the battle with the world, instead of being a burden themselves. I think their wasted energy will continue to be destructive to their husbands, to their children, and to themselves until it is used in their own battle with the world. But when women as well as men emerge from biological living to realize their human selves, those left-over halves of life may become their years of greatest fulfilment.[15]

When their mothers' fulfilment makes girls sure they want to be women, they will not have to 'beat themselves down' to be feminine; they can stretch and stretch until their own efforts will tell them who they are. They will not need the regard of boy or man to feel alive. And when women do not need to live through their husbands and children, men will not fear the love and strength of women, nor need another's weakness to prove their own masculinity. They can finally see each other as they are. And this may be the next step in human evolution.

Who knows what women can be when they are finally free to become themselves? Who knows what women's intelligence will contribute when it can be nourished without denying love? Who knows of the possibilities of love when men and women share not only children, home, and garden, not only the fulfilment of their biological roles, but the responsibilities and passions of the work that creates the human future. It has barely begun, the search of women for themselves. But the time is at hand when the voices of the feminine mystique can no longer drown out the inner voice that is driving women on to become complete.

NOTES

CHAPTER I

The Problem that Has No Name

1. See the Seventy-fifth Anniversary Issue of *Good Housekeeping*, May 1960, 'The Gift of Self', a symposium by Margaret Mead, Jessamyn West, *et al.*
2. Lee Rainwater, Richard P. Coleman, and Gerald Handel, *Working-man's Wife*, New York, 1959.
3. Betty Friedan, 'If One Generation Can Ever Tell Another', *Smith Alumnae Quarterly*, Northampton, Mass., Winter 1961. I first became aware of 'the problem that has no name' and its possible relationship to what I finally called 'the feminine mystique' in 1957, when I prepared an intensive questionnaire and conducted a survey of my own Smith College classmates fifteen years after graduation. This questionnaire was later used by alumnae classes of Radcliffe and other women's colleges with similar results.
4. Jhan and June Robbins, 'Why Young Mothers Feel Trapped', *Redbook*, September 1960.
5. Marian Freda Poverman, 'Alumnae on Parade', *Barnard Alumnae Magazine*, July 1957.

CHAPTER 2

The Happy Housewife Heroine

1. Betty Friedan, 'Women Are People Too!' *Good Housekeeping*, September 1960. The letters received from women all over the United States in response to this article were of such emotional intensity that I was convinced that 'the problem that has no name' is by no means confined to the graduates of the women's Ivy League colleges.
2. In the 1960s, an occasional heroine who was not a 'happy housewife' began to appear in the women's magazines. An editor of *McCall's* explained it: 'Sometimes we run an offbeat story for pure entertainment value.' One such novelette, which

was written to order by Noel Clad for *Good Housekeeping* (January 1960), is called 'Men Against Women'. The heroine – a happy career woman – nearly loses child as well as husband.

CHAPTER 3

The Crisis in Woman's Identity

1. Erik H. Erikson, *Young Man Luther, A Study in Psychoanalysis and History*, New York, 1958, pp. 15 ff. See also Erikson, *Childhood and Society*, New York, 1950, and Erikson, 'The Problem of Ego Identity', *Journal of the American Psychoanalytical Association*, Vol. 4, 1956, pp. 56–121.

CHAPTER 4

The Passionate Journey

1. See Eleanor Flexner, *Century of Struggle: The Woman's Rights Movement in The United States*, Cambridge, Mass., 1959. This definitive history of the woman's rights movement in the United States, published in 1959 at the height of the era of the feminine mystique, did not receive the attention it deserves, from either the intelligent reader or the scholar. In my opinion, it should be required reading for every girl admitted to a U.S. college. One reason the mystique prevails is that very few women under the age of forty know the facts of the woman's rights movement. I am much indebted to Miss Flexner for many factual clues I might otherwise have missed in my attempt to get at the truth behind the feminine mystique and its monstrous image of the feminists.

2. See Sidney Ditzion, *Marriage, Morals and Sex in America – A History of Ideas*, New York, 1953. This extensive bibliographical essay by the librarian of New York University documents the continuous interrelationship between movements for social and sexual reform in America, and, specifically, between man's movement for greater self-realization and sexual fulfilment and the woman's rights movement. The speeches and tracts assembled reveal that the movement to emancipate women was often seen by the men as well as the women who led it in terms of 'creating an equitable balance of power

between the sexes' for 'a more satisfying expression of sexuality for both sexes'.

3. ibid., p. 107.
4. Yuri Suhl, *Ernestine L. Rose and the Battle for Human Rights*, New York, 1959, p. 158. A vivid account of the battle for a married woman's right to her own property and earnings.
5. Flexner, *op. cit.*, p. 30.
6. Elinor Rice Hays, *Morning Star, A Biography of Lucy Stone*, New York, 1961, p. 83.
7. Flexner, op. cit., p. 64.
8. Hays, op. cit., p. 136.
9. ibid., p. 285.
10. ibid., p. 73.
11. Hays, op. cit., p. 221.
12. Flexner, op. cit., p. 117.
13. ibid., p. 235.
14. ibid., p. 173.
15. Ida Alexis Ross Wylie, 'The Little Woman', *Harper's*, November 1945.

CHAPTER 5

The Sexual Solipsism of Sigmund Freud

1. Clara Thompson, *Psychoanalysis: Evolution and Development*, New York, 1950, pp. 131 ff:

Freud not only emphasized the biological more than the cultural, but he also developed a cultural theory of his own based on his biological theory. There were two obstacles in the way of understanding the importance of the cultural phenomena he saw and recorded. He was too deeply involved in developing his biological theories to give much thought to other aspects of the data he collected. Thus he was interested chiefly in applying to human society his theory of instincts. Starting with the assumption of a death instinct, for example, he then developed an explanation of the cultural phenomena he observed in terms of the death instinct. Since he did not have the perspective to be gained from knowledge of comparative cultures, he could not evaluate cultural processes as such. ... Much which Freud believed to be biological has been shown by modern research to be a reaction to a certain type of culture and not characteristic of universal human nature.

2. Richard La Piere, *The Freudian Ethic*, New York, 1959, p. 62.

NOTES

3. Ernest Jones, *The Life and Work of Sigmund Freud*, New York, 1953, Vol. I, p. 384.
4. ibid., Vol II (1955), p. 432.
5. ibid., Vol. I, pp. 7–14, 294; Vol. II, p. 483.
6. Bruno Bettelheim, *Love Is Not Enough: The Treatment of Emotionally Disturbed Children*, Glencoe, Ill., 1950, pp. 7 ff.
7. Ernest L. Freud, *Letters of Sigmund Freud*, New York, 1960, Letter 10, p. 27; Letter 26, p. 71; Letter 65, p. 145.
8. ibid., Letter 74, p. 60; Letter 76, pp. 161 ff.
9. Jones, *op. cit.*, Vol. I, pp. 176 f.
10. ibid., Vol II, p. 422.
11. ibid., Vol. I, p. 271:

> His descriptions of sexual activities are so matter-of-fact that many readers have found them almost dry and totally lacking in warmth. From all I know of him, I should say that he displayed less than the average personal interest in what is often an absorbing topic. There was never any gusto or even savour in mentioning a sexual topic. ... He always gave the impression of being an unusually chaste person – the word 'puritanical' would not be out of place – and all we know of his early development confirms this conception.

12. ibid., Vol. I, p. 102.
13. ibid., Vol. I, pp. 110 ff.
14. ibid., Vol. I, p. 124.
15. ibid., Vol. I, p. 127.
16. ibid., Vol. I, p. 138.
17. ibid., Vol. I, p. 151.
18. Helen Walker Puner, *Freud, His Life and His Mind*, New York, 1947, p. 152.
19. Jones, *op. cit.*, Vol. II, p. 121.
20. ibid., Vol. I, pp. 301 ff. During the years Freud was germinating his sexual theory, before his own heroic self-analysis freed him from a passionate dependence on a series of men, his emotions were focused on a flamboyant nose-and-throat doctor named Fliess. This is one coincidence of history that was quite fateful for women. For Fliess had proposed, and obtained Freud's lifelong allegiance to, a fantastic 'scientific theory' which reduced all phenomena of life and death to 'bisexuality', expressed in mathematical terms through a periodic table based on the number 28, the female menstrual cycle. Freud looked forward to meetings with Fliess 'as for the satisfying of hunger and thirst'. He wrote to him: 'No one can replace the

intercourse with a friend that a particular, perhaps feminine side of me, demands.' Even after his own self-analysis, Freud still expected to die on the day predicted by Fliess' periodic table, in which everything could be figured out in terms of the female number 28, or the male 23, which was derived from the end of one female menstrual period to the beginning of the next.

21. ibid., Vol. I, p. 320.
22. Thompson, op. cit., p. 133.
23. Sigmund Freud, 'The Psychology of Women', in *New Introductory Lectures on Psychoanalysis*, tr. by W. J. H. Sprott, New York, 1933, pp. 170 f.
24. ibid., p. 182.
25. ibid., p. 184.
26. Thompson, op. cit., pp. 12 f:

> The war of 1914–18 further focused attention on ego drives. . . . Another idea came into analysis around this period . . . and that was that aggression as well as sex might be an important repressed impulse. . . . The puzzling problem was how to include it in the theory of instincts. . . . Eventually Freud solved this by his second instinct theory. Aggression found its place as part of the death instinct. It is interesting that normal self-assertion, i.e., the impulse to master, control or come to self-fulfilling terms with the environment, was not especially emphasized by Freud.

27. Sigmund Freud, 'Anxiety and Instinctual Life', in *New Introductory Lectures on Psychoanalysis*, p. 149.
28. Marynia Farnham and Ferdinand Lundberg, *Modern Woman: The Lost Sex*, New York and London, 1947, pp. 142 ff.
29. Ernest Jones, op. cit., Vol. II, p. 446.
30. Helene Deutsch, *The Psychology of Women – A Psychoanalytical Interpretation*, New York, 1944, Vol. I, pp. 224 ff.
31. ibid., Vol. I, pp. 251 ff.
32. Sigmund Freud, 'The Anatomy of the Mental Personality', in *New Introductory Lectures on Psychoanalysis*, p. 96.

CHAPTER 6

The Functional Freeze, The Feminine Protest, and Margaret Mead

1. Henry A. Bowman, *Marriage for Moderns*, New York, 1942, p. 21.

2. ibid., pp. 22 ff.
3. ibid., pp. 62 ff.
4. ibid., pp. 74–6.
5. Talcott Parsons, 'Age and Sex in the Social Structure of the United States', in *Essays in Sociological Theory*, Glencoe, Ill., 1949, pp. 223 ff.
6. Talcott Parsons, 'An Analytical Approach to the Theory of Social Stratification', *op. cit.*, pp. 174 ff.
7. Mirra Komarovsky, *Women in the Modern World, Their Education and Their Dilemmas*, Boston, 1953, pp. 52–61.
8. ibid., p. 66.
9. ibid., pp. 72–4.
10. Mirra Komarovsky, 'Functional Analysis of Sex Roles', *American Sociological Review*, August 1950. See also 'Cultural Contradictions and Sex Roles', *American Journal of Sociology*, November 1946.
11. Kingsley Davis, 'The Myth of Functional Analysis as a Special Method in Sociology and Anthropology', *American Sociological Review*, Vol. 24, No. 6, December 1959, pp. 757–72. Davis points out that functionalism became more or less identical with sociology itself. There is provocative evidence that the very study of sociology, in recent years, has persuaded college women to limit themselves to their 'functional' traditional sexual role. A report on 'The Status of Women in Professional Sociology' (Sylvia Fleis Fava, *American Sociological Review*, Vol. 25, No. 2, April 1960) shows that while most of the students in sociology undergraduate classes are women, from 1949 to 1958 there was a sharp decline in both the number and proportion of degrees in sociology awarded to women (4,143 B.A.s in 1949 down to a low of 3,200 in 1955, 3,606 in 1958). And while one half to two thirds of the undergraduate degrees in sociology were awarded to women, women received only 25 to 43 per cent of the masters' degrees, and only 8 to 19 per cent of the Ph.D.s. While the number of women earning graduate degrees in all fields has declined sharply during the era of the feminine mystique, the field of sociology showed, in comparison to other fields, an unusually high 'mortality' rate.
12. Margaret Mead, *Sex and Temperament in Three Primitive Societies*, New York, 1935, pp. 279 f.
13. Margaret Mead, *From the South Seas*, New York, 1939, p. 321.
14. Margaret Mead, *Male and Female*, New York, 1955, pp. 16–18.
15. ibid., p. 26.

I did not begin to work seriously with the zones of the body until I went to the Arapesh in 1931. While I was generally familiar with Freud's basic work on the subject, I had not seen how it might be applied in the field until I read Geza Roheim's first field report, 'Psychoanalysis of Primitive Culture Types' ... I then sent home for abstracts of K. Abraham's work. After I became acquainted with Erik Homburger Erikson's systematic handling of these ideas, they became an integral part of my theoretical equipment.

16. ibid., pp. 50 f.
17. ibid., pp. 72 ff.
18. ibid., pp. 125 ff.
19. ibid., pp. 135 ff.
20. ibid., pp. 274 ff.
21. ibid., pp. 278 ff.
22. ibid., pp. 276–85.
23. Margaret Mead, Introduction to *From the South Seas*, New York, 1939, p. xiii. 'It was no use permitting children to develop values different from those of their society ...'
24. Marie Jahoda and Joan Havel, 'Psychological Problems of Women in Different Social Roles – A Case History of Problem Formulation in Research', *Educational Record*, Vol. 36, 1955, pp. 325–33.

CHAPTER 7

The Sex-Directed Educators

1. Mabel Newcomer, *A Century of Higher Education for Women*, New York, 1959, pp. 45 ff. The proportion of women among college students in the U.S. increased from 21 per cent in 1870 to 47 per cent in 1920; it had declined to 35.2 per cent in 1958. Five women's colleges had closed; 21 had become co-educational; 2 had become junior colleges. In 1956, 3 out of 5 women in the co-educational colleges were taking secretarial, nursing, home economics, or education courses. Less than 1 out of 10 doctorates were granted to women, compared to 1 in 6 in 1920, 13 per cent in 1940. Not since before the First World War have the percentages of American women receiving professional degrees been as consistently low as in this period. The extent of the retrogression of American women can also be measured in terms of their failure to develop to their own potential. According to *Womanpower*, of all the young women *capable* of

doing college work, only one out of four goes to college, compared to one out of two men; only one out of 300 women capable of earning a Ph.D. actually does so, compared to one out of 30 men. If the present situation continues, American women may soon rank among the most 'backward' women in the world. The U.S. is probably the only nation where the proportion of women gaining higher education has decreased in the past 20 years; it has steadily increased in Sweden, Britain, and France, as well as the emerging nations of Asia and the communist countries. By the 1950s, a larger proportion of French women were obtaining higher education than American women; the proportion of French women in the professions had more than doubled in fifty years. The proportion of French women in the medical profession alone is five times that of American women; 70 per cent of the doctors in the Soviet Union are women, compared to 5 per cent in America. See Alva Myrdal and Viola Klein, *Women's Two Roles – Home and Work*, London, 1956, pp. 33–64.

2. Mervin B. Freedman, 'The Passage through College', in *Personality Development During the College Years*, ed. by Nevitt Sanford, *Journal of Social Issues*, Vol. XII, No. 4, 1956, pp. 15 f.

3. John Bushnel, 'Student Culture at Vassar', in *The American College*, ed. by Nevitt Sanford, New York and London, 1962, pp. 509 f.

4. Lynn White, *Educating our Daughters*, New York, 1950, pp. 18–48.

5. ibid., p. 76.

6. ibid., pp. 77 ff.

7. See Dael Wolfle, *America's Resources of Specialized Talent*, New York, 1954.

8. Cited in an address by Judge Mary H. Donlon in proceedings of 'Conference on the Present Status and Prospective Trends of Research on the Education of Women', 1957, American Council on Education, Washington, D.C.

9. See 'The Bright Girl: A Major Source of Untapped Talent', *Guidance Newsletter*, Science Research Associates Inc., Chicago, Ill., May 1959.

10. See Dael Wolfle, op. cit.

11. John Summerskill, 'Dropouts from College', in *The American College*, p. 631.

12. Joseph M. Jones, 'Does Overpopulation Mean Poverty?' Center for International Economic Growth, Washington,

1962. See also *United Nations Demographic Yearbook*, New York, 1960, pp. 580 ff. By 1958, in the United States, more girls were marrying from 15–19 years of age than from any other age group. In all of the other advanced nations, and many of the emerging underdeveloped nations, most girls married from 20–24 or after 25. The U.S. pattern of teenage marriage could only be found in countries like Paraguay, Venezuela, Honduras, Guatemala, Mexico, Egypt, Iraq, and the Fiji Islands.

13. Nevitt Sanford, 'Higher Education as a Social Problem', in *The American College*, p. 23.

14. Elizabeth Douvan and Carol Kaye, 'Motivational Factors in College Entrance', in *The American College*, pp. 202–6.

15. ibid., pp. 208 f.

16. Esther Lloyd-Jones, 'Women Today and Their Education', *Teachers' College Record*, Vol. 57, No. 1, October 1955; and No. 7, April 1956. See also Opal David, *The Education of Women – Signs for the Future*, American Council on Education, Washington, D.C., 1957.

17. Mary Ann Guitar, 'College Marriage Courses – Fun or Fraud?' *Mademoiselle*, February 1961.

18. Helene Deutsch, op. cit., Vol. I, p. 290.

19. Mirra Komarovsky, op. cit., p. 70. Research studies indicate that 40 per cent of college girls 'play dumb' with men. Since the ones who do not include those not excessively over-burdened with intelligence, the great majority of American girls who are gifted with high intelligence evidently learn to hide it.

20. Jean Macfarlane and Lester Sontag, Research reported to the Commission on the Education of Women, Washington, D.C., 1954, (mimeo MS.).

21. Harold Webster, 'Some Quantitative Results', in *Personality Development During the College Years*, ed. by Nevitt Sanford, *Journal of Social Issues*, 1956, Vol. 12, No. 4, p. 36.

22. Nevitt Sanford, *Personality Development During the College Years*, *Journal of Social Issues*, 1956, Vol. 12, No. 4.

23. Mervin B. Freedman, 'Studies of College Alumni', in *The American College*, p. 878.

24. Lynn White, op. cit., p. 117.

25. ibid., pp. 119 f.

26. Max Lerner, *America As a Civilization*, New York, 1957, pp. 608–11:

The crux of it lies neither in the biological nor economic disabilities of women but in their sense of being caught between a man's world which they have no real will to achieve and a world of their own in which they find it hard to be fulfilled. ... When Walt Whitman exhorted women 'to give up toys and fictions and launch forth, as men do, amid real, independent, stormy life', he was thinking – as were many of his contemporaries – of the wrong kind of equalitarianism. ... If she is to discover her identity, she must start by basing her belief in herself on her womanliness rather than on the movement for feminism. Margaret Mead has pointed out that the biological life cycle of the woman has certain well-marked phases from menarche through the birth of her children to her menopause; that in these stages of her life cycle, as in her basic bodily rhythms, she can feel secure in her womanhood and does not have to assert her potency as the male does. Similarly, while the multiple roles that she must play in life are bewildering, she can fulfil them without distraction if she knows that her central role is that of a woman. ... Her central function, however, remains that of creating a life style for herself and for the home in which she is life creator and life sustainer.

27. See Philip E. Jacob, *Changing Values in College*, New York 1957.
28. Margaret Mead, 'New Look at Early Marriages', interview in *U.S. News and World Report*, 6 June 1960.

CHAPTER 8

The Mistaken Choice

1. See the *United Nations Demographic Yearbook*, New York, 1960, pp. 99–118, 476–90, and 580. The annual rate of population increase in the U.S. in the years 1955–9 was far higher than that of other Western nations, and higher than that of India, Japan, Burma, and Pakistan. In fact, the increase for North America (1.8) exceeded the world rate (1.7). The rate for Europe was .8; for the U.S.S.R. 1.7; Asia 1.8; Africa 1.9; and South America 2.3. The increase in the underdeveloped nations was, of course, largely due to medical advances and the drop in death rate; in America it was almost completely due to increased birth rate, earlier marriage, and larger families. For the birth rate continued to rise in the U.S. from 1950 to 1959, while it was falling in countries like France, Norway, Sweden, the U.S.S.R., India, and Japan. The U.S. was the only so-called

'advanced' nation, and one of the few nations in the world where, in 1958, more girls married at ages 15–19 than at any other age. Even the other countries which showed a rise in the birth rate – Germany, Canada, the United Kingdom, Chile, New Zealand, Peru – did not show this phenomenon of teenage marriage.

2. See 'The Woman with Brains (continued)', *New York Times Magazine*, 17 January 1960, for the outraged letters in response to an article by Marya Mannes, 'Female Intelligence – Who Wants It?' *New York Times Magazine*, 3 January 1960.

3. See National Manpower Council, *Womanpower*, New York, 1957. In 1940, more than half of all employed women in the U.S. were under 25, and one fifth were over 45. In the 1950s peak participation in paid employment occurs among young women of 18 and 19 – and women over 45, the great majority of whom hold jobs for which little training is required. The new preponderance of older married women in the working force is partly due to the fact that so few women in their twenties and thirties now work, in the U.S. Two out of five of all employed women are now over 45, most of them wives and mothers, working part time at unskilled work. Those reports of millions of American wives working outside the home are misleading in more ways than one: of all employed women, only one third hold full-time jobs, one third work full time only part of the year – for instance, extra saleswomen in the department stores at Christmas – and one third work part time, part of the year. The women in the professions are, for the most part, that dwindling minority of single women; the older untrained wives and mothers, like the untrained 18-year-olds, are concentrated at the lower end of the skill ladder and the pay scales, in factory, service, sales, and office work. Considering the growth in the population, and the increasing professionalization of work in America, the startling phenomenon is not the much-advertised, relatively insignificant increase in the numbers of American women who now work outside the home, but the fact that two out of three adult American women do *not* work outside the home, and the increasing millions of young women who are not skilled or educated for work in any profession. See also Theodore Caplow, *The Sociology of Work*, 1954, and Alva Myrdal and Viola Klein, *Women's Two Roles – Home and Work*, London, 1956.

4. Edward Strecker, *Their Mothers' Sons*, Philadelphia and New York, 1946, pp. 52–9.
5. ibid., pp. 31 ff.
6. Farnham and Lundberg, *Modern Woman: The Lost Sex*, p. 271. See also Lynn White, *Educating Our Daughters*, p. 90.

Preliminary results of the careful study of American sex habits being conducted at the University of Indiana by Dr A. C. Kinsey indicate that there is an inverse correlation between education and the ability of a woman to achieve habitual orgastic experience in marriage. According to the present evidence, admittedly tentative, nearly 65 per cent of the marital intercourse had by women with college backgrounds is had without orgasm for them, as compared to about 15 per cent for married women who have gone no further than grade school.

7. Alfred C. Kinsey, *et al.*, Staff of the Institute for Sex Research, Indiana University, *Sexual Behavior in the Human Female*, Philadelphia and London, 1953, pp. 378 f.
8. Lois Meek Stolz, 'Effects of Maternal Employment on Children: Evidence from Research', *Child Development*, Vol. 31, No. 4, 1960, pp. 749–82.
9. H. F. Southard, 'Mothers' Dilemma: To Work or Not?' *New York Times Magazine*, 17 July 1960.
10. Stolz, op. cit. See also Myrdal and Klein, op. cit., pp. 125 ff.
11. Benjamin Spock, 'Russian Children Don't Whine, Squabble or Break Things – Why?' *Ladies' Home Journal*, October 1960.
12. David Levy, *Maternal Overprotection*, New York, 1943.
13. Arnold W. Green, 'The Middle-Class Male Child and Neurosis', *American Sociological Review*, Vol. II, No. 1, 1946.

CHAPTER 9

The Sexual Sell

1. The studies upon which this chapter is based were done by the Staff of the Institute for Motivational Research, directed by Dr Ernest Dichter. They were made available to me through the courtesy of Dr Dichter and his colleagues, and are on file at the Institute, in Croton-on-Hudson, New York.
2. Harrison Kinney, *Has Anybody Seen My Father?*, New York, 1960.

CHAPTER 10

Housewifery Expands to Fill the Time Available

1. Jhan and June Robbins, 'Why Young Mothers Feel Trapped', *Redbook,* September 1960.

2. Carola Woerishoffer Graduate Department of Social Economy and Social Research, 'Women During the War and After', Bryn Mawr College, 1945.

3. Theodore Caplow points out in *The Sociology of Work,* p. 234, that with the rapidly expanding economy since 1900, and the extremely rapid urbanization of the United States, the increase in the employment of women from 20.4 per cent in 1900 to 28.5 per cent in 1950 was exceedingly modest. Recent studies of time spent by American housewives on housework, which confirm my description of the Parkinson effect, are summarized by Jean Warren, 'Time: Resource or Utility', *Journal of Home Economics,* Vol. 49, January 1957, pp. 21 ff. Alva Myrdal and Viola Klein in *Women's Two Roles – Home and Work* cite a French study which showed that working mothers reduced time spent on housework by thirty hours a week, compared to a full-time housewife. The work week of a working mother with three children broke down to 35.2 hours on the job, 48.3 hours on housework; the full-time housewife spent 77.7 hours on housework. The mother with a full-time job or profession, as well as the housekeeping and children, worked only one hour a day longer than the full-time housewife.

4. Robert Wood, *Suburbia, Its People and Their Politics,* Boston, 1959.

5. See 'Papa's Taking Over the P.T.A. Mama Started', *New York Herald Tribune,* 10 February 1962. At the 1962 national convention of Parent–Teacher Associations, it was revealed that 32 per cent of the 46,457 P.T.A. presidents are now men. In certain states the percentage of male P.T.A. heads is even higher, including New York (33 per cent), Connecticut (45 per cent), and Delaware (80 per cent).

6. Nanette E. Scofield, 'Some Changing Roles of Women in Suburbia: A Social Anthropological Case Study', transactions of the New York Academy of Sciences, Vol. 22, No. 6, April 1960.

7. Mervin B. Freedman, 'Studies of College Alumni', in *The American College*, pp. 872 f.
8. Murray T. Pringle, 'Women Are Wretched Housekeepers', *Science Digest*, June 1960.
9. See *Time*, 20 April 1959.
10. Edith M. Stern, 'Women are Household Slaves', *American Mercury*, January 1949.
12. Russell Lynes, 'The New Servant Class', in *A Surfeit of Honey*, New York, 1957, p. 49–64.

The Sex-Seekers

1. Several social historians have commented on America's sexual preoccupation from the male point of view. 'America has come to stress sex as much as any civilization since the Roman,' says Max Lerner (*America as a Civilization*, p. 678). David Riesman in *The Lonely Crowd* (New Haven, 1950, p. 172 ff.) calls sex 'the Last Frontier'.

More than before, as job-mindedness declines, sex permeates the daytime as well as the playtime consciousness. It is viewed as a consumption good not only by the old leisure classes but by the modern leisure masses. ...

One reason for the change is that women are no longer objects for the acquisitive consumer but are peer-groupers themselves. ... Today, millions of women, freed by technology from many household tasks, given by technology many aids to romance, have become pioneers with men on the frontiers of sex. As they become knowing consumers, the anxiety of men lest they fail to satisfy the women also grows ...

It is mainly the clinicians who have noted that the men are often less eager now than their wives as sexual 'consumers'. The late Dr Abraham Stone, whom I interviewed shortly before his death, said that the wives complain more and more of sexually 'inadequate' husbands. Dr Karl Menninger reports that for every wife who complains of her husband's excessive sexuality, a dozen wives complain that their husbands are apathetic or impotent. These 'problems' are cited in the mass media as additional evidence that American women are losing their 'femininity' – and thus provide new ammunition for the mystique. See John Kord Lagemann, 'The Male Sex', *Redbook*, December 1956.

2. Albert Ellis, *The Folklore of Sex*, New York, 1961, p. 123.

3. See the amusing parody, 'The Pious Pornographers', by Ray Russell, in *The Permanent Playboy*, New York, 1959.

4. Nathan Ackerman, *The Psychodynamics of Family Life*, New York, 1958, pp. 112–27.

5. Kinsey, *et al.*, *Sexual Behavior in the Human Female*, pp. 353 ff., 426.

6. Doris Menzer-Benaron M.D., *et al.*, 'Patterns of Emotional Recovery from Hysterectomy', *Psychosomatic Medicine*, XIX, No. 5, September 1957, pp. 378–88.

7. The fact that 75 per cent to 85 per cent of young mothers in America today feel negative emotions – resentment, grief, disappointment, outright rejection – when they become pregnant for the first time has been established in many studies. In fact, the perpetuators of the feminine mystique report findings to reassure young mothers that they are only 'normal' in feeling this strange rejection of pregnancy – and that the only real problem is their 'guilt' over feeling it. Thus *Redbook* magazine, in 'How Women Really Feel about Pregnancy' (November 1958), reports that the Harvard School of Public Health found 80 to 85 per cent of 'normal women reject the pregnancy when they become pregnant'; Long Island College Clinic found that less than a fourth of women are 'happy' about their pregnancy; a New Haven study finds only 17 of 100 women 'pleased' about having a baby. Comments the voice of editorial authority:

> The real danger that arises when a pregnancy is unwelcome and filled with troubled feelings is that a woman may become guilty and panic-stricken because she believes her reactions are unnatural or abnormal. Both marital and mother–child relations can be damaged as a result.... Sometimes a mental-health specialist is needed to allay guilt feelings.... Nor is there any time when a normal woman does not have feelings of depression and doubt when she learns that she is pregnant.

Such articles never mention the various studies which indicate that women in other countries, both more and less advanced than the United States, and even American 'career' women, are less likely to experience this emotional rejection of pregnancy. Depression at pregnancy may be 'normal' for the housewife-mother in the era of the feminine mystique, but it is not normal to motherhood. As Ruth Benedict said, it is not biological necessity, but our culture, which creates the discomforts, physical and psychological, of the female cycle. See her *Continuities and Discontinuities in Cultural Conditioning*.

8. See William J. Goode, *After Divorce*, Glencoe, Ill., 1956.

9. A. C. Kinsey, *et al.*, *Sexual Behavior in the Human Male*, Philadelphia and London, 1948, p. 259, pp. 585–8.

10. The male contempt for the American woman, as she has moulded herself according to the feminine mystique, is depressingly explicit in the July 1962 issue of *Esquire*, 'The American Woman, A New Point of View'. See especially 'The Word to Women – "No"', by Robert Alan Aurthur, p. 32. The sexlessness of the American female sex-seekers is eulogized by Malcolm Muggeridge ('Bedding Down in the Colonies', p. 84):

> How they mortify the flesh in order to make it appetizing! Their beauty is a vast industry, their enduring allure a discipline which nuns or athletes might find excessive. With too much sex to be sensual, and too ravishing to ravish, age cannot wither them nor custom stale their infinite monotony.

11. Kinsey, *et al.*, *Sexual Behavior in the Human Male*, p. 631.

12. See Donald Webster Cory, *The Homosexual in America*, New York, 1960, preface to second edition, pp. xxii ff. Also Albert Ellis, *op. cit.*, pp. 186–90. Also Seward Hiltner, 'Stability and Change in American Sexual Patterns', in *Sexual Behavior in American Society*, Jerome Himelhoch and Sylvia Fleis Fava, eds., New York, 1955, p. 321.

13. Sigmund Freud, *Three Contributions to the Theory of Sex*, New York, 1948, p. 10.

14. Birth out of wedlock increased 194 per cent from 1956 to 1962; venereal disease among young people increased 132 per cent (*Time*, 16 March 1962).

15. Kinsey, *et al.*, *Sexual Behavior in the Human Male*, pp. 348 ff., 427–33.

16. Kinsey, *et al.*, *Sexual Behavior in the Human Female*, pp. 293, 378, 382.

17. Clara Thompson, 'Changing Concepts of Homosexuality in Psychoanalysis', in *A Study of Interpersonal Relations, New Contributions to Psychiatry*, Patrick Mullahy, ed., New York, 1949, pp. 218 f.

18. Erich Fromm, 'Sex and Character: the Kinsey Report Viewed

from the Standpoint of Psychoanalysis', in *Sexual Behavior in American Society*, p. 307.

19. Carl Binger, 'The Pressures on College Girls Today', *Atlantic Monthly*, February 1961.

20. Sallie Bingham, 'Winter Term', *Mademoiselle*, July 1958.

CHAPTER 12

Progressive Dehumanization: The Comfortable Concentration Camp

1. Marjorie K. McCorquodale, 'What They Will Die for in Houston', *Harper's*, October 1961.

2. See David Riesman, *The Lonely Crowd*; also Erich Fromm, *Escape From Freedom*, New York and Toronto, 1941, pp. 185–206. Also Erik H. Erikson, *Childhood and Society*, p. 239.

3. David Riesman, introduction to Edgar Friedenberg's *The Vanishing Adolescent*, Boston, 1959.

4. Harold Taylor, 'Freedom and Authority on the Campus', in *The American College*, pp. 780 ff.

5. David Riesman, introduction to Edgar Friedenberg's *The Vanishing Adolescent*.

6. See Eugene Kinkead, *In Every War But One*, New York, 1959. There has been an attempt in recent years to discredit or soft-pedal these findings. But a taped record of a talk given before the American Psychiatric Association in 1958 by Dr William Mayer, who had been on one of the Army teams of psychiatrists and intelligence officers who interviewed the returning prisoners in 1953 and analysed the data, caused many pediatricians and child specialists to ask, in the words of Dr Spock: 'Are unusually permissive, indulgent parents more numerous today – and are they weakening the character of our children?' (Benjamin Spock, 'Are We Bringing Up Our Children Too "Soft" for the Stern Realities They Must Face?' *Ladies' Home Journal*, September 1960.) However unpleasantly injurious to American pride, there must be some explanation for the collapse of the American G.I. prisoners in Korea, as it differed not only from the behaviour of American soldiers in previous wars, but from the behaviour of soldiers of other nations in Korea. No American soldier managed to escape from the enemy prison camps, as they had in every other war. The shocking 38 per cent death rate was not explainable, even according to military

authorities, on the basis of the climate, food, or inadequate medical facilities in the camps, nor was it caused by brutality or torture. 'Give-up-itis' is how one doctor described the disease the Americans died from; they simply spent the days curled up under blankets, cutting down their diet to water alone, until they were dead, usually within three weeks. This seemed to be an American phenomenon. Turkish prisoners, who were also part of the U.N. force in Korea, lost no men by disease or starvation; they stuck together, obeyed their officers, adhered to health regulations, cooperated in the care of their sick, and refused to inform on one another.

7. Edgar Friedenberg, *The Vanishing Adolescent*, pp. 212 ff.

8. Andras Angyal, M.D., 'Evasion of Growth', *American Journal of Psychiatry*, Vol. 110, No. 5, November 1953, pp. 358–61. See also Erich Fromm, *Escape from Freedom*, pp. 138–206.

9. See Richard E. Gordon and Katherine K. Gordon, 'Social Factors in the Prediction and Treatment of Emotional Disorders of Pregnancy', *American Journal of Obstetrics and Gynecology*, 1959, 77:5, pp. 1074–1083; also Richard E. Gordon and Katherine K. Gordon, 'Psychiatric Problems of a Rapidly Growing Suburb', *American Medical Association Archives of Neurology and Psychiatry*, 1958, Vol. 79; 'Psychosomatic Problems of a Rapidly Growing Suburb', *Journal of the American Medical Association*, 1959, 170:15; and 'Social Psychiatry of a Mobile Suburb', *International Journal of Social Psychiatry*, 1960, 6:1, 2, pp. 89–99. Some of these findings were popularized in the composite case histories of *The Split Level Trap*, written by the Gordons in collaboration with Max Gunther (New York, 1960).

10. Richard E. Gordon, 'Sociodynamics and Psychotherapy', *A.M.A. Archives of Neurology and Psychiatry*, April 1959, Vol. 81, pp. 486–503.

11. Adelaide M. Johnson and S. A. Szurels, 'The Genesis of Antisocial Acting Out in Children and Adults', *Psychoanalytic Quarterly*, 1952, 21:323–43.

12. ibid.

13. Beata Rank, 'Adaptation of the Psychoanalytical Technique for the Treatment of Young Children with Atypical Development', *American Journal of Orthopsychiatry*, XIX, 1 January 1949.

14. ibid.

15. ibid.

16. Beata Rank, Marian C. Putnam, and Gregory Rochlin, M.D., 'The Significance of the "Emotional Climate" in Early

Feeding Difficulties', *Psychosomatic Medicine*, X, 5 October 1948.

17. Richard E. Gordon and Katherine K. Gordon, 'Social Psychiatry of a Mobile Suburb', op. citp., p. 89–100.

18. ibid.

19. Oscar Sternbach, 'Sex Without Love and Marriage Without Responsibility', an address presented at the 38th Annual Conference of The Child Study Association of America, 12 March 1962, New York City (mimeo MS.).

20. Bruno Bettelheim, *The Informed Heart – Autonomy in a Mass Age*, Glencoe, Ill., 1960.

21. ibid., p. 265.

CHAPTER 13

The Forfeited Self

1. Rollo May, 'The Origins and Significance of the Existential Movement in Psychology', in *Existence, A New Dimension in Psychiatry and Psychology*, Rollo May, Ernest Angel, and Henri F. Ellenberger, eds., New York, 1958, pp. 30 f. (See also Erich Fromm, *Escape from Freedom*, pp. 269 ff.; A. H. Maslow, *Motivation and Personality*, New York, 1954; David Riesman, *The Lonely Crowd*.)

2. Rollo May, 'Contributions of Existential Psychotherapy', in *Existence, A New Dimension in Psychiatry and Psychology*, p. 87.

3. ibid., p. 52.

4. ibid., p. 53.

5. ibid., pp. 59 f.

6. See Kurt Goldstein, *The Organism, A Holistic Approach to Biology Derived From Pathological Data on Man*, New York and Cincinnati, 1939; also *Abstract and Concrete Behavior*, Evanston, Ill., 1950; *Case of Idiot Savant* (with Martin Scheerer), Evanston, 1945; *Human Nature in the Light of Psychopathology*, Cambridge, 1947; *After-Effects of Brain Injuries in War*, New York, 1942.

7. Eugene Minkowski, 'Findings in a Case of Schizophrenic Depression', in *Existence, A New Dimension in Psychiatry and Psychology*, pp. 132 f.

8. O. Hobart Mowrer, 'Time as a Determinant in Integrative Learning', in *Learning Theory and Personality Dynamics*, New York, 1950.

9. Rollo May, 'Contributions of Existential Psychotherapy', pp. 31 f. In Nietzsche's philosophy, human individuality and dignity are 'given or assigned to us as a task which we ourselves

must solve'; in Tillich's philosophy, if you do not have the 'courage to be', you lose your own being; in Sartre's, you *are* your choices.

10. A. H. Maslow, *Motivation and Personality*, p. 83.

11. A. H. Maslow, 'Some Basic Propositions of Holistic–Dynamic Psychology', an unpublished paper, Brandeis University.

12. ibid.

13. A. H. Maslow, 'Dominance, Personality and Social Behavior in Women', *Journal of Social Psychology*, 1939, Vol. 10, pp. 3–39; and 'Self Esteem (Dominance-Feeling) and Sexuality in Women', *Journal of Social Psychology*, 1942, Vol. 16, pp. 259–94.

14. A. H. Maslow, 'Dominance, Personality and Social Behavior in Women', *op. cit.*, pp. 3–11.

15. ibid., pp. 13 f.

16. ibid., p. 180.

17. A. H. Maslow, 'Self-Esteem (Dominance-Feeling) and Sexuality in Women', pp. 288. Maslow points out, however, that women with 'ego insecurity' pretended a 'self-esteem' they did not actually have. Such women had to 'dominate', in the ordinary sense, in their sexual relations, to compensate for their 'ego insecurity'; thus, they were either castrative or masochistic. As I have pointed out, such women must have been very common in a society which gives women little chance for true self-esteem; this was undoubtedly the basis of the man-eating myth, and of Freud's equation of femininity with castrative penis envy and/or masochistic passivity.

18. A. H. Maslow, *Motivation and Personality*, pp. 200 f.

19. ibid., pp. 214.

20. ibid., pp. 242 f.

21. ibid., pp. 257 f. Maslow found that his self-actualizing people 'have in unusual measure the rare ability to be pleased rather than threatened by the partner's triumphs. ... A most impressive example of this respect is the ungrudging pride of such a man in his wife's achievements even where they outshine his.' (ibid., p. 252.)

22. ibid., p. 245.

23. ibid., p. 255.

24. A. C. Kinsey, *et al.*, *Sexual Behavior in the Human Female*, pp. 356 ff.; Table 97, p. 397; Table 104, p. 403.

Decade of Birth *v.* Percentage of Marital Coitus Leading to
Orgasm

IN FIRST YEAR OF MARRIAGE, PERCENTAGE OF FEMALES

Percentage of marital coitus with orgasm	Decade of birth			
	Before 1900	1900– 1909	1910– 1919	1920– 1929
None	33	27	23	22
1–29	9	13	12	8
30–59	10	22	15	12
60–89	11	11	12	15
90–100	37	37	38	43
Number of cases	331	589	834	484

IN FIFTH YEAR OF MARRIAGE, PERCENTAGE OF FEMALES

Percentage of marital coitus with orgasm	Decade of birth			
	Before 1900	1900– 1909	1910– 1919	1920– 1929
None	23	17	12	12
1–29	14	15	13	14
30–59	14	13	16	19
60–89	12	13	17	19
90–100	37	42	42	36
Number of cases	302	489	528	130

25. ibid., p. 355.
26. See Judson T. Landis, 'The Women Kinsey Studied', George
Simpson, 'Nonsense about Women', and A. H. Maslow and
James M. Sakoda, 'Volunteer Error in the Kinsey Study', in
Sexual Behavior in American Society.
27. Ernest W. Burgess and Leonard S. Cottrell, Jr, *Predicting
Success or Failure in Marriage*, New York, 1939, p. 271.
28. A. C. Kinsey, *et al.*, *Sexual Behavior in the Human Female*, p. 403.
29. Sylvan Keiser, 'Body Ego During Orgasm', *Psychoanalytic
Quarterly*, 1952, Vol. XXI, pp. 153–66:

Individuals of this group are characterized by failure to develop adequate egos.... Their anxious devotion to, and lavish care of, their bodies belies the inner feelings of hollowness and inadequacy.... These patients have little sense of their own identity and are always ready to take on the personality of someone else. They have few personal convictions, and yield readily to the opinions of others.... It is chiefly among such patients that coitus can be enjoyed only up to the point of orgasm.... They dared not allow themselves uninhibited progression to orgasm with its concomitant loss of control, loss of awareness of the body, or death.... In instances of uncertainty about the structure and boundaries of the body image, one might say that the skin does not serve as an envelope which sharply defines the transition from the self to the environment; the one gradually merges into the other; there is no assurance of being a distinct entity endowed with the strength to give of itself without endangering one's own integrity.

30. Lawrence Kubie, 'Psychiatric Implications of the Kinsey Report', in *Sexual Behavior in American Society*, pp. 270 ff:

> This simple biologic aim is overlaid by many subtle goals of which the individual himself is usually unaware. Some of these are attainable; some are not. Where the majority are attainable, then the end result of sexual activity is an afterglow of peaceful completion and satisfaction. Where, however, the unconscious goals are unattainable, then whether orgasm has occurred or not, there remains a post-coital state of unsated need, and sometimes of fear, rage or depression.

31. Erik H. Erikson, *Childhood and Society*, pp. 239–83, 367–80. See also Erich Fromm, *Escape from Freedom and Man for Himself*; and David Riesman, *The Lonely Crowd*.

32. See Alva Myrdal and Viola Klein (*Women's Two Roles*), who point out that the number of American women now working outside the home seems greater than it is because the base from which the comparison is usually made was unusually small: a century ago the proportion of American women working outside the home was far smaller than in the European countries. In other words, the woman problem in America was probably unusually severe because the displacement of American women from essential work and identity in society was far more drastic – primarily because of the extremely rapid growth and industrialization of the American economy. The women who had grown with the men in the frontier days were banished almost overnight to *anomie* – which is a very expressive sociological name for that sense of non-existence or non-identity suffered by one who has no real place in society –

when the important work left the home, where they stayed. In contrast, in France where industrialization was slower, and farms and small family-size shops are still fairly important in the economy, women a century ago still worked in large numbers – in field and shop – and today the majority of French women are not full-time housewives in the American sense of the mystique, for an enormous number still work in the fields, in addition to that one out of three who, as in America, work in industry, sales, offices, and professions. The growth of women in France has much more closely paralleled the growth of the society, since the proportion of French women in the professions has doubled in fifty years. It is interesting to note that the feminine mystique does not prevail in France, to the extent that it does here; there is a legitimate image in France of a feminine career woman and feminine intellectual, and Frenchmen seem responsive to women sexually, without equating femininity either with glorified emptiness or that man-eating castrative mom. Nor has the family been weakened – in actuality or mystique – by women's work in industry and profession. Myrdal and Klein show that the French career women continue to have children – but not the great number the new educated American housewives produce.

33. Sidney Ditzion, *Marriage, Morals and Sex in America, A History of Ideas*, New York, 1953, p. 277.
34. William James, *Psychology*, New York, 1892, p. 458.

CHAPTER 14

A New Life Plan for Women

1. See 'Mother's Choice: Manager or Martyr', and 'For a Mother's Hour', *New York Times Magazine*, 14 January 1962, and 18 March 1962.
2. The sense that work has to be 'real', and not just 'therapy' or busywork, to provide a basis for identity becomes increasingly explicit in the theories of the self, even when there is no specific reference to women. Thus, in defining the beginnings of 'identity' in the child, Erikson says in *Childhood and Society* (p. 208):

The growing child must, at every step, derive a vitalizing sense of reality from the awareness that his individual way of mastering experience (his ego synthesis) is a successful variant of a group identity and is in accord with its space–time and life plan.

In this children cannot be fooled by empty praise and condescending encouragement. They may have to accept artificial bolstering of their self-esteem in lieu of something better, but their ego identity gains real strength only from wholehearted and consistent recognition of real accomplishment – i.e., of achievement that has meaning in the culture.

3. Nanette E. Scofield, 'Some Changing Roles of Women in Suburbia: A Social Anthropological Case Study', transactions of the New York Academy of Sciences, Vol. 22, 6 April 1960.

4. Polly Weaver, 'What's Wrong with Ambition?' *Mademoiselle*, September 1956.

5. Edna G. Rostow, 'The Best of Both Worlds', *Yale Review*, March 1962.

6. Ida Fisher Davidoff and May Elish Markewich, 'The Post-parental Phase in the Life Cycle of Fifty College-Educated Women', unpublished doctoral study, Teachers College, Columbia University, 1961. These fifty educated women had been full-time housewives and mothers throughout the years their children were in school. With the last child's departure, the women suffering severe distress because they had no deep interest beyond the home included a few whose actual ability and achievement were high; these women had been leaders in community work, but they felt like 'phonies', 'frauds', earning respect for 'work a ten-year-old could do'. The authors' own orientation in the functional-adjustment school makes them deplore the fact that education gave these women 'unrealistic' goals (a surprising number, now in their fifties and sixties, still wished they had been doctors). However, those women who had pursued interests – which in every case had begun in college – and were working now in jobs or politics or art, did not feel like 'phonies', or even suffer the expected distress at menopause. Despite the distress of those who lacked such interests, none of them, after the child-bearing years were over, wanted to go back to school; there were simply too few years left to justify the effort. So they continued 'woman's role' by acting as mothers to their own aged parents or by finding pets, plants, or simply 'people as my hobby' to take the place of their children.

The interpretation of the two family-life educators – who

themselves became professional marriage counsellors in middle age – is interesting:

> For those women in our group who had high aspirations or high intellectual endowment or both, the discrepancy between some of the values stressed in our success-and-achievement oriented society and the actual opportunities open to the older, untrained women was especially disturbing. ... The door open to the woman with a skill was closed to the one without training, even if she was tempted to try to find a place for herself among the gainfully employed. The reality hazards of the work situation seemed to be recognized by most, however. They felt neither prepared for the kind of job which might appeal to them, nor willing to take the time and expend the energy which would be required for training, in view of the limited number of active years ahead. ... The lack of pressure resulting from reduced responsibility had to be handled. ... As the primary task of motherhood was finished, the satisfactions of volunteer work, formerly a secondary outlet, seemed to be diminishing. ... The cultural activities of the suburbs were limited. ... Even in the city, adult education ... seemed to be 'busy work', leading nowhere. ...
>
> Thus, some women expressed certain regrets: 'It is too late to develop a new skill leading to a career.' 'If I had pursued a single line, it would have utilized my potential to the full.'

But the authors note with approval that 'the vast majority have somehow adjusted themselves to their place in society'.

> Because our culture demands of women certain renunciations of activity and limits her scope of participation in the stream of life, at this point being a woman would seem to be an advantage rather than a handicap. All her life, as a female, she had been encouraged to be sensitive to the feelings and needs of others. Her life, at strategic points, had required denials of self. She had had ample opportunities for 'dress rehearsals' for this latest renunciation ... of a long series of renunciations begun early in life. Her whole life as a woman had been giving her a skill which she was now free to use to the full without further preparation ...

7. Nevitt Sanford, 'Personality Development During the College Years', *Journal of Social Issues*, 1956, Vol. 12, No. 4, p. 36.
8. The public flurry in the spring of 1962 over the sexual virginity of Vassar girls is a case in point. The real question, for the educator, would seem to me to be whether these girls were getting from their education the serious lifetime goals only education can give them. If they are, they can be trusted to be responsible for their sexual behaviour. President Blanding

indeed defied the mystique to say boldly that if girls are not in college for education, they should not be there at all. That her statement caused such an uproar is evidence of the extent of sex-directed education.

9. The impossibility of part-time study of medicine, science, and law, and of part-time graduate work in the top universities has kept many women of high ability from attempting it. But in 1962, the Harvard Graduate School of Education let down this barrier to encourage more able housewives to become teachers. A plan was also announced in New York to permit women doctors to do their psychiatric residencies and postgraduate work on a part-time basis, taking into account their maternal responsibilities.

10. Virginia L. Senders, 'The Minnesota Plan for Women's Continuing Education', in 'Unfinished Business – Continuing Education for Women', *The Educational Record*, American Council on Education, October 1961, pp. 10 ff.

11. Mary Bunting, 'The Radcliffe Institute for Independent Study', ibid., pp. 19 ff. Radcliffe's president reflects the feminine mystique when she deplores 'the use the first college graduates made of their advanced educations. Too often and understandably, they became crusaders and reformers, passionate, fearless, articulate, but also, at times, loud. A stereotype of the educated women grew up in the popular mind and concurrently, a prejudice against both the stereotype and the education.' Similarly she states:

> That we have not made any respectable attempt to meet the special educational needs of women in the past is the clearest possible evidence of the fact that our educational objectives have been geared exclusively to the vocational patterns of men. In changing that emphasis, however, our goal should not be to equip and encourage women to compete with men. ... Women, because they are not generally the principal breadwinners, can be perhaps most useful as the trail blazers, working along the bypaths, doing the unusual job that men cannot afford to gamble on. There is always room on the fringes even when competition in the intellectual market places is keen.

That women use their education today primarily 'on the fringes' is a result of the feminine mystique, and of the prejudices against women it masks; it is doubtful whether these remaining barriers will ever be overcome if even educators are going to discourage able women from becoming 'crusaders

and reformers, passionate, fearless, articulate' – and loud
enough to be heard.

12. *Time*, November 1961. See also 'Housewives at the $2 Win-
dow', *New York Times Magazine*, 1 April 1962, which describes
how baby-sitting services and 'clinics' for suburban housewives are now being offered at the race tracks.

13. See remarks of State Assemblywoman Dorothy Bell Lawrence,
Republican, of Manhattan, reported in the *New York Times*, 8
May 1962. The first woman to be elected a Republican district
leader in New York City, she explained: 'I was doing all the
work, so I told the county chairman that I wanted to be chairman. He told me it was against the rules for a woman to hold
the post, but then he changed the rules.' In the Democratic
'reform' movement in New York, women are also beginning
to assume leadership posts commensurate with their work, and
the old segregated 'ladies' auxiliaries' and 'women's committees' are beginning to go.

14. Among more than a few women I interviewed who had, as the
mystique advises, completely renounced their own ambitions
in order to become wives and mothers, I noticed a repeated
history of miscarriages. In several cases, only after the woman
finally resumed the work she had given up, or went back to
graduate school, was she able to carry to term the long-desired
second or third child.

15. American women's life expectancy – 75 years – is the longest of
women anywhere in the world. But as Myrdal and Klein point
out in *Women's Two Roles*, there is increasing recognition that,
in human beings, chronological age differs from biological age:
'At the chronological age of 70, the divergencies in biological
age may be as wide as between the chronological ages of 50 and
90.' The new studies of ageing in humans indicate that those
who have the most education and who live the most complex
and active lives, with deep interests and readiness for new
experience and learning, do not get 'old' in the sense that
others do. A close study of 300 biographies (see Charlotte
Buhler, 'The Curve of Life as Studied in Biographies', *Journal
of Applied Psychology*, XIX, August 1935, pp. 405 ff.) reveals
that in the latter half of life, the person's productivity becomes
independent of his biological equipment, and, in fact, is often
at a higher level than his biological efficiency – that is, *if the
person has emerged from biological living*. Where 'spiritual factors'
dominated activity, the highest point of productivity came in

the latter part of life; where 'physical facts' were decisive in the life of an individual, the high point was reached earlier and the psychological curve was then more closely comparable to the biological. The study of educated women cited above revealed much less suffering at menopause than is considered 'normal' in America today. Most of these women, whose horizons had not been confined to physical housekeeping and their biological role, did not, in their fifties and sixties feel 'old'. Many reported in surprise that they suffered much less discomfort at menopause than their mothers' experience had led them to expect. Therese Benedek suggests (in 'Climacterium: A Developmental Phase', *Psychoanalytical Quarterly*, XIX, 1950, p. 1) that the lessened discomfort, and burst of creative energy many women now experience at menopause, is at least in part due to the 'emancipation' of women. Kinsey's figures seem to indicate that women who have by education been emancipated from purely biological living experience the full peak of sexual fulfilment much later in life than had been expected, and in fact, continue to experience it through the forties and past menopause. Perhaps the best example of this phenomenon is Colette – that truly human, emancipated French woman who lived and loved and wrote with so little deference to her chronological age that she said on her eightieth birthday: 'If only one were 58, because at that time one is still desired and full of hope for the future.'

Index